Fantastic Metamorphoses, Other Worlds

THE CLARENDON LECTURES
IN ENGLISH 2001

Frontispiece Hieronymus Bosch, *The Garden of Earthly Delights*, detail, *c*.1504, Prado, Madrid.

Fantastic Metamorphoses, Other Worlds

Ways of Telling the Self

MARINA WARNER

OXFORD
UNIVERSITY PRESS

OXFORD

UNIVERSITY PRESS

Great Clarendon Street, Oxford OX2 6DP

Oxford University Press is a department of the University of Oxford.
It furthers the University's objective of excellence in research, scholarship,
and education by publishing worldwide in

Oxford New York

Auckland Bangkok Buenos Aires Cape Town Chennai
Dar es Salaam Delhi Hong Kong Istanbul Karachi Kolkata
Kuala Lumpur Madrid Melbourne Mexico City Mumbai Nairobi
São Paulo Shanghai Taipei Tokyo Toronto

Oxford is a registered trade mark of Oxford University Press
in the UK and in certain other countries

Published in the United States
by Oxford University Press Inc., New York

British Library Cataloguing in Publication Data
Data available

Library of Congress Cataloging in Publication Data
Warner, Marina, 1946–
Fantastic metamorphoses, other worlds : ways of telling the self / Marina Warner.
p. cm.
Includes bibliographical references.
1. Metamorphosis in literature. I. Title.
PN56.M53 W37 2002   809'.93353—dc21   2002029058
ISBN 0-19-818726-2

3 5 7 9 10 8 6 4 2

Typeset in Centaur MT
by SNP Best-set Typesetter Ltd., Hong Kong
Printed in Great Britain
on acid-free paper by
Biddles Ltd, Guildford and King's Lynn

For Hermione

But all the story of the night told over,
And all their minds transfigur'd so together,
More witnesseth than fancy's images,
And grows to something of great constancy.

A Midsummer Night's Dream

Thanks and Acknowledgements

Exchanges of many kinds helped me write these lectures. Conversations, letters, emails, word-of-mouth, have contributed to their making, and the resulting debt I owe friends and colleagues is very great. Many showed quite startling generosity in sharing information and opinions. I have been steered, guided, gently directed here and there by many hands, as in some friendly, enjoyable game of blind man's buff. The blindnesses remain my own.

I would like to thank especially Peter Hulme, who lent me his copy of Ramón Pané at the beginning of my hunt, directed further reading, and commented later on work in progress; David Richards, who shared his wide-ranging knowledge of cross-cultural encounters; Jonathan King, who showed me relevant material in the British Museum; Debbie Lee, whose emails opened up new references; Tim Fulford, who shared his perceptions into Romanticism; Mary Douglas, who was severe but all the more helpful for it. Richard Buxton, who has himself written insightfully on metamorphosis, guided more of my reading. During the lectures themselves, Hermione Lee was my constant tutor and my friend, keeping her critical ear alert to edit me with rigour; her care in this and many other ways transformed the lectures and my experience at Oxford. To her, all salutations and thanks, always. Adrian Poole read the drafts before I worked on them for publication, and I have followed his suggestions as closely as I could because they showed such sympathy in criticism, and such clarity in advice. Kenneth Gross also read parts, to inspirational effect, and I am indebted to him for numerous connections; Karl Miller has offered me advice and encouragement, which I greatly value. Sarah Bakewell threw light on the project from the start from a different perspective and also commented most helpfully on the drafts.

During the Michaelmas term I spent in Oxford, Roy Foster was an incomparable ally and friend; he also read some of the material in draft; Terence Cave inspired the direction of my thinking as ever; Meg Bent at All Souls added incomparable wit, thoughtfulness, and generosity to my period there as a Visiting Fellow. I am very grateful to her for her friendship. I was helped by numerous comments and suggestions by many of the Fellows: Myles Burnyeat gave a draft of one lecture exhilaratingly close scrutiny; Derek Parfit and Hannah Pickard both kindly also read parts, emending my non-philosophical vagueness; James Walmsley responded with a thoughtful challenge to my arguments in the first lecture. I was proud and delighted to be a member of the college for the term, and thank the Warden and the Dean of Visiting Fellows, Martin West, Ian Maclean, and others involved in my coming. I much appreciated the cheerful support of Julie Edwards at the college and, in the English faculty, Melanie Clancy. Sophie Goldsworthy was a great supporter of the idea and the series throughout; also at OUP, Frances Whistler and Sarah Hyland have seen the book through with scrupulous care, enthusiasm, and kindness.

At an earlier stage, the staff of the Wren Library, Trinity College, Cambridge, were most helpful, and Jean Khalfa ever a wise counsellor. I began giving a seminar on Metamorphosis at Stanford University, where Terry Castle was an inspiration; so were the students in the class, though it was unfortunately cut short by illness. This gave me a chance to read for several months, and I can never thank enough Irene Andreae who looked after me then without a word of impatience. I've also benefited from giving lectures or seminars, and writing essays which have given me a chance to develop my ideas. The Fundación de los Amigos del Prado and its director, Ines Cobo, prompted my voyage of discovery when they invited me to contribute to their lecture series on Immortal Stories; my research into Bosch's *Garden of Earthly Delights* became the starting point for the whole series of lectures. Also in Madrid, Mercedes García-Arenal became a friend and inspiration. I am also grateful to Neil Corcoran at St Andrews, Gillian Beer at Cambridge, Oliver Taplin at Oxford, Stanley Wells, and Jonathan Bate, for the invitation to the International Shakespeare Association biennial conference, in Valencia, Spain; to the British Museum, and to Dan Hade who invited me to Penn State to a summer school; to James Lingwood of Artangel, London; to the History Department at Swansea for the honour of giving the Ernest Hughes Memorial lecture; to Jenny Uglow at the University of Kent for the invitation to give the Ian Gregor Memorial Lecture, and to Robert Fowler at the Bristol Institute of Hellenic and Roman Studies. The commission to select a show on the topic from Ken Arnold, of the Wellcome Institute, gave me access to another rich vein of material.

I know there are many people whom I have omitted, but my thinking about metamorphosis was enriched and refined by the insights of John Barnard, Tony Nuttall, Megan Vaughan, Stuart Clark, Claudia Swan, Peter Brooks, Francis Celoria, Elizabeth Edwards, Pamela Thurschwell, Joseph Koerner, Robert Crawford, Mark Haworth-Booth, Gillian Beer, John Beer, Lindsay Smith, Ibrahim Muhawi, Steven Lukes, Charles Fernyhough, Londa Schiebinger, Nicholas Roe, Nick Groom, Randal Keynes, Mark Dorrian, Lyn Innes, Nicholas Penny, Carolyn Kunin, Wendy Doniger, Darryl Pinckney, Edward Said, and Louise Neri. Jacqueline Rose, whom I am proud to follow as a Clarendon Lecturer, was, as ever, incisive, witty, and tonic.

The research was made all the more enjoyable by Sheila O'Connell, at the British Museum, by the staff of the British Library, by Clive Hurst and Julie Anne Lambert at the Bodleian, by the staff at Rhodes House, Oxford, and the Wellcome Library, London, and by Tony Smith of Magdalen College, Oxford, who kindly led me to some of the illustrated materials in the library there. Helena Ivins, Megan McInnes, Kate Hencher have helped invaluably at various stages. Imogen Cornwall-Jones has proved a most ingenious and active sleuth. And I am as always very grateful for the support of Gill Coleridge, and the judgement, warmth, and interest of Alison Samuel.

The translation of Heine's poem (pp. 161–2) is reproduced by kind permission of Richard Stokes; the lines from 'One need not be a Chamber . . . ' (p. 164), are reprinted by kind permission of the publishers and the Trustees of Amherst College from *The Poems of Emily Dickinson*, ed. Thomas H. Johnson, Cambridge, Mass.: The Belknap Press of Harvard University Press, Copyright © 1951, 1955, 1979 by the President and Fellows of Harvard College; the passage on p. 61 is from Ted Hughes, *Tales from Ovid*, and is reprinted by kind permission of the Estate of Ted Hughes and Faber & Faber Ltd. and Farrar Straus & Giroux.

M. W.

Kentish Town
2002

Contents

List of Illustrations

Introduction

'ALL THINGS ARE CHANGING . . .': METAMORPHOSIS AND THE TRANSMIGRATION OF SOULS

Ovid opens the *Metamorphoses* with the ringing claim 'My intention is to tell of bodies changed | To different forms . . .' ('In nova fert animus mutatas dicere formas | corpora . . .'); he continues with a prayer, 'you gods, who made the changes | Will help me—or I hope so' ('. . . di, coeptis (nam vos mustastis et illas) | adspirate meis . . .').[1] The theme of transformation then expands, through fifteen books, from particular case histories until it encompasses the whole wheeling universe itself, and the poem closes with an eloquent, vigorous, metaphysical hymn, in which the ancient sage Pythagoras gives voice to the poem's overarching philosophy. He invokes creation dynamically moving to a cyclical rhythm of generation, emergence, decay, and re-emergence:

> omnia mutantur, nihil interit: errat et illinc
> huc venit, hinc illuc, et quoslibet occupat artus
> spiritus eque feris humana in corpora transit
> inque feras noster, nec tempore deperit ullo,
> utque novis facilis signatur cera figuris
> nec manet ut fuerat nec formam servant eandem,
> sed tamen ipsa eadem est, animam sic semper eandem
> esse, sed in varias doceo migrare figuras.

> (All things are always changing,
> But nothing dies. The spirit comes and goes,

Is housed wherever it wills, shifts residence
From beasts to men, from men to beasts, but always
It keeps on living. As the pliant wax
Is stamped with new designs, and is no longer
What once it was, but changes form, and still
Is pliant wax, so do I teach that spirit
Is evermore the same, though passing always
To ever-changing bodies.)[2]

The blurring here between art and nature, as in the imagery of wax moulding (as used for sculpture casting), in order to convey the migrating forms of life, recurs in the long poem with significant frequency: in this vision, metamorphosis is the principle of organic vitality as well as the pulse in the body of art. This concept lies at the heart of classical and other myths, and governs the practice and scope of magic; it also, not coincidentally, runs counter to notions of unique, individual integrity of identity in the Judaeo-Christian tradition.[3] This is the theme of the lecture series collected here in book form. For metamorphosis survived, through all looks askance and disapproval and censure; it is thriving more than ever in literature and in art. When I chose the theme, *Fantastic Metamorphoses, Other Worlds: Ways of Telling the Self,* for the Clarendon Lectures in the Michaelmas term, 2001, I wanted to explore further and deeper the unstable, shape-shifting personae and plots I had come across in fairy tales, myths, and their literary progeny, in order to uncover the contexts in which ideas of personal transformation emerged and flourished, and to offer some historical background to the current high incidence of the phenomena, in poetry, fiction, films, video games. I set out to find out about the types and processes of metamorphosis that were described in the tradition and to read them in order to throw light on changing ideas about persons and personhood.

But in what ways did the spirit come and go in Ovid's scheme? In what way was the soul 'mutable' in this mythology?

First and foremost, it was an actually movable entity, changing its habitation, from body to body:

> morte carent animae semperque priore relicta
> sede novis domibus vivunt habitantque receptae …
>
> (Our souls are deathless; always, when they leave our bodies,
> They find new dwelling places …)[4]

Furthermore, these bodies themselves were in the process of changing shape. Thus Ovidian shape-shifting belongs on the one hand to the broad rubric of metempsychosis, the Pythagorean doctrine, which holds that the soul, or essence of something or some person, migrates from one body to another. Forms do not only take on different forms; the whole of nature evolves through the creative power of shape-shifting and this transmigration of souls.

In the course of the poem, Ovid rings his own changes on material he found in his Greek predecessors; he refashioned, transformed, and, in many instances, reconfigured ancient myths as well as inventing new ones. He provides the earliest surviving source for several favourite classical stories which have retroactively acquired a 'Greek' character. His poem is, needless to say, a literary achievement of extraordinary fertility, vitality, and invention, and his stories have inspired works of art since medieval times, and wave upon wave of different reinterpretations and approaches.[5]

Through the whole intricate scoring of the poem run hundreds of stories of ever-changing bodies: to notate and number them resembles one of those fairy-tale tasks, such as sifting peas and lentils. By the standard of working taxonomy today, the classes of forms that exist are porous, and morph into one another: animal, vegetable, mineral fuse and meld; higher and lower—rocks, flowers, trees, every variety of beast and fowl as well as human beings— are transformed one into the other. There is permanence as well as flux in the Ovidian cosmos: the extreme fixed state of petrification even brings to an end the animate existence of several of fate's victims, turned to stone for their crimes and misdemeanours, others fixed in the heavens as new constellations. Sometimes Ovid's imagination focuses on geography: in the course of dramatizing one story, such as Medea's, he'll strike chords from many, many others in passing: from the ground of the landscape over which Medea flies in her dragon chariot spring figure after figure of earlier metamorphoses, for example, features of the landscape, explained through stories. Souls inhabit everything, and human passions, erupting at moments of crisis, often transmute the very nature of nature:

> nos quoque, pars mundi, quoniam non corpora solum,
> verum etiam volucres animae sumus, inque ferinas
> possumus ire domos pecudumque in pectora condi . . .
>
> (We, part of creation, also
> Must suffer change. We are not bodies only,
> But wingéd spirits, with the power to enter
> Animal forms, house in the bodies of cattle.)[6]

So on the one hand, Ovidian metamorphosis belongs to the vast, biological scheme of things, occupying a universal plane in cosmic time and catching up human lives into its timeless and vast perspective. It expresses eternal flux, a prevailing law of mutability and change. But on the other hand, Ovid does not merge himself wholly with the figure of Pythagoras, and hundreds of the dramatic episodes that he recounts do finalize phenomena in a single shape. He studs his rich tapestry with just-so stories about the origins of natural phenomena—these are the tales of individual transformation which have inspired writers and artists for two millennia. When Daphne is turned into a laurel tree (Pl. V) and a young man called Cycnus becomes a swan, when the fates of Hyacinthus and Narcissus offer a story behind the flowers, the subjects achieve final personality in this new form: from the perspective of creation and the life force, the shape into which they shift more fully expresses them and perfects them than their first form.

Ovid's picture of natural generation, assuming a universe that's unceasingly progenitive, multiple, and fluid, organizes the relationships between creatures according to axioms of metaphorical affinity, poetic resonance, and even a variety of dream punning. Linnaeus would come along much later—more than two millennia after the ancient philosophers who influenced Ovid had elevated flux to the prime mover of nature. He would propose, to the scandal of his contemporaries, that phenomena should be classified by their sex organs; it was this principle, he argued, the ability to unite and procreate, that determined identity of species. It is still the basis of species differentiation today.

But in Ovid, no such limitations impede the energies of nature or interrupt the vital continuum of all phenomena. Ovid's biological metamorphoses include any number of disruptions of these borders: rocks turn into men and women, when Deucalion and Pyrrha create a new generation of humans by tossing stones over their shoulders which spring up into life (Fig. 1), and vice versa, as when Niobe, first punished for her maternal conceit by the deaths of all her children is then turned into a mountain, weeping rivers of tears. The young girls gathering flowers when Proserpina is raped and carried off by Pluto cry out, begging to wander the world in search for her, and are changed, in Ovid, into the sirens. The fifteenth-century illuminator in one, richly illustrated folio volume was aware of the classical tradition that the sirens were bird-formed, but because he also knew northern legends about mermaids, he struck a compromise and showed them as flying fishes (Fig. 2). In other episodes of Ovidian metamorphosis, trees give birth to the beautiful youth, Adonis, after his mother Myrrha has been changed into the bitter myrrh tree for falling in love with her own father and seducing him. In the famous story of Pygmalion, the sculptor finds that his longing for a woman unlike any of the real ones he knows of incidentally brings to life a statue of Galatea he is making. Occasionally, simple *visual* puns on morphology can inspire one variety of botanical metamorphosis: for example, when

Fig. 1 After the flood in Ovid's Metamorphoses, the only survivors, Deucalion and Pyrrha, re-people the devastated world by throwing their 'mother's bones'—rocks from the earth—over their shoulder (*La Bible des poètes*, 1493).

Perseus lays down the Gorgon's head, the seaweed on the shore hardens at contact and turns into coral.

Some tales are cautionary: the penalty fits the crime. Lycaon, who serves up a cannibal meal to Zeus, is turned into a werewolf; Arachne, who boasts about her weaving skills, is condemned to live for ever as a spider (Fig. 3); when a group of peasants, cutting rushes on a lakeshore, refuse to allow the goddess Latona to bathe and purify herself after giving birth to the divine twins, Apollo and Diana, Ovid lingers on Latona's revenge. She prays to the gods,

Fig. 2 The Sirens appear in the form of birds on Greek vases, but in northern folklore are fish-tailed; this artist squared the circle and pictured them as flying fishes (*La Bible des poètes*, 1493).

and inflicts on them a punitive metamorphosis by punning analogy: she curses them,

> 'Aeternum stagno' dixit 'vivatis in isto!'
> ('May you live for eternity in that pond')

The curse works: they turn into frogs (Fig. 4).[7]

In other stories, sudden transmutation snatches someone up into another form, not to inflict punishment but to effect an astonishing reprieve: Tereus, Procne, and Philomela are all suddenly changed—into birds—before they wreak more havoc on one

Fig. 3 On the terrace of the proud in Purgatory, Dante and Virgil see 'poor mad Arachne' who was changed into a spider for rashly taking on the goddess Minerva in a contest of weaving skills (from Gustave Doré's illustrated *Divine Comedy*, Paris, 1861).

Fig. 4 The goddess Latona curses her attackers who prevent her bathing, and they are turned into frogs (from an Italian allegorized Ovid, seventeenth century).

another. Ted Hughes commented that Ovid was interested in 'passion where it combusts, or levitates, or mutates into an experience of the supernatural', but that Tereus' tale is one in which 'mortal passion makes the breakthrough by sheer excess, without divine intervention'.[8]

Ovid's fables can also display a certain perverse comedy, characteristic of the magical casuistry intrinsic to oracles and to fairy boons: the goddess Aurora, in love with the moral Tithonus, asks the gods to give him immortal life. But because she has forgotten to ask for immortal youth as well, he grows older and more and more decrepit, so she tires of him and, eventually, turns him into a grasshopper (Fig. 5).

Many of the most terrible metamorphoses are inflicted by the gods in cruel revenge, frequently unprovoked: Actaeon is changed into a stag, for coming upon Diana bathing, and is then torn apart

TITHON

11

Tithon fils de Laomedon Roy de Troye, obtient de l'Aurore qui l'auoit tant aimé en sa ieunesse pour sa beau-
té, d'estre changé en Cigalle, ne pouuant ni rajeunir, ni cesser de viure. *Homere hymne 3. Properce. l. 2. Bleg. 18.*
C. Dauid sculp. *Auec priuilege du Roy* P. Mariette le fils escudit

Fig. 5 When the goddess of the dawn, Aurora, fell in love with Tithonus, she asked the gods to give him immortality but forgot to ask for endless youth; when he grew decrepit, she turned him into a grasshopper (here rather wasp-like, in Pierre Mariette's seventeenth-century engraving).

by his own pack of hounds (Fig. 6). The enchantress Circe, who figures far more malevolently in Ovid than in Homer, acts as a kind of ambitious society hostess cum woman scorned: out of pure spite, she turns the lovely and chaste Scylla into a frightful sea monster (Fig. 7), and, when the king, Picus, rejects her advances, she changes him into a woodpecker (drolly captured in the fifteenth-century illustrated *Ovide moralisé* (Pl. IV)).

The processes of continual flux on the one hand and the storybook accounts of the formation of phenomena embody contradictory principles: Arachne is sentenced to remain a spider forever, and loses any ability to mutate or be housed in another shape later. No matter: the verve of the poem carries the reader past such inconsistencies. With infectious energy, wit, style, and intense empathy, Ovidian metamorphoses turn themselves to various ends, endowing the form of the long poem with a protean character, itself rooted not in natural processes, but in the irruption of the marvellous.

For some changes of shape in the Ovidian cosmos are reversible: the gods, unlike mortals, are not condemned to remain in their altered form, but are endowed with irrepressible powers of metamorphosis, constitutive of their divinity, their deathlessness. Zeus' polymorphousness, as he assaults nymphs and mortal women alike, have become familiar stories, chiefly through Renaissance interpreters who drew inspiration directly from Ovid. Many of these episodes of rape and insemination lie at the foundation of cultures and nations in Greek and Roman thought—hence Europa. Danae was imprisoned in a tower by her fearful father, but Zeus/Jupiter spirited himself inside in a shower of gold: the hero Perseus was their offspring. To assault 'Olympia', he changed into a serpentine figure—leaving much besides that was human, as Giulio Romano's explicit fresco piece for his patron the Duke of Ferrara, at the Palazzo del Tè, Mantua, makes clear (Fig. 8). Io, who was wooed by the god in the form of a divine cloud, was painted by Correggio for his series on the Loves of the Gods. She was then changed

Fig. 6 Actaeon out hunting chances upon the goddess Diana and her nymphs bathing; furious, she changes him into a stag; his own dogs no longer know him and tear him apart (from Parmigianino's fresco, Fontanellato).

Fig. 7 Glaucus the sea-god, with dark green beard and fish tail, falls in love with the nymph Scylla; out of jealousy, Circe turns her into a monstrous hybrid, with a girdle of snapping dogs' heads at her waist (from George Sandys's English translation of Ovid's poem, 1632).

Fig. 8 'A god's embrace is never fruitless', says one victim of Olympian lust in the *Odyssey*: for the gods, metamorphosis chiefly offered opportunities for disguise and seduction (here Jupiter and 'Olympia', vividly imagined by Giulio Romano, for the Palazzo del Tè, Mantua).

into a heifer (Fig. 9), but unusually survived and became human again, the ancestress of the Argives—the Greeks themselves. Leda, whom Jupiter seduced in the form of a swan, became one of the most popular subjects of Italian high Renaissance art, as I explore in the second chapter, on 'Hatching'.

Besides the immortals, a small group of prodigious beings are, by nature, perpetual shape-shifters, and inspire Ovid towards self-identification: Proteus, for instance, who gives his name to the English adjective protean, meaning polymorphous, ever changing, unstable, and the Old Man of the Sea, Peleus, who assaults another creature of ocean, Thetis the sea nymph, and holds on to her as she struggles and twists from his grasp in one form then another. Ovid changes from third person description to the voca-tive to address Thetis as he tells of her mutating from bird to tree to spotted pard ('forma ... maculosae tigridis'). In this shape, she scares off Peleus—on this occasion.

These sequences of struggles are called, in the folklore tradition, witches' duels: they feature in many fairy tales, and indeed bear in their very structure the marks of oral repetition and symmetrical patterning and narrative expansion.

The wrought metaphors—of art and figuration, of *making*—which Ovid uses, confuse not only the status of Thetis' transform-ations (which are substantive and actual in the text, not illusory), but the very status of image-language, which performs here an analogous office of making picture-flesh. Her various forms are personae, in the sense of mask, as well as personae in the sense of person. Significantly, in this passage, Ovid echoes the opening of the whole poem, for Thetis, more than so many of his characters, is a body who changes into other forms.:

> quod nisi venisses variatis saepe figuris
> ad solitas artes, auso foret ille potitus . . .

(And hadst thou not, by changing oft thy form, had recourse to thine accustomed arts, he would have worked his daring will on thee.)[9]

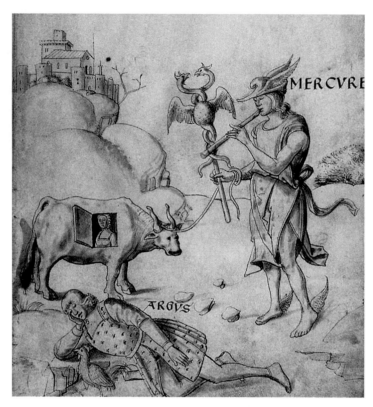

Fig. 9 Io was turned into a heifer to prevent Jupiter's courtship, and many-eyed Argus was set to watch over her, but Mercury lulled him to sleep. A sixteenth-century illustrator, anxious that Io should be identifiable, shows her through a window in the cow's flank.

In Ovid, metamorphosis often breaks out in moments of crisis, as expressions of intense passion, as Hughes points out; but, as a literary figure, it refuses to settle between the states of metaphorical evocation to actual description and embodies the condition of writing itself.[10]

Both forms of change however put up resistance to time and forgetting: the last emphatic word of the poem, 'vivam'—'I shall live' condenses the proud assertion of inextinguishable vitality that the poet issues—against ruin, against disappearance. Ovid did live on through his book: its influence was all the more profound because so much of his fantasy and beliefs were heterodox and there emanated from them the fascinating flavour of the prohibited. At the end of the fifteenth century, when for the first time Europeans came across the metamorphic beliefs of pagans who were not remote progenitors, but contemporaries, they grasped at understanding them through a pre-existent vision of metamorphosis, mediated through Ovid, and through Ovid's medieval interpreters, including Dante. The two principles, soul migration on the one hand and bodily transformation on the other, identifiable as the core of pagan belief, inform fantastic literature; Ovid has been and continues to be an inexhaustible granary; these chapters can only pick out a scattering from the poem's plenty.

CROSSING AND RECROSSINGS: THE TRANSMIGRATION OF STORIES

As I attempted to hold steady to the shifting, dazzling body of metamorphoses, Ovidian and later, my moorings lay with studies of the Western tradition, such as Charles Taylor's seminal book, *Sources of the Self*, and Ian Hacking's *Rewriting the Soul*.[11] However, through my reading of fantastic literature, I intimated that tales of metamorphosis often arose in spaces (temporal, geographical, and mental) that were crossroads, cross-cultural zones, points of interchange on the intricate connective tissue of communications between cultures. It is no accident that fairy tales were first written down, for example, all round the edge of the Mediterranean, in Egypt and in the great ports of Venice and Naples, and travelled along trade routes from far and wide, circulating via the bazaars and caravanserai of the Middle East, the diplomatic bags of early empire-builders and proselytizers, specimen-hunters and cartographers, figures who are themselves often situated at turning points in

culture and at moments of clash and conflict between one intellectual hegemony and another: it is characteristic of metamorphic
writing to appear in transitional places and at the confluence of traditions and civilizations. I was looking for 'congeners', materials
through which one culture interacts with and responds to another,
conductors of energies that may themselves not be apparent or
directly palpable in the resulting transformations. The congener
is a concept Peter Hulme usefully introduces in his book *Colonial
Encounters* to add a different nuance to the idea of a source or of an
analogue, or, I would add, to characterize a way of looking and
understanding. 'Congeners', he writes, 'can cast light by virtue of
their deeper similarities, independently of any putative influence
… The object of study is the common coinage, not a numbered
account.'[12] I found my congeners mostly in an oddly neglected
branch of literature, early ethnography, and its subset of scientific
inquiry, into entomology, botany, and biology.

Metamorphosis is a defining dynamic of certain kinds of
stories—myths and wonder tales, fairy stories and magic realist
novels. In this kind of literature, it is often brought about by
magical operations; but, as I discovered in the course of my reading, magic may be natural, not supernatural, and the languages of
science consequently profoundly affect visions of metamorphic
change. The estimate of metamorphosis as a prodigious inter-
ruption of natural development, and, by contrast to this, metamorphosis as an organic process of life itself keeps shifting: I became
very involved in asking, what thinking lay behind these changes?
What helped modify the value and weight of metamorphosis as an
event in a story?

Transformations bring about a surprise, and among the many
responses story solicits from us, is surprise. The breaking of rules
of natural law and verisimilitude creates the fictional world with its
own laws—even Ovid, as he develops his Pythagorean mysteries,
situates the changes in a fictive past where the rules of generation
and death were differently disposed. There is an intrinsic pleasure

in the reader or listener's given freedom to enter that world, inhabit it, move inside it. Moreover, some kinds of metamorphosis play a crucial part in anagnorisis, or recognition, the reversal fundamental to narrative form, and so govern narrative satisfaction: when the beggar maid turns out to be the foundling princess—Perdita in *The Winter's Tale* for example, any number of Cinderellas, in opera, novels, as well as classic fairy tales, or when the beast or the pet bird or the stricken deer turns out to be a prince under a spell. Stories of this kind promise us change, too.

In the four lectures, I tried to pick up some of the frequencies at which this energy of metamorphosis has travelled, the ways it communicated principles and ideas and transformed their receivers and readers. Beginning with the mutations in Ovid's great poem, my thoughts then evolved through the imagery of the three processes that emerged as dominant in the processes of metamorphosis: first hatching, then splitting; splitting opens up into the concept of doubling. I looked to match these metamorphic processes with fertile points of interchange, where a way of thinking about people met another, through an achieved work of literature or a collectively held story, and I tried to identify different, critical points in time, to draw an overview of the shifts that have taken place in understanding the possible permutations of personal identity. I tried to remain alert to the changing character of the concepts themselves: how ideas about hatching, for example, were altered by discoveries in natural history.

The encounter with the Americas seems to me one of the most transformative experiences of history, and not only on the original peoples there, whose lives were utterly altered—and in so many ways shattered and destroyed. That side of the story cannot be overlooked or sidelined or evaded, but it is not the whole story. On this theme, I took my cue from another phrase, one used by the maverick historian Peter Lamborn Wilson: 'positive shadow'. He introduces it, in reference to the Europeans who 'turned Turk', to characterize the ways colonized or repudiated cultures can still

exercise a fascination, a 'perfume of seduction' over their new masters, and thereby produce a series of reciprocal transformations.[13]
More examples of this cultural hall of mirrors, in which reflections
of one culture are refracted through another, would include the
Jesuits in sixteenth- and seventeenth-century China, when the
Christian missionaries became profoundly interested and affected
by Confucian philosophy; another, more familiar incidence, which
will surface briefly in my last chapter, occurred when subcon-
tinental Indian mystical thought interfused nineteenth-century
Theosophists and Spiritualists. These exchanges have come under
greater study than the psychological and literary effects of the early
imperial venture in the Americas. But they reveal how the new and
the strange do not always shock; they can lure, they can delight. The
Other in history has exercised a huge power of attraction, not
repulsion, and overturning the metaphors of shock, alarm, terror,
and recoil that trammel critical discussion of this inaugural con-
frontation of modernity can change the way memory-work reckons
up the balance of the past. The change in itself can then stretch and
deepen the language of pleasure.[14]

I also take my cue from Paul Gilroy, who, in *The Black Atlantic*,
argues for redrafting a history made in common after the migra-
tions caused by empire and slavery; his approach moves away from
a model of clashing oppositions to one of coalescence—turbulent,
disgraceful, riven with inequalities, of course, but nevertheless
mutual in the sense that those who are done to, also do—and rather
more than it might seem from existing historiography. Within the
broad Atlantic and the vast question of European and American
contacts and exchange, the geographical zone of the Caribbean
constitutes a smaller, but rich historical arena of mutation and
change, and a space most propitious to the play of imagination.[15]
In English, the word Creole designates indigenous, native-born
white West Indians; in French, the culture of the Caribbean and of
the francophone southern states of America, before the Louisiana
purchase of 1803, a delta where meet rivers flowing from Africa,

Spain, Britain, France as well as the productive silt of the Meso-American aboriginal peoples. The territories of the African diaspora in the Americas became 'a cross-cultural space',[16] a mercantile and political confluence of heterogeneous peoples, histories, and languages, a shifting, metamorphic, and phantasmal zone, where 'le merveilleux créole' (the creole marvellous) made its appearance in different languages and different genres.

Gilroy's perspective builds on Ashis Nandy's crucial insights in *The Intimate Enemy*, into 'colonialism as a shared culture' and 'a psychological state rooted in earlier forms of social consciousness in both the colonizers and the colonized'.[17] These cultural critics contributed to my exploring into the affinities between the reading of Ovid in the early Renaissance and the reception of Indian, or Taino, legends in the 1490s, which I discuss in the first chapter.

The argument that the contemptuous depiction of savage rites and superstitions gave the oppressor permission to oppress the subaltern as an inferior, a child, a barbarian does not take into account sufficiently the continuing and ever-increasing fascination above all with stories of metamorphosis and magic in evidence in ethnographic and literary texts. The emphasis on repression does not suffice either, it seems to me: the confluence of ideas and the resulting current offers more direct intellectual and cultural exchanges.[18] It produced, during those momentous early encounters, rich new materials to think with; this form of mental and imaginative adventure itself represents another form of plunder, and one which, no less than the territorial profits, also fashioned the history and the self-portrait of Europe's identity. The metamorphic processes that animate Taino tales—hatching and splitting—become signs of difference that sharpen Christian taxonomies of justice and truth, deviance and delinquency; their incidence in 'wild thought'—Lévi-Strauss's *la pensée sauvage*—helped develop the metaphors by which, in Toni Morrison's phrase, the colonizers 'played in the dark' and defined their distinctiveness.[19]

But a review of the written evidence from the region—necessarily limited, before the nineteenth century, to missionaries, planters, historians, and scientists—allows a picture to form of enchanted personality, of powers to alter states and take possession of others' spirits; this picture of occult powers lies embedded in a broader imaginary, orientalist map of power and wisdom: this map places Hellenistic Egypt in pride of place, as epitomized by the hybrid mystagogue and romancer Apuleius, whose alter ego, Lucius, becomes a priest of Isis at the end of his book *The Metamorphoses of Lucius, or The Golden Ass*. In the language of myths and fairy tales, Egypt means magic and Egypt is African, or rather Moorish, and this superimposition colours modern representations of transformed, enchanted personality. But the notion of Egyptian occult wisdom is far-flung and deep rooted. For example, Paul Muldoon, my immediate predecessor as Clarendon Lecturer, began his odyssey through Irish poetry with the hero Amergin, founder of Celtic riddling and occult bardism, the first Irish glee-man, identifying his mother as an Egyptian Pharoah's daughter, Scota. Her father's name is given as Nectanebes: this name is borrowed across from the *Romance of Alexander*, the wonder-packed panegyric to Alexander the Great, which was written in the third century BC and disseminated throughout medieval Christendom. [20] Nectanebo, in this truly popular fantastic history, is Egyptian, and a wizard, and the real, though secret father of Alexander; Nectanebo can change his shape, tell the future, and work spells, and has transfused his magical powers, it is implied, to his natural son who does not know it. So does orientalizing myth-making wind even Alexander the Great into the web of fantasies about Africa. These fantasies will above all interact with the history and experience of peoples in the African diaspora brought about by slavery.

In the first chapter, 'Mutating', I focus on the first document written about the native peoples of the Caribbean and their beliefs, by a monk—Fray Ramón Pané—who was left behind by

Christopher Columbus precisely to find out about the locals' stories and religion. These tales of metamorphosis were set down at the end of the fifteenth century, and must have been read, as I have said, in the light of metamorphoses rather more familiar to European imagination. I then turn to one of the most fascinating riddles in the history of art, the contemporary triptych by Hieronymus Bosch, known as *The Garden of Earthly Delights*, and I propose an interpretation in the light of the encounter with the Taino Indians' myths of origin and transformation.

Bosch paints many monsters, some absurd, some terrifying, and both kinds are associated with eggs and with hatching. According to the 'logic of the imaginary', egg-laying reptiles and ambiguous, spawning, shape-changing amphibians suit magical operations most particularly, as Macbeth's second witch knows well when she stirs into the cauldron, 'Fillet of a fenny snake . . . Eye of newt and toe of frog . . .' (IV. i).[21] Hatching provides a fertile mythopoeic figure in itself, and in the second chapter, I unfold some of its transformations, beginning with Maria Merian's studies of butterflies' life cycle, made in the Dutch colony of Suriname at the turn of the seventeenth century, in order to throw light on the changing view of human personality and its unfolding over time and changes in the course of an individual life. The idea that a series of metamorphoses develops the form of an individual underlies the misadventures of the protagonist Lucius in Apuleius' *The Golden Ass*, written in the second century and widely read from the fifteenth century onwards all over Europe. This story of metamorphosis differs profoundly from Ovid's victims because Lucius, after being changed into a donkey by a miscarriage of magic, manages to return to his shape as a man; its wonderful narrative offspring, starting with Francesco Colonna's romance of 1499, *The Strife of Love in a Dream*, includes *A Midsummer Night's Dream* and fairy tales of the Beauty and the Beast kind. With this narrative of positive transformation in mind, I put the case in the second lecture that a linear concept of progress through a series of shed skins, as it were, to an ultimate

perfected outcome, released from disfigurement or transmogrification, comes under pressure from the empirical observation of
insects, in which each stage, however grubby, however inconsistent
and incongruous, expresses the full creature under another shape;
furthermore, the monstrosity of being hatched, as in the myth
of Leda and the swan, fades within this fresh understanding of
natural development. I then suggest that Kafka, followed by
Nabokov, absorbed the metaphorical process of hatching in order
to tell of a different kind of human person, who is precisely
manifest in the larva, nymph, and cocoon.

In the third chapter, 'Splitting', I offer a genealogy of the zombie, and argue that this concept of the living dead, introduced into
English through the nation's colonies, served to characterize a new,
recognizable psychological state of being in the late eighteenth century. Coleridge is one of the earliest writers to convey the condition
of spellbound vacancy; he does not actually adopt the zombie per
se, though it is a word he comments on and glosses, as I discovered.

The turn towards the uncanny and the supernatural that
happened within the Enlightenment might not be satisfactorily
diagnosed as a cultural bipolar disorder, an irrational euphoria
detonated by the sobriety and limits of empiricism and reasonable
inquiry; nor does it need be construed as a return of the repressed,
a counter-Enlightenment negation of sense and rationality, a drive
towards excitation and frenzy in revolt against law and order and
moderation. Instead, if one bears in mind the tone of mocking
dissent that permeates Gothic, an alternative, politicized interpretation becomes possible: taking in the expansion of commercial
and political power in this period, and, turning on its head the
governing notion of Otherness, it could be proposed that the discovery and definition of zombie personality represents an extension of the spirit of empirical inquiry, that a new psychology was
developing by observation and investigation, which was to have
a significant influence. As Debbie Lee has written, in an important article on the Romantics and Voodoo, 'African-European

encounters were fraught with the politics of domination that ultimately threatened the self. What one culture lost in identity, the other possessed in power.'[22] The imperial enterprise was an incubus, and it recognized the lineaments of its work in the zombie; loss of soul was a precondition—and a consequence—of slavery, and not only for its first victims. The zombie is not simply a product of a different psychological approach to mental illness; it is a literary expression of political clashes and their effects.

Uncanny fictions and poetry gather in mass and intensity and even velocity of dissemination from the 1760s to the 1840s, in chronological symbiosis, if not in actual intellectual engagement, with the ethnography of new territories, and within the material conflicts caused by French and English empire-building. The dominant settings are not strange, only *estranged* by supernatural forces. The reason that the fever of Gothic begins to spike at this time could derive from economic and political energies: the metamorphoses inflicted by occupation, slavery, and the getting of wealth abroad incited a literature of metamorphic identity as the apt vehicle of the changing times. Celtic lore had always been there, for example, as had peasants' and balladeers' legends and *contes de fées*. But they had not moved into popular, high literature. Why do stories of faerie, of doublings and soul murder, in Scotland and England and farther afield, take root in James Hogg in the early nineteenth century and come to brilliant expression in the stories of Robert Louis Stevenson towards its close? Why, in American literature, do local tales of hauntings, of horror and dread from the bayous and the levées of the Mississippi inspire Edgar Allan Poe in mid-century, and why do the magic capers, vanishings, and enchantments that feature in Count Anthony Hamilton's ironic orientalist fairy tales, then spur William Beckford to write *Vathek*?

In the case of Poe and Beckford, there are personal, direct creole connections, through Poe's Louisiana years, and Beckford's Jamaican fortune. But the biographies of the writers are not necessary to the argument for imperial fascination and its Gothic effect.

The introduction of zombies per se into storytelling in English falls to an eccentric figure, the much travelled Helleno-Irishman Lafcadio Hearn at the turn of the nineteenth century, in his collections of creole fairy tales, as I discuss in the third chapter, and the zombie as contemporary life form makes its first fully achieved literary appearance in Jean Rhys's masterpiece, *Wide Sargasso Sea*. The novel dramatizes the deadly conflict over possession—possession in both the sense of wealth and of haunting—at a profoundly personal, inward level, through the juxtaposed first person accounts of Antoinette Mason and the Mr Rochester figure from *Jane Eyre*. But throughout, its passions spread rings outwards to encompass the larger historical issue of identities that remain after colonial power has swept through, on and past.

To trace a genealogy of the concept, such as the zombie, offers a way of seeing, it seems to me, new metamorphoses of persons increasingly explored in nineteenth- and twentieth-century evocations of character. Some of this literature has been categorized as magic realism, whose progenitors number many writers of the larger Caribbean and the Americas, but the term denotes highly colourful, often picaresque tales of preternatural and prodigious events, and excludes the eerie, haunted, and spectral psychological depictions of split, spellbound, or multiple personality that concern me in the last two chapters.

The figure of the double resonates in fantastic stories written from Venice to Prague to Edinburgh to Louisiana, *pari passu* with a growing interest in the supernatural, in multiple spirits, soul travel and soul theft, from the late eighteenth century onwards, influenced by exchanges and encounters at the confluence of cultures, as in the case of zombies. Tales of metamorphosis proliferated, themselves multi-limbed, protean, polymorphous: the era of secularization, scientific inquiry, epistemological adventures in the pursuit of clear Reason saw a bubbling spate of fables, dramas, romances, fancies, and harlequinades in which animals turn into human beings and vice versa, in which magic spells and talismans bring about a myriad transformations; in which souls leave living bodies to fly to other dimensions of existence and return; or depart from their fleshly host to take up occupation of another: poems and stories told of identities doubling and redoubling through body-hopping, body-squatting, or spirit travels, also known as the shaman's flight.

This kind of metamorphosis—shape-shifting—breaks the rules of time, place, of human reproduction and personal uniqueness; it became a highly popular, much elaborated motive force in fantastic fictions, exploding in full bizarre bloom in western Europe first in the tales of Gian Battista Basile, published in Naples in 1633–6, and their close cousins, *The Arabian Nights*, which were translated into French in 1702; *Le Cabinet des fées*, a collection of fairy tales and fantastic fables, begins with Charles Perrault's pioneering book of 1697, and includes Antoine Galland's translation of the *Arabian Nights*. The *Cabinet* fills an astonishing forty-one volumes and was published in 1785–9, first in Paris, but later in the series, on account of certain coincidental *évènements* at the time, in Amsterdam and Geneva.[23]

The vogue for such blithe, fantastic fictions began running very strongly indeed during the era of revolutionary upheaval; captive ghosts, stolen souls, and the vampiric supernatural gained a fresh vitality and significance. In Venice, Carlo Gozzi's theatre, drawing on *commedia dell'arte* conventions, plundered strange new material about body-hopping and wandering spirits from the orientalist fairy tales in increasing circulation. Key works of the supernatural, such as the Polish-Austrian Jan Potocki's extravagant and wonderful ghoulish farrago, *The Manuscript Found in Saragossa*, were also written during this turbulent time.[24] The theme reached a new seriousness and pitch of unease in the Gothic romance and the modern novel.

In the last chapter, I follow the throng of possessed or split selves to discover the gathering host of doubles, doppelgängers, and alter egos who haunt fiction, not only in ghost and horror stories, but in the little-read late works of Lewis Carroll, *Sylvie and*

Bruno and its sequel, *Sylvie and Bruno Concluded,* written as the nine-teenth century was drawing to its close. The influence of imperial and colonial contacts still informs the thriving presence of doppel-gängers in psychology and in imaginative literature, especially in the work of Scottish authors and thinkers, and they interact with another, scientific episteme, the development of optical media of duplication and projection and their considerable and enduring impact on ideas of individual integrity. Through Lewis Carroll's photography, I follow the intertwining of optical developments with theories of bundles of selves in a single person; the possibili-ties of technical duplication converged with beliefs in shamanic displacement and bodily projection encountered in other worlds, and seemed to materialize them, to confirm them, to make them real. Science and magic converge in ways of thinking about shad-ows, ghosts, and out-of-body experiences, in a uniquely Victorian amalgam of spiritual quest and rationality.

The lecture hall makes possible a certain profligacy, with slides and asides (and the occasional attempt at a joke); for this published version, I have had to strip away many images, and repress some of the profusion. I have also rearranged the material, writing this introduction to set out the background to my explorings, and closing with some thoughts about contemporary writing and the direction that metamorphoses are now taking, in remarkable new mythologies being written, ostensibly for children, for example. The questions that metamorphosis raises in relation to the consis-tency of the self are as controversial as they were when Ovid was moralized for polite consumption; but in an era when individual agency is so highly prized, they have taken a different direction. The history of changes in the manifestations and meanings of metamorphic myths can throw some light on the phenomenon's continuing vitality, in the search for personal identity and the indestructible pleasure of making up—and reading—stories.

I

Mutating

RAMÓN PANÉ: *An Account of the Antiquities of the Indians*

I, brother Ramón, poor hermit of the order of St Jerome, by the order of our illustrious Lord Admiral, Viceroy and Governor of the islands and the mainland of the Indies, write what I have been able to learn and know of the belief and the idolatry of the Indians, and how they observe their gods . . .[1]

The act of witness that follows catches across a great gap of time some fragments of the creation myth and other tales of generation and metamorphosis that were told by the Taino, the indigenous people of the Caribbean archipelago at the moment of first encounter between the old and the newly discovered Mundo Otro, or Other World, as Columbus first called the Americas.[2]

Pané's account opens with a cosmological myth: the sea was made, he reports, when a certain man, called Giaia, killed his son, Giaiael, after the son had plotted against him, and placed his bones in a gourd and hung it from the roof of his house; one day, wanting to look at his son's remains, he opened the gourd and fishes came streaming from it. He and his wife were wondering whether to eat them or not when four brothers, born as identical quadruplets from the body of their dead mother, came upon the gourd and feasted their fill on the fish that had been Giaiael's bones. Hearing the boy's father approaching, they tried to put the gourd back, but spilled it: 'and so,' writes Pané, 'they hold that the sea came into being.'

This shifting sequence of stories features one of the quadruplet brothers, the founding hero of Taino culture, Deminan Caracaracol, and tells how houses were first built by him with his brothers after he was hit between his shoulder blades, and the wound swelled up till he could bear it no longer but begged to be released; they cut him open with a stone, rather like an oyster, and he gave birth to a live, female turtle.

In another part of *An Account of the Antiquities of the Indians*, another trickster type hero, Guahayona, manages to abduct all the wives of his brothers, abandon their children, and confine the women on an island. The children cry out, and are then all turned into 'tona'—a kind of toad.

So, in spite of frequent disgusted protests at the contents he is relaying, Pané does seem to have gathered some marvellous stories, which, though highly unusual in detail, are certainly reminiscent of classical myths and metamorphoses for receivers of his reports then (echoes of Saturn devouring his children, for example). They continue to tell of the adventures of Caracaracol and other heroes, and of fundamental aspects of creation: the sacralization of various places, objects, and practices; the division of the past into periods of time, the development of language, the establishment of dietary laws, the ranking of rulers and authorities, and, most significantly as we shall see, the coming of women.[3]

Fray Ramón Pané, this important early witness, hardly figures in the chronicles: he was an otherwise unknown Catalan friar, who was left behind by Christopher Columbus on the island of Hispaniola, which now comprises Haiti and the Dominican Republic, where the first Spanish settlement in the Americas—Isabella—was established.[4] Pané was probably deposited in the course of Columbus' second voyage, Columbus having ordered him to learn the languages of the local 'Indians' as he called the Taino, and 'investigate and set down in writing all that might further be learned about the rites and religion and antiquities of the peoples of this island'.[5] Uniquely Pané was not instructed primarily to talk, but to listen; though conversion was one of his aims, unusually it was not the prime burden of his mission.

Pané complied, not with very good grace, first in one province and one local language, then moving, still under orders, to another, more populous part of the island. He was relieved in 1498 and returned to Spain.[6] Columbus later prided himself that he 'took great pains to understand what they [Indians] believe and if they know where they go after they are dead'.[7] Ramón Pané was his agent; he was to inquire on his patron's behalf into ideas about gods, spirits, the afterlife, and magic. He complains, at rhythmic intervals, that he cannot make head or tail of what he is being told, and that this is not his fault, but the fault of these 'ignorant people', who cannot read or write and, because they do not have books, cannot even agree on the stories they tell him: he was coming across the plural, labile oral tradition.

His informants included above all the old people, 'especially the leaders . . . because they believe such fables more certainly than the others: in this respect, they, like the Moors, have their law redacted in ancient songs, by which they are governed, in the same way as the Moors use [their] scripture'.[8] In this aside, Pané lets us glimpse two premises that are crucial to our understanding of him now: he assumed that the myths were interrelated to the rule of law, and the governance of the society, and he therefore cast the Indians' stories as religious, rather than aesthetic or diverting. Consequently, from his clerical point of view, they became infidel, erroneous, mistaken. Second, he instinctively assumes similarity to the Moors, the bitter enemy within the newly unified Spanish Catholic state. Pané is writing just before the fall of Granada, but his account began to circulate in manuscript copies after his return in 1498, thus during and after the Catholic kings' determined crusade against Islam in Europe.

Much interference and distortion consequently inflects Fray Ramón Pané's tale telling, but his testimony to those momentous years of first exchanges is the first ethnographical document extant on the Americas. It is surprising how little it has been noticed and discussed, though perhaps this oversight offers an indication, 500 years on, of a certain heedlessness over the collision of different cultures and its consequences.

Pané's *Account of the Antiquities of the Indians*—less than thirty printed pages—has enjoyed an odd history. The original Spanish manuscript is lost, and it only survives as part of the biography of Christopher Columbus written by his son, Fernando, which was published for the first time in Venice, in 1571 (thirty-two years after Fernando's death in 1539 and sixty-five after Columbus' in 1506)— and then only in a clumsy Italian version.[9] But it is appropriate that the surviving version of the friar's first-hand witness should be a translation of a translation: Ramón Pané's account not only contains many stories of translation between worlds, between sexes, between cultures, but it also constitutes in itself a kind of forensic exhibit for the metamorphic encounter with the Americas. In his evident struggle to set down, without benefit of go-between, confusing stories in which characters shed names and change shapes, he keeps straying onto his own home ground, the Catholic faith. Towards the end, his tale swerves into a conversion narrative— another form of translation, between faiths—and incidents of a miraculous nature.

Although Ramón Pané's Indian stories of metamorphosis were not published independently when he wrote them, there was a lively interest in his descriptions and the manuscript was probably copied several times; furthermore, the biography of Columbus, in which it was embedded, left its mark on all the early historians of the New World.[10]

Among them was the Lombard-born humanist, soldier, ecclesiastic, and chronicler Pietro Martire d'Anghiera (1459–1526), official chronicler at the court of Ferdinand and Isabella, the Queen's chaplain, tutor to the royal children, and the overarching founding father of American historiography for his contemporaries and their successors. Peter Martyr de Angleria, as he is commonly called in English, drew on Pané's *Account* for the first volume of his influential book, *De Orbe Novo* (*Of the New World*).[11] His closeness to the Queen and to her double project of global conversion and imperial expansion can be felt in an anonymous sixteenth-century altarpiece, now in the Prado, *La Virgen de los reyes católicos*, in which the historian and courtier appears behind his queen and the royal children, in the guise of his namesake and patron saint, St Peter Martyr (d. 1252).[12]

From these intimate positions, the influence exercised by Peter Martyr, as he is called for short, was profound. He fought in the battles for Granada between 1492 and 1501, and acted as intermediary between Christendom and Islam during the ensuing period of triumphal hostilities and deep, righteous intolerance. Among the many high honours he was awarded by his masters, *los reyes católicos*, the Catholic kings, he was given the abbotship of the new parish of Jamaica. Though he never made the voyage there, he wrote of the New World with authority and passion and imagination and irony. But he remained entirely reliant on others' reports; in this he sets a precedent much honoured by chroniclers of the Americas.

Peter Martyr de Angleria's history of the first three Columbine voyages first appeared in a pirate edition in 1504 in Venice, and only later, in its full form, when it enjoyed a huge, international success, going through nineteen editions in seven languages besides Latin before 1563. The historian of early America, Kirkpatrick Sale comments, '[It] was for a long time the most important work on the New World . . . the centrepiece—sometimes lifted *in toto* . . . for other important books on America in the first half of the century'.[13] All the other significant early historians of this epoch also draw on the humble friar: Gonzalus Ferdinandus Oviedo (1535),[14] for example. Fray Bartholomé de Las Casas even spoke with Pané in person and then worked from his manuscript.[15] Las

Casas calls him 'simple and well-meaning'[16] and has kind words for Pané's efforts, but, like a weary schoolmaster, seems to feel he could have done better: 'He says some other things that are confused and of little substance, as a simple person . . . and therefore it is better not to relate these things'.[17] This disparagement of Pané reflects a certain anxiety of influence, since Las Casas himself goes on to draw on his account *in extenso*—and so a certain ashamed dependence may lie behind the inexplicable neglect surrounding Pané's unique, rich material. Samuel Purchas, *His Pilgrims*, gathered these historical sources together for the English reading audience. And here we begin to enter more familiar terrain for us, as anyone who has read *The Tempest* in any annotated edition will know, because Shakespeare used Richard Eden's translation of Peter Martyr, published in 1555, and echoes from this version resonate strongly in the play—sometimes verbatim—in ways that are deeply interfused with its poetic themes of magic, trance, and transformation.[18]

Numerous variations on metamorphosis occur—frequently—inside the stories the 'poor hermit' sets down, and in the process of writing, impatiently, less than coherently, leaving rather a lot to be desired by the standards of vivid storytelling or literary craft, the collector, listener, interpreter acts as the agent of the forces of change of another sort. But, as set out in the last chapter, metamorphosis did not only travel in one direction: however much Fray Ramón Pané declares his disgust and scorn for the myths he is struggling to take down, his writing begins to fall under 'the positive shadow' cast by their subjects. His 'Indians' and in turn his vision inflects the vision of metamorphosis at the beginning of the sixteenth century.

At the same time as Peter Martyr was gathering material for his chronicle of the first decades of cross-cultural encounter in North America, and dwelling on the bipolar fantasies of cannibal terror and earthly paradise, Hieronymus Bosch was painting the triptych known as *The Garden of Earthly Delights*; it is dated to around 1504; it strikingly displays a cornucopia of metamorphoses that may owe their originality to the cross-fertilization of Old World and New World mythologies. As Joseph Koerner has convincingly shown, 'Europe's unexpected encounter with America made surprises more expectable.' The New World was not only a zone of discovery, but also of fantasy: it offered extraordinary possibilities for *thinking differently*. With this in mind, it is rewarding, even exciting, to look more closely at the remarkable collection of native myths first circulating in the years that Bosch was painting *The Garden of Earthly Delights*; it gives a way of revisiting the myth of the Golden Age and the picture's particular envisioning of it, in the earliest reports on the inhabitants of the Caribbean.[19]

However, before I return to look at the painting closely, I shall look at the principal cultural filters through which the Taino myths were sieved by their early recipients—Dante's *Inferno*, or *Hell*, and Ovid's great poem in fifteen books, *The Metamorphoses*, in its medieval revisions—and describe their treatment of transformations. For Fray Ramón's way of listening in—his way of reading—fantastic stories, myths, and metamorphoses can be taken most profitably in conjunction with the prevailing didactic approach to reading pagan and Christian myths of metamorphoses, as relayed by the most vivid, spirited, compelling writers of poetic myths.

DANTE: INFERNAL METAMORPHOSES

The scandalous behaviour of the deathless but nevertheless superseded gods cast a long shadow on the Christian iconography of good and bad behaviour; their protean energies of transformation and sexuality were translated into hellish imagery. In medieval eschatology, metamorphosis by almost any process belongs to the devil's party; devils, and their servants, witches, are monstrously hybrid themselves in form, and control magic processes of mutation. Within the Judaeo-Christian tradition, metamorphosis has marked out heterodoxy, instability, perversity, unseemliness, monstrosity. As a philosophical and literary trope, as a theological principle, as cosmic and biological explanation, it distinguishes good from evil, the blessed from the heathen and the damned: in the Christian heaven, nothing changes, whereas in hell, everything combines and recombines in terrible amalgams, compounds, breeding hybrids, monsters—and mutants.

In the *Inferno*, Dante envisions for the damned highly inventive and fantastical processes by which the sinners are condemned to lose identity in an eternal cycle of annihilation; in the Eighth Circle of the Malebolge, deep in the pit of hell, liars, pimps, seducers, and flatterers are ceaselessly tormented by change. Later, in Cantos XXIV–XXV, Dante consciously sets about surpassing Ovid's descriptive powers, in order to realize, in word pictures, a 'novità' in the literary tradition of 'mutare e transmutare.'[20] In the circle of the thieves, Dante describes how a snake fastens on a sinner, intertwines his multiple limbs about him, and mingles so deeply with his being that his prey ceases to be an entity at all but merges into an 'imagine perversa' (a perverse image).[21] The sinners exclaim at the sight of the awesome beast with two heads, one at each end of its body, in defiance of due order and nature:

> . . . e ciascuno
> gridava: 'Ohmè, Agnel, come ti muti!
> Vedi che già non se' nè due nè uno.'

(. . . and each one cried out, 'Oh my, how you change! See how you're already neither two [beings] nor one!')[22]

Then Dante openly sets out to surpass his inspiration:

> Taccia di Cadmo et d'Aretusa Ovidio;
>   chè se quello in serpente e quella in fonte
>   converte poetando, io non lo 'nvidio;
> chè due nature mai a fronte a fronte
>   non trasmutò sì ch'amendue le forme
>   a cambiar lor matera fosser pronte.

(Ovid can hold his tongue about Cadmus and Arethusa; if in his poetry he turned one into a snake and the other into a fountain, I feel no envy; for he never transmuted two natures confronted one by the other so that both their forms were ready to exchange their matter.)[23]

In practice, in this very passage, Dante borrows from the celebrated sexual dynamics of Salmacis and Hermaphroditus as they fuse in Book IV of *Metamorphoses*.[24] But whereas Ovid dramatizes the generation of a new being through Salmacis' ardour, and dwells on her total incorporation of her love object, instituting metamorphosis as the origin of the marvellous phenomena nature gives birth to, Dante stages an inverted transubstantiation, making the claim that, in the afterlife of the damned, morphing utterly reduces identity and integrity.

As Satan is the monstrous ape of God, so hellishness can be expressed by a horrific, parodic inversion of good things, of the Christian tropes of resurrection, eternity, vitality, nourishment. The language that conceptualized *maleficium* or witchcraft in early modern thought came into being within a structure of paired 'contrareities', or polarities, which systematically apportioned value against one side in favour of another, often its inverted double.[25] The deadly commingling of the sinners in Dante's hell not only embodies a perversion of natural, sexual congress, but also blasphemes against ideals of human union with God's nature by taking it to extremes: the punished lose their natures as their matter is changed, exchanged, transmuted. This protracted story of dissolution obliterates personhood to degree zero, a point never reached or even contemplated by the Pythagorean credo, which holds that 'nothing dies' and somehow Daphne lives on in the laurel tree. 'Dante employs metamorphosis', comments Caroline Walker Bynum, 'where no traces [of identity] endure in a way that shows us the impossibility of identity perduring (in any logical sense) without the survival of vestiges of body or "shape"'.[26]

Dante's ingenious scheme of torments in *Inferno* culminates in the most natural, fundamental metabolic process of all: digestion. Consumption wholly occupies Satan in the frozen pit of hell, where Dante finds him, ceaselessly devouring traitors; the self here is annihilated by passing through the devil's guts to be excreted through his anus: a natural process of transformation conceived as the ultimate eschatological penalty.

Dante's fertility of imagination provided artists of the afterlife with a wonderfully graphic range of metamorphic punishments; Sandro Botticelli's concentrated meditation on Dante's poem takes the ferocious tortures of the thieves stage by stage, almost like an animator drawing a sequence of cels today; the sinner's tormentors are themselves diabolical in their hybridity and heterogeneity of limb and feature: a centaur who erupts onto the page, an explosion of furious tails and crests and horns and hair, or a shaggy lion-headed devil with a bat's wings, a unicorn tusk, fangs, multiple dugs, the long tongue of a lizard, scales, webbed or horned paws, and, finally, hairy pendulous scrotum and a huge curved penis like a horn.[27]

Furthermore, the curls and spirals and twists and turns of the sepia lines manage remarkably to communicate the kinetic energy of mutation processes even in the stilled and motionless medium of drawing. Here, metamorphosis of one kind or another signifies perdition.

The grotesqueness of Botticelli's *Drawings to Dante*, shown in 2001 at the Royal Academy, London, astonished many viewers who are more familiar with his Madonnas and his *poesie*, the harmonious, Neoplatonist visions of *The Birth of Venus* and the *Primavera*; he began the sequence around 1480 and finished it around twenty years later, when Hieronymus Bosch's analogous vision of devils, enfleshed in several apocalyptic paintings, crystallized the growing affinities between somatic, indeed visceral transmutation, eternal damnation, and the terminal, but ever repeated agony of losing the self.[28] Botticelli's drawings for *The Divine Comedy* can be usefully brought in as context for Bosch's phantasmagoria. The major work on the series was done around 1494–5, that is around a decade before *The Garden of Earthly Delights* (Figs. 10 and 11).

These hellish, Christian twists on Ovidian metamorphosis provide, first, the brooding metaphysical context within which Ramón Pané's account of the Indians' cosmic mythology was received, and second, an indication of later conflicts over the portrayal of change in human personality. In Catholic doctrine, transubstantiation involves a transformation of substance, but not appearance: bread and wine changes miraculously into the body and blood of Christ. In pagan metamorphosis, species—outward appearances—are all changed, but the inner spirit remains the same: it inverts the wonder, profanely. Furthermore, in opposition to Ovid and to the Pythagorean view of change, the irreducibility of the person forms the core of soul; when one becomes two and two one, as in the obscene clutches of Dante's thieves, this constitutes a vision of diabolical untruth, a *détournement* of order.

OVID MORALIZED: DISFIGUREMENTS
OF THE SPIRIT

Because metamorphosis expressed a profound and contrary position, and because Ovid's poem is filled with erotic, violent, even lurid stories evoked with consummate sophistication, a way had to be found to make reading Ovid permissible for good Christians, if he was to be read at all and his stories to continue to live. Metamorphosis and its premises, the migration of souls, remained stubborn obstacles, alluring and forbidding at once, but it is a tribute to human ingenuity that Ovid's material did find a way of surviving. Ovid's moral sense does not direct the reader; indeed he often seems remarkably indifferent to responsibilities and judgement; didacticism is utterly alien to him. However, through his profoundly ironical fatalism, he frequently appears to be enjoying

Fig. 10 In the pit of hell, the thieves fuse with diabolical snakes in a hideous, continual sequence of comminglings: losing their identity is their eternal punishment. Sandro Botticelli, Dante's *Inferno*, Canto XXV.

Fig. 11 Hybrid, exaggerated bestial and sexual features—horns, bat's wings, hooves, tails—characterize medieval devils, here marshalled by their leader Barbariccia to push sinners back into the boiling pitch of hell. Sandro Botticelli, Dante's *Inferno*, Canto XXII.

unmasking divine cruelty, caprices, and revenges, and he engages mordantly with human capacities for wickedness, for rape, incest, murder. So it proved not impossible to twist him into Christian shape, by using the kind of sophistry at the schoolmen's command. The *Moralized Ovid* was a curious medieval effort: a laboured paraphrase in jigging couplets of Ovid's great poem. First composed in the early fourteenth century, around the same time as Dante's *Divine Comedy*, it is one of the earliest vernacular mutations of the *Metamorphoses*, and it probes the poem for hidden, moral, Christian meanings.[29] Many imitators of this approach followed suit, and these mutants enjoyed inexplicable success in the eyes of contemporary readers, since they turn the poem all to dust—Ovid's brilliant supple verse, vital imagery, narrative energy, dramatic tempos and irony, all are reduced to prolix, incoherent sermonizing. Adding strained, lengthy glosses in columns running alongside and below the poem became a subterfuge to evade disapproval, even censorship: it extended to the pagan poem the devices of biblical scholars, who disinfected the Song of Songs by allegorical deviousness. The scholars managed to give Ovid's abundant, sexy cornucopia of stories a lofty moral tone.

Such a text was sumptuously and even wittily illustrated for a folio edition, known as *La Bible des poètes*, published in Paris by Antoine Verard before 1500; the British Library has two splendid copies of this publication, one of those incunabula that look just like a Gothic manuscript.[30] As late as the seventeenth century, Karel van Mander, the highly influential author of the *Schilder-boeck*, excused the pagan poet his lubricious matter, by casting him as an apostle of reason to combat lust. Transformation itself, he asserts, constitutes an 'external disfigurement of the spirit' to which Ovid draws attention.[31] The tradition persisted: the celebrated edition first published in Oxford in 1632, translated by George Sandys, with plates at the start of each Book, includes pages of introductory matter citing authorities in defence of Ovid (Fig. 7).[32]

Nobody reads these versions today. But their existence reveals how in the Christian context, metamorphosis exercised a fascination that could only be disciplined and contained by conscientious and elaborate didacticism. Some explanations came easily: transformations, such as Arachne into a spider, read as fitting, divine retribution for sin. Dante and Virgil find 'poor mad Arachne' on the terrace of the Proud, in purgatory, a proper fate for overambitious females (Fig. 3).[33] Lycaon, who served up a cannibal feast to Zeus, and so became the first werewolf, excites a spontaneous, compassionate outburst in one commentator: Lycaon foreshadows 'all avaricious persons, bailiffs, prefects, usurers, robbers and all merchants who over the course of time are all harmful to poor people'.[34]

At other times, the 'sens moral' is a little more ingenious: for example, after the Flood, when Deucalion and Pyrrha create a new generation of humans by tossing stones over their shoulders which spring up into life, a gloss informs us that just as Jesus Christ turns sinners into good men, so the rocks were softened by contrition to be born anew (Fig. 1). Of Picus' transmogrification into a magpie, the author suggests, 'this bird . . . has a hard beak and a long tongue so that it can thrust it among ants and . . . swallow them by drawing it in . . . So let us say that this Circe, full of poison, signifies the devil or the sin of lust . . . and so he [Picus] is turned into a bird, that is to say light and destitute of reason and discretion because the poisonous enchantments of Circe are to be fled and carefully avoided.' (Pl. IV)[35] In Venice, in 1676, the commentator managed to interpret the passionate embraces by which the nymph Salmacis fuses into her love object, Hermaphroditus, into a type of divine grace working on the soul (no Dantesque use of union as a metaphor for sin).[36]

However, commenting on the last book of Ovid's poem, one author cannot help betray a certain longing to accommodate Ovid within the fold of Christian precursors, yet he cannot quite achieve it: 'it is a matter worth marvelling at that a pagan should have . . . already sensed that the soul is immortal, as it is, but not movable in the way he held. . . .' The writer tails off worriedly, 'His sayings are very special and filled with great mystery . . . all things in this world are vanity and lie under vanity and that there is nothing that is stable.'[37]

The trouble that wrapped metamorphosis, inspiring Dante to describe heavy penalties in its terms, and driving Ovidian commentators and translators to wriggle out of its manifest heterodoxy, develops into apocalyptic vision in the great triptych of Hieronymus Bosch, a painting which dazzlingly condenses the themes I am tackling in this book. The picture dramatizes numerous transformations as it confronts dissenting and different ideas about the world, about people and persons, about good and evil, which were beginning to circulate through sources such as Ramón Pané's *Account*.

THE LOST GOLDEN AGE: HIERONYMUS BOSCH

Standing in front of *The Garden of Earthly Delights* in the Prado one day last spring, I heard numerous tour guides drawing their group's attention to Hieronymus Bosch's fantastic triptych (Pl. I). As they drifted by, the word 'moralizing' echoed again and again, in variants from several languages around the world. *Moralizante, moralizad, moral*. Pointing to a man with a flower peeping out of his bottom, 'Look, sodomy,' said one guide, confidently. This seems to be the consensus: as the wall label says, 'the message it [the painting] transmits is that of the frailty and ephemeral character of sinful pleasures'. I will try and look here at the language and imagery of those sins, those earthly delights and pleasures, to see if the transformations Bosch limns in this compelling and inexhaustible work can allow glimpses of deeper transformations taking place on earth, in the society of his day—above all, the revelation of an Other World, one that offered startling challenges to ideas of identity and psychological continuity.

The extraordinary metamorphic energy and inventiveness of the artist and the persistent enigma of his unforgettable fantasies have all combined over the last hundred years to inspire some notable interpretations, linguistic, astrological, theological, and alchemical. Different, brilliant, exegetical approaches include Dirk Bax's detailed correlation of Bosch's imagery to Dutch puns and proverbs (1949), Wilhelm Fraenger's millenarian analysis (relating the painting's story and images to the thought of the Brethren of the Common Life, who were active in Bosch's native town), Laurinda Dixon's detailed study of Bosch's alchemical imagery, and Michel de Certeau's scrupulous meditation on meaninglessness as significant in itself.[38]

Bosch is dangerous territory: many a brave seeker has lost the path and disappeared. Nevertheless, I am still going to suggest another story behind the idiosyncratic mutations and conjunctions, the unexpected population and pleasures of the *Garden of Earthly Delights*. Far from being split by the irrational and wayward operations of fantasy they could be firmly spliced within a historical and cultural set of events.

The feasting and play in the painting involves above all weird acts with fruit: this is a vegetarian party, even a fruitarians' bacchanal, without wine or other liquor, an orgy that is oddly unfleshed and ethereal, involving neither roasted meats nor any kind of flesh at all, but only berries, cherries, strawberries, blackberries, flowers, and sloes (Fig. 12). Several of the naked throng are feasting on giant strawberries, a group of bathers is grazing in a circle at a blackberry; another giant fruit of the same kind appears near the foreground (Fig. 13). Round red cherry-like fruits are scattered throughout the scene: sometimes worn as hats, as on the head of a slender black maiden in the left foreground, and sometimes bursting open, showing a bird perched inside, as between the legs of the

Fig. 12 The spontaneous bounty of nature: dwellers in the earthly paradise play among several varieties of giant fruits, wearing them, crawling inside them, and feasting on them: no meat-eating or cooking is taking place here.

Fig. 13 Berries, which are not harvested but grow wild, dominate the pleasures freely available, as they do in the classical dream of the Golden Age, when humans did not plough or labour or ever fall ill or grow old.

upside-down figure in the pond on the left. There are scarce signs of any other sources of nourishment. A fish or two is being carried and patted, but none is being cooked or eaten. A group on the right-hand edge towards the top have caught some kind of reptile and are holding it aloft on a staff, while, high in the sky on the left, another reptile dangles from the talons of a winged hybrid, half bluebird, half lion or stag, that is flying through the air. But if hunting is going on, the hunters are principally pursuing bright red currant-like orbs, cherries, and other fruits as their quarry: several figures are holding up these vivid spoils in triumph.

Another cluster of people, on the farthest shore, sits under and around a gigantic strawberry, surely the largest fruit of all in a painting that features numerous fruit of gargantuan dimensions. That is, the fruits are colossal, if the creatures besporting themselves are taken to be human size and not miniature sprites or elves. The dislocations of scale, which estrange the scene depicted, could belong in a fairyland, where the birds are bird sized, but the inhabitants are small.[39] We shall see that in some stories disseminated at the time, people rather than fairies are indeed born from flowers and fruits.

Some of the mysterious frolickers are twisted in odd, antic positions: these fantastical groupings give the scene its character as a Boschian drollery, since they could not be performed in this world by ordinary human beings: huddles of figures upside down, partying scrimmages under a shell, or a bird, or a fruit, joyous capers and cavorting (Pl. II). There is comedy, but no violence; acrobatics and exhibitionism, but no combat. Besides, these displays are often taking place in the distance, while the foreground figures are less riotous.

The whole scene is restless, and syncopated, though, with the central cavalcade of fabulous beasts and riders whirling widdershins in the background, against a turbulent scurrying of different clusters of bathers, more riders, long arc-tailed mer-folk, and boating couples. From the water, a swarm of naked figures is streaming *into* a cracked egg, reversing the natural course of hatching. Bosch's decorative fancy piles pinnacle on rock, pierces pillars of coral with crystal tubes, crowns a spur of pink with a curling tendril like the whisker of a prawn, or with a perched, dancing figure. His drolleries move to a spiky, jagged rhythm, the scatter of vignettes pulling the viewer here and there, harum-scarum, as the eyes scan the profusion of data, trying to find a pattern, a meaning. As Certeau has described: 'This painting plays on our need to decipher. It enlists in its service a Western drive to *read*.'[40]

Many groups in the painting are whirling round: the very phrase that signifies bafflement, perturbation, delirium, dizziness, and loss of reason; they are huddled in circles or riding a carousel, as if taking part in roundelays or choruses, or even games that involve packs or scrums; the foreground includes six large globes or spheres of different materials, one enclosing a pair of lovers in a veined bubble, dusted by a gorgeous, ornate thistle-like flower; a bell jar shelters one trio, another similar translucent glass cover or cloche tops the elaborate pavilion on the right, and the painting features, besides the central floating orb in the lake in the background and the spiked, spherical rock on the right, several other vessels of a globular shape—suggestions of alembics and flasks. A blue porcupine blooms inside a transparent bubble, held like a child's balloon by one of the riders in the cavalcade; many calyxes and seed pods, flower heads, buds, and berries extend this internal system of globular pattern and order and repeat. Hatching shells, spilling fruits, and split drupes, all reveal richly coloured roes (Pl. III).[41]

Some of the ovules are hard, spiny, and delicate as sea creatures, coralline and crustacean; others invoke the shells of bird eggs directly. But it is only on the left-hand wing, among the prelapsarian creatures in Eden, that nature is spawning (Fig. 14). Eggs are associated here with lizards and newts from nature and dragons from legend, while in the background, a flock of crow-like birds enter another shell-cavity (Fig. 15). It is in Eden also that a kill or two is taking place, for a lion has seized a deer in the background, a

Fig. 14 In the Garden of Eden, God presents the newly born Eve to Adam joining them in the first marriage; but there are hints of trouble to come, including the Dragon Palm on the left, a tree which, according to legend, drips blood.

Fig. 15 From the pond in Eden, monsters are hatching, announcing the devil's work of perversion and falsity.

cat has caught a mouse in the foreground, and in the distance, a boar is threatening a stoat. Still, it is surprising that Bosch introduces these scenes into the garden of Eden, and ominously depicts monsters dwelling there: a hacksaw-beaked bird with a frog dangling, and no less than two tricephalous birds—this kind of freak a sign of discord and *diablerie*, looking forward to the forked tongue and double dealing of the devil, and thence to the Fall.

The spheres, the floating orbs, the globular matrix enclose the whole conception of the picture, in the floating world painted on the outside shutters, where the disc of the earth's surface, seen in perspective inside the liquid jelly sac of the globe itself, bears certain husks and pods that have apparently yielded their contents, as well as one floating eggshell-like container, sprouting a stalk and berry. The chain of images that in Bosch's visual vocabulary links shells and pods and spawn to the planetary orb also leads to the orb of the eye and the symbol of the all-seeing One. Joseph Koerner has argued eloquently and lucidly that Bosch's paintings use the

Fig. 16 At the centre of a harsh, moralizing painting of the Seven Deadly Sins, attributed to Bosch, Christ the Redeemer appears in the pupil of God's all-seeing eye, a promise of salvation from the consequences of divine omniscience.

roundel as a compositional device to reverse the angle of view: in *The Seven Deadly Sins*, an eye with a huge central iris, and the inscription 'Cave cave deus videt', is looking out at the spectator, who is caught in the ambit of its gaze, as if discovered among scenes illustrating wrongdoing (Fig. 16).[42] Similarly, the closed outer shutters of the *Garden of Earthly Delights* form a huge floating eyeball, staring at us, and placing us in an outsider's vantage, enjoying something like the Olympian, total view of the Creator who appears so tiny up on the left-hand side (Fig. 17). The visual rhyme— orb/world/eye—invites us to partake in its angle of view, to use it as an instrument, so that when the wings open to the spectacle of other worlds inside it is as if they were revealed by a magnifying lens, as were in use by jewellers and gem cutters and lens grinders in the Netherlands.

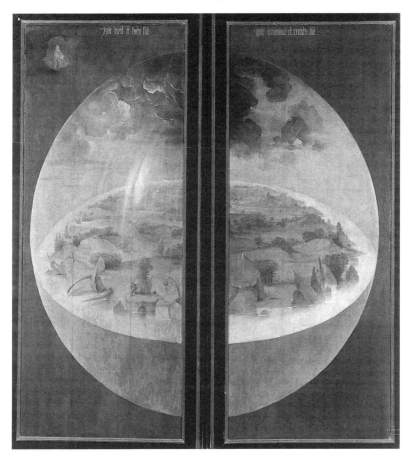

Fig. 17 The closed outer wings of the triptych show the world in mid-creation as a monochrome, floating sphere of light and darkness, land and waters, like a huge eyeball.

The relative perspectives of macrocosm to the central revelatory microcosm require only a slight step backwards for the two ellipses to conform—the disc of the earth's surface on the third day, after the separation of light from dark and land from sea, is reprised in little by the central pool and meadow of the centrepiece. This *enfilade* of circles and apertures contributes forcefully to the effect of Bosch's continual play with exits and entrances. The circular bathing pool lies just above the centre, while above that, through the round aperture in the side of the orb, a mooning bottom can be seen to one side of a couple embracing. These openings proceed along a string which suggests to the viewer that inside every pavilion, every vessel, every shell or gall or berry something more is happening. The *Garden* is crammed with emergent and submerged figures, who keep their secrets. It is dark on the outside looking in (this is medieval cinema)—this primordial, monochrome, uninhabited universe must be so rendered to suggest the colourless lack of vitality before the coming of people. Inside, a riot of pinks, azures, ivory white, and pale greens vivify the throng of revellers.

The meaning of the central panel develops however in relation to the wings; it is a mistake to overlook the oppositions which Bosch articulates. On the right inside wing, Bosch contrived more *cadavres exquis* from the template of an ovoid shape or a pierced ball: the dominant 'tree man' in hell on the right wing, with his haunting, phantom-white, egg-like exoskeleton; while on the left nearer the foreground, a bird-headed devil is defecating a globule of blue tissue like the amniotic sac or the soft-skinned egg of a snake, in which figures of the damned are being recycled (Fig. 18).

On this right wing, the usual infernal permutations of devouring, regurgitating, excreting, which serve to dramatize so horrifyingly the punishment of sinners in apocalyptic literature, from the early Christian apocrypha through to Dante's *Inferno*, are elaborated by Bosch with his unsurpassed originality and fantasy. Not till Kafka's terrifying short story 'In the Penal Colony' has anyone imagined torment with such dark and subtle and ghastly comic ingenuity. Again violence done to one body by another keeps the artist's imagination busy, and he shows the damned being burned, cut up, butchered, disembowelled, cooked, ingested, as well as frozen in a kind of diabolical kitchen. At least three colossal carving knives appear in the painting, and numerous other spikes and

Fig. 18 The tree man, a phantom giant with an egg-like torso, looms over the horrors and torments of the damned: a hell's kitchen, where the dead are carved up, roasted, devoured, regurgitated, and even defecated by devils (Bosch, Hell, right inside wing).

prods and prongs and nails and spears: this is an age when metal has certainly been invented and harnessed for war and punishment, as in the legendary Age of Silver that followed the lost Golden Age.

Yet it would be a mistake to let the characteristic grotesques of Bosch's hell seep into the ways of looking at the rest of him; however, because some of his most celebrated and dazzling compositions include several paintings of *The Temptation of St Anthony*, in which he uses his imagination to produce monsters, Bosch's eloquence in communicating pleasure—blissful, paradisal, serene festivity—has been sidelined. It is moreover difficult to look at Bosch without looking through the long telescope of time in which his grilli-type demons, his fantastic conjugations of heterogeneous parts and limbs, have spawned the common denizens of Sabbaths and other scenes of pandemonium in the works of his imitators, Bruegel above all, who deliberately adopt ugliness and deformity to represent folly and sin.

Followers, admirers, epigones reduce the characteristics of the originator as in a stockpot, and produce a stronger flavour than the original; indeed, Bosch himself can be less Bosch-like perhaps than his reputation claims, or his followers have conveyed, at least with regard to the *Garden of Earthly Delights*, for in the central panel the only preternatural creatures and peculiar hybrids seem rather more light-hearted than condemnatory, such as the famous jigging couple, wound with briars, who have hidden their heads in a pink eggshell with an owl impassively staring from the top (Frontispiece), or the blue-bottomed threesome in the background whose legs are peeping from a shrimp-like shell born on the backs of some of the other nudists.

Above all, however, there is a major difference between *The Garden of Earthly Delights* and other moralized representations of sin, spiritual death, and damnation that communicated, in Bosch's footsteps, the working of evil through a repertory of physical freakishness. The nudes Bosch paints in the *Garden* are not hideously aged, bloated, disfigured; they don't have exaggerated sexual characteristics. This differs profoundly from the conventions of representation that obtained when concupiscence was at issue. Botticelli's drawings for *The Divine Comedy*, with their monstrous devils, can be usefully brought in as comparisons (Bosch is unlikely to have seen them, but he might conceivably have seen Baccio Bandini's suite of prints after the illustrations to the first books of the *Inferno* (1481–7).)[43] Botticelli shows the sodomites for example with dumpy limbs, fat bellies, bald heads, heavy, withered dugs, and other marks of human ageing.[44] It is not a difference in degrees of skill that distinguishes the characterization of Bosch's carnival crowd from Botticelli's sufferers, but a difference of context and of significance. It may be surprising that Botticelli's grimacing devils anticipate Bosch's hellish tormentors, but this affinity between them reveals that in the central panel of *The Garden of Earthly Delights* Bosch is representing another world besides the grotesque world of lust and damnation.

In the painting of *The Seven Deadly Sins*, attributed to Bosch, the lustful are being assailed by demons crawling onto and into their bed, while a woman in the centre of the picture has a toad-like monster clamped to her sex, according to the medieval tradition. By contrast to this punitive monstrosity, Bosch's Adam and Eve, at the moment of their union on the left wing, in all naked purity and innocence, are depicted with the same Gothic lineaments and glabrous pallor as most of the throng of couples in the centre panel of the *Garden of Earthly Delights*. Approximately the same age, size, weight, body type (black and white figures alike), they all seem to be blessed with the kind of physical well-being and equilibrium of the blessed; indeed they share the same physique as the just rising from their graves to be gathered up to heaven, in Bosch's imagery of the Last Judgement. Uniform, slender, asexual nakedness stands in for a state of disincarnate, ethereal timelessness, and is used to characterize the souls of the dead in medieval iconography; the tradition edges the cast of hundreds in the *Garden* out of time into an imaginary dimension (Pl. I).[45] But does this time lie in the future, like the resurrection of the dead? Or in the past? When we follow the gaze of the huge floating eye on the outer wings into the vision, are we travelling beyond the bounds of time-space into a kind of dream nowhere, a heterotopia, a zone of dreams? This Other World, this playground of these Others, where does it lie?

And are these couples, these groups lovers? Are they to be wedded, like Adam and Eve? If they are, what is the character of their embraces? They are undressed, of course, and it is consequently assumed that all their activities are somehow all involved with voluptuous sins of one kind or another, and the antinomian tenets of milleniarists have been discussed to explain their congress. They show no shame at their state, do not cover their genitals or pose provocatively, beckoning attention to their beauty as young witches do in Bosch's paintings of the period.

There are several pairs of lovers in the picture: most notably the pair enclosed in the bubble, floating on the water near the foreground on the left and dusted by the gorgeous stamen-rich flower head. The man in another pairing, in the bathing pool near the flock of birds, is looking back out of the frame, as he pushes the woman in a kind of tango motion (Pl. II). His is one of several faces who look out of the painting to interpellate the viewer; the device recurs in Bosch's compositions, sometimes complicitly, sometimes warningly. In this way, Bosch effectively compresses the distance in time and space, which separates us, the viewers, from the represented events, and pulls the scene into the here and now where we are standing in contemplation. Eyeing the onlooker, the painter also looks at himself in the mirror of the work. This kind of suggestive self-portraiture would seem to inspire the features of another man in the *Garden*, in the lower right-hand side of the centrepiece, who is also glancing out, and pointing to a woman beside him in the pit—he is one of the very few clothed characters in the composition (though it might be that he is a wild man, with a hairy pelt)

(Pl. III). If he is indeed wearing a poor hermit's habit, as it would appear, then Bosch might be making an important connection, to which I shall come later.

As to the presence of sexual play: there are four legs waving from the mussel shell, and, in the central orb, in the deep background, love-making does seem to be taking place, and one or two of the women have the rounded abdomens so admired in the nude of International Gothic, which might indicate pregnancy: for example, the indigo-blue-black woman sitting with a man on the drake's back under the kingfisher, on the left. But otherwise the scene does not reveal an orgy of sexual embraces and union going on—rather an orgy of eating, of tasting, picking, sucking, munching, as well as hiding in, riding on, playing with, dressing up in—flora, fauna, and fruit.

The metaphorical reverberations of flowers and fruit can be sexual, of course. The role of forbidden fruit in the Fall and temptation lies at the centre of the Christian story. Their presence conjures pleasure, striking notes of feasting and merry-making, and here, the painting of berries erupting from between a man's legs, or a blue jay feeding berries to an eager, greedy group of upturned faces, or, in the foreground, a duck popping another little red berry like a sweet into the mouth of a man sitting inside a kind of Fabergé egg, all hint at subtle, deviant, erotic connoisseurship. But taken alongside the carnivorous assaults and even cannibal gorging that is going on in both Eden and Hell on the wings, this courtly picnicking does communicate a mood rather different from sinful lust.

The semantic substitutions between sex and food, sin and death that govern the language of Christian eschatology shift into another order of equivalences in Bosch's imagery and give a different moral charge: the exchanges between the sexes take place according to vegetable, not animal procedures: these beings are being fertilized and then germinating—like plants.

The fruits that the orgiasts are sampling are seeds, or clusters of seeds: in the case of strawberries, they bear achenes, or small hard pips on their exteriors. Several pods are bursting and spilling seed; the largest husks and galls are hatching people, and some pupa-like casings in the foreground are splitting open, as if human beings belonged to a natural non-sexual food chain involving birds, insects, and fruits, not animal husbandry or even pastoralism. The cracks and fissures suggest penetration, and birds are fertilizing the plants, in the same way as they pollinate and cross-fertilize plants in their own search for food. At very nearly the dead centre of the picture a butterfly is drinking nectar from a thistle—and of course gathering pollen by the way. However, the role of birds and insects in the propagation of plants was not fully understood till much later—so it would be anachronistic to see fully understood representation of natural reproduction, although Bosch, a most delicate and accurate observer, might well be picturing more than he knew.

According to the classic Lévi-Straussian polarity, this scene of natural abundance precedes cooking, and excludes meat—raw or cooked. We are participating as spectators at a pre-sacrificial banquet, both with regard to nourishment and to ritual. The few flesh eaters that do appear include the owls, crows, and the kingfisher among the delightful parliament of fowl on the left, but in spite of this inconsistency, *The Garden of Earthly Delights* predominantly portrays other forms of reproduction and nourishment besides copulation and ingestion, and their extreme, analogous permutations, sodomy and cannibalism. You may object that Bosch in his time could not have been more explicit in his depictions of sex than this, and the scene simply offers highly original substitutions. But I would counter this by arguing that the different choices he makes in these substitutions point in another direction. Generation, growth, metamorphosis are taking place according to laws imagined to obtain elsewhere.

Laurinda Dixon has demonstrated with acuity and profound learning how many of Bosch's images are modelled, even copied, from illustrations in medieval alchemical manuscripts. She makes a very powerful case for the iconographic debt, and argues

eloquently that the activities of the dwellers in the *Garden* dramatize
an early stage of commingling in the alchemical process, known as
'child's play', by which means adepts sought to recover the secret of
immortal life lost through the Fall.[46] However, the organic energies
that seem to bring about transformation and abundance in the
Garden—cross-pollination, ovulation, hatching—do not tally with
the elaborate chemical processes of transformation—distilling,
combusting, and condensing—that the work of alchemy pre-
scribes. Nor does the efflorescence—the 'vegetable love'—which
the painting limns correspond to the *putrefactio, decoctio,* and *exaltatio*
of the alchemical stages. Alchemy concentrates above all on the
transmutation of metals, not in evidence at all in Bosch—no fires,
no smelting or calcinating or refining or crystallizing moves the
action in the *Garden.* There are no metal tools or weapons or jewels.
The processes of metamorphosis that are under way belong in
nature's autonomous ecology, not to human scientific intervention;
they cannot be fitted into a sacrificial economy, unlike the depiction of hell on the right. No ashes, no waste, no residue remains:
the gyre turns on itself, in accordance with the Pythagorean concept of cyclical generation. Nothing dies.

The artist also puts the imagery to work towards another moral
significance. This harmony and equilibrium, this variety of self-
generating, spontaneous metamorphosis, rather than human copulation and birthing, are among the mythic qualities of a primordial
time of bliss and innocence imagined in mythologies the world
over. The participants are not working towards a forfeited state
of perfection, but their practices and the landscape they dwell in
embody it.

Ernst Gombrich pointed out the affinity of Bosch's vision
to classical evocations of the Golden Age, found in Hesiod and
then, insistently, in Ovid; this dream was much repeated and
reworked in medieval literature and thought.[47] For example, the
philosopher Eriugena's vision of the earthly paradise in the twelfth
century imagines 'a nature beyond sexual partition or division'—

reproducing without differentiation.[48] He was expanding on an ancient poetic vision: Hesiod writes that in the Golden Age,

> all good things
> Were theirs [humanity's]; ungrudgingly, the fertile land
> Gave up her fruits unasked.[49]

Vegetarianism is one of the salient qualities of this lost time, of its natural foison and abundance, its innocence and its justice. As Ovid puts on the lips of the sage Pythagoras:

> 'At vetus illa aetas, cui fecimus aurea nomen,
> fetibus arboreis et, quas humus educat, herbis
> fortunata fuit nec polluit ora cruore.
> tunc et aves tutae movere per aera pennas,
> et lepus inpavibus mediis erravit in arvis,
> nec sua credulitatas piscem suspenderat hamo:
> cuncta sine insidiis nullamque timentia fraudem
> plenaque pacis erant.'

> ('There was a time, the Golden Age, we call it,
> Happy in fruits and herbs, when no men tainted
> Their lips with blood, and birds went flying safely
> Through air, and in the fields the rabbits wandered
> Unfrightened, and no little fish was ever
> Hooked by its own credulity: all things
> Were free from treachery and fear and cunning,
> And all was peaceful.')[50]

These lines come towards the end of Ovid's *Metamorphoses*, when the philosopher Pythagoras is expounding his views of metempsychosis, as quoted earlier: nothing in nature dies, but passes on into other forms in a perpetual living cycle of transformations ('Our souls are deathless; always, when they leave our bodies, | They find new dwelling places . . .').[51] For this reason, because the soul can take up habitation in a beast or other form, as well as in fruits and rocks and stones, Pythagoras harks back to the vegetarianism of the Golden Age, and forbids meat eating.

At the beginning of Ovid's poem, however, the associations with Bosch's vision of prelapsarian pleasures become closer, for it makes precise references to strawberries, as well as to blackberries and other berries and fruits, what George Sandys lyrically renders as 'Wildings'.[52]

> Aurea prima sata est aetas, quae vindice nullo,
> sponte sua, sine lege fidem rectumque colebat . . .
> ipsa quoque inmunis rastroque intacta nec ullis
> saucia vomeribus per se dabat omnia tellus,
> contentique cibis nullo cogente creatis
> *arbuteos* fetus montanaque *fraga* legebant
> cornaque et in duris haerentia *mora* rubetis . . .
> ver erat aeternum, placidique tepentibus auris
> mulcebant zephyri *natos sine semine* flores;
> mox etiam fruges tellus inarata ferebat,
> nec renovatus ager gravidis canebat aristis;
> flumina iam lactis, iam flumina nectaris ibant
> flavaque de viridi stillabant ilice mella.

Here in Ted Hughes's version, in that idyllic time:

> Men needed no weapons.
> Nations loved one another.
> And the earth, unbroken by plough or by hoe,
> Piled the table high. Mankind
> Was content to gather the abundance
> Of whatever ripened.
> *Blackberry or strawberry*, mushroom or truffle,
> Every kind of nut, figs, apples, cherries,
> Apricots and pears, . . .
> Spring weather, the airs of spring
> All year long brought blossom.
> The unworked earth
> Whitened beneath the bowed wealth of the corn.
> Rivers of milk mingled with rivers of nectar.
> And out of the black oak oozed amber honey.[53]

The Golden Age stages its purity through parthenogenesis, just as Christian salvation later imagines beginnings in immaculate conception and virgin birth: flowers blossom *sine semine*, without seed, without semen, without sexual congress, emissions, and organs. (The parthenogenetic character of this foison would have been unexceptionable to the painting's early viewers because the sexual reproduction of plants would not be understood until later.) Hieronymus Bosch's painting of a lost, golden nowhere or *heterotopia* draws on the Golden Age, its classical qualities and charms: no meat, no weapons, no hierarchy or sovereignty, and, above all, no dying. This myth can be taken together with the first reports coming out of the New World at the end of the fifteenth century.

RAMÓN PANÉ: THE COMING OF WOMEN AND THE COMPANY OF GHOSTS

'They seeme to live in that golden worlde of the whiche olde wryters speak so muche,' wrote Peter Martyr of the new found land, America;[54] he was one of several writers who read Ramón Pané and understood the newly encountered inhabitants of the 'Other World' through the cultural filter of classical myths. In the early years after colonization began, it continued to be common to compare the Indians of Hispaniola and other islands to the lost innocents of the Age of Gold. Bosch's several black men and women do not conform to prevailing ideas about the appearance of the Indians, as they more closely resemble Moors from Africa, like the most resplendent of the three Magi in the *Adoration of the Magi* triptych. This in itself might place the picture in a Spanish context, for, as mentioned earlier, its making coincides with the Catholic crusade against Moorish Islam. Needless to say, this is taking place before iconographic conventions of representing native Americans became entrenched.[55]

In the early years after colonization began, it was common to invoke antique precursors to position the Indians' beliefs and rites: Peter Martyr, after recounting Pané's description of the drugged trances of an Indian Boitio, or shaman, exclaims to his patron cardinal Ludovico of Aragon, 'Come, illustrious prince, after this, how are you to stand amazed at the spirit of Apollo who brandishes his words with immense fury? And you thought that superstitious antiquity had ended!'[56] The historian Bartholomé de las Casas, who remains far more sympathetic in tone, writes, 'They had a thousand tall tales, apparently like the fables feigned by the poets among the ancient Greeks and Romans . . .'[57] The specific legend of the lost innocents of the Age of Gold came to several minds, as Gonzalo's yearning invocation of a dream commonwealth recalls in *The Tempest* (II. i. 144–56). His speech about 'the plantation of this isle' invokes the peace and plenty to surpass the fabled Golden Age; one of the qualities of the Golden Age, its foison and abundance, its spontaneous bounty and its idleness, its innocence and its justice, lay in the absence of bloodshed:

> Had I plantation of this isle, my lord,— . . .
> I'th'commonwealth I would, by contraries,
> Execute all things; for no kind of traffic
> Would I admit; no name of magistrate;
> Letters should not be known; riches, poverty,
> And use of service, none; contract, succession,
> Bourn, bound of land, tilth, vineyard, none;
> No use of metal, corn, or wine, or oil;
> No occupation, *all men idle, all;*
> *And women too, but innocent and pure;*
> No sovereignty— . . .
> All things in common Nature should produce
> Without sweat or endeavour: treason, felony,
> Sword, pike, knife, gun, or need of any engine,
> Would I not have; but Nature should bring forth,
> Of its own kind, all foison, all abundance,
> To feed my innocent people . . .

I would with such perfection govern, sir,
T'excel the Golden Age. [Emphasis added]

The vision owes a celebrated debt to Montaigne's *Les Cannibales*, but it is also suffused with the Columbine blend of idealism and self-aggrandizement. The same mythical imagery of prelapsarian spontaneity reverberates through the patriotic Marvell's later idyllic encomium to the God who gave humanity the Bermudas (also mentioned in *The Tempest*) and guided the English boats to its bounty:

> He gave us this eternal spring,
> Which here enamels everything;
> And sends the fowls to us in care,
> On daily visits through the air.
> He hangs in shades the orange bright,
> Like golden lamps in a green night . . .
> He makes the figs our mouths to meet,
> And throws the melons at our feet . . .[58]

Humanist chroniclers and translators like Richard Eden in England had however altered the emphasis of the material they plundered from Ramón Pané: where he sounds exasperated, they sentimentalize, while he held off moralizing, even while disapproving, they offer ways of thinking about the material that suffuses it with nostalgia, nostalgia for a lost, classical paradise.[59] In Richard Eden, Shakespeare would have come across these Ovidian echoes of the Golden Age, and later, the translator of Peter Martyr makes an explicit link with the Roman poet's philosophy when he lifts Pané's description of the local magicians' fasting and invokes Pythagoras by name: they 'led their lyfe in silence and abstinence,' he wrote, 'more straightly than ever dyd the philosophers of Pithagoras secte, absteinying in lyke maner from the eating of all thinges that lyve by blood, contented onely with such fruites, hearbes, and rootses, as the desartes and woods mynistred unto them to eate . . .'[60]

This is the key motif: Pythagoreans and native Hispanolian priests refuse 'all things that live by blood'. The Taino heroic ancestors thrive by exchanges that do not involve bloodshed or sacrifice, nor do the ghosts of the dead live by blood, but only on fruit, as we shall see shortly. Cannibalism is the shadow that descends to lose them from view; the Golden Age the time before it fell across the scene. Both are reverse sides of the utopian fantasies that energize conquerors and settlers.

Two of Pané's stories set up particular reverberations of a most intriguing kind with the *Garden of Earthly Delights*: his stumbling, fragmentary report about a pre-existent scheme of generation in which outlandish transmogrifications commonly take place, and his account of a parallel spirit world from which the dead visit the living, also in transformed shapes of one kind or another. These could have been read, indeed would have been read, by Spanish and other members of the new colonial powers (including the Dutch) through their own beliefs as coded in romances and legends from ancient Greek and Roman mythology: one of these, about the lost Age of Gold reverberates strongly, as mentioned already, in some of the later encomia to the 'noble savages' in the newly conquered parts of the world.

The first story concerns that all-important step in culture mentioned earlier: the coming of women. The hero and founder of Taino civilization, Guahayona, of the primordial order that preexisted human society, is able to survive exposure to the sun, unlike his fellows who have to remain hidden in a grotto in the dark; he carries off all the females of his own kind and conducts them to an island, where he abandons them, severing them from their offspring. These last begin to cry for hunger, and this is when they are turned into toads, as described before. Guahayona continues on his quest, stealing more women—the wives of his brother-in-law in this case—until there are none left for other men, who begin to feel the lack acutely. While bathing in a heavy rainstorm which has washed away the footprints of the departed women, so that the men do not know where to look for them, there falls around their bathing place, gathering under the boughs, 'una certa forma di persona' (a certain form of person) 'which were neither men nor women'.[61] The men try to catch them but they slip from their grasp 'as if they were eels'. Only four men, who had 'very rough bodies' ('il corpo molto aspero'), were able to seize hold of them, 'but then they did not know how to make them women'.

Fray Ramón goes on: 'They looked for a bird, . . . called a wood-pecker, "*pico*" in our language, and they took those women with neither male nor female nature, and bound their feet and their hands, and took the aforesaid bird, and tied it to their bodies, and [the bird] taking them for beams of wood, began his usual work, and pecked and burrowed in the usual place where a woman's nature would be. In this way therefore, the Indians say they obtained women, according to what the oldest of them relate.' He then apologizes, as he does many times in his work, and gives an interesting glimpse into the difficulties of keeping up with a storyteller in the early days, long before tape recordings: 'But because I wrote in a hurry and did not have enough paper, I couldn't write down in its right place that which I took down mistakenly in another, but in spite of this, I have not been misleading, because they still believe everything just as I have written it down.'[62]

The coming of human women involves something that falls from trees—like fruit, like cones; the changes that take place involve swelling and opening, bursting and cracking and spilling, more akin to vegetable propagation and ripening than to human sexual coupling and parturition. The agent of this transformation does not apply mammalian forms of generation and reproduction, but, as in several other Taino myths, deliberate, incongruous interventions, such as pecking, slitting, shattering, pupating; and these activities result in offspring that bear no resemblance to their matrix or originating matter, and demand counter-intuitive leaps across the boundaries of species and external appearance, such as flowers into people, bones into water, indeterminate fruits or perhaps berries into available, sexualized women. The very disruptions of natural processes, as experienced empirically, guarantee within the stories their intrinsic character of being wonderful; this astonishing, preternatural quality makes them out of this world, from where they can project another dimension of mythical time-space.

Legends about woodpeckers persisted in the region and the bird's magical powers infuse a set of hopes and dreams recounted by the classical scholar and poet George Sandys in his important translation and edition of Ovid's *Metamorphoses*. For it is noteworthy that Sandys's brother, Sir Edwin Sandys, was secretary to the Virginia Company in its American colony, and that George worked on his Ovid translation on his passage to America in 1621 —'amongst the roreing of the seas, the rustling of the Shrowdes, and Clamour of Saylers . . .' (*sic*) as he rather dramatically puts it.[63] He was sailing to join his brother and work for him as the Company's treasurer. In his idiosyncratic and anecdotal running commentary on the poem, he frequently introduces incidents and stories he picked up in the troubled English outpost (the Virginia Company was dissolved in 1624). Glossing the meanings of Picus, the king who is turned into a woodpecker by the enchantments of Circe, Sandys writes of the birds: 'They weill clamber up trees like Cats: and by jobbing against the bark do know if the worme lye under. They breed in round holes . . . these being stopt with pins of Iron, they will open them again with a certain hearb which being put to the key-hole would make the lock fly back: whereby not seldome he had entred mens houses, and opened their Coffers.' He then relates a mysterious story from the Caribbean: 'And I knew a fellow, who sixe or seven yeares had been a slave to the Spaniard in the West-Indies, who with desperate oathes would averre, how such an hearb was common in those countries; insomuch as the shackles would often unbolt, and fall from the feet of the horses, as they fed in the pastures; and how himself therewith had often opened a passage to the stuffing of his emptie belly.'[64] It is hard to understand exactly

what these properties mean: Sandys's way with pronouns is slap-
dash. Did the slave escape his shackles and find food with the help
of the herb? Did a woodpecker bring him the herb, as the elision of
the two parts of the tale might suggest? Whatever, Sandys's report
gives a glimpse into the lore, stories, natural wonders, and beliefs
that flourished when America still was 'a new found land'. As
Raphael Lyne comments in his lively study of Ovid in English
translations, the strangeness in the poem gave a way of looking at
the new strangenesses in incipient modernity.[65]

So does the strangeness of Bosch's *Garden of Earthly Delights*.
The central panel of the *Garden* represents, in wonderfully observed
detail, a flock of birds, which includes a robin, a goldfinch, a
hoopoe, a mallard, a kingfisher, and one of the picture's lovely owls.
This flock also boasts a splendid woodpecker. Near the centre of
the picture, a carefully observed great-tit hangs from a stem. The
birds are almost all gathered on the edge of a bathing pool, or are
half launched on to the shallows of one of the sheets of water in
the scene, and there, several couples are discovering each other, in
different pairings; on the other side, on a tussock that forms the
roof of one of the curious edifices, another couple are lying, the
man gazing at the head of his companion, who through the pale-
ness of her flesh would seem to be a woman but has a head in the
form of a blue damson (Pl. III). This drupe would seem to me the
closest allusion to the story in Pané, that women were born as fruit.

The second, even more weird and wonderful story in Pané's gal-
limaufry brings us back once more to fruit, and to the imagery that
Hieronymus Bosch develops in this variation on a godless paradise.
In the section dealing with 'the forms which, they say, the dead
take',[66] Pané relates how 'the dead, they say, stay shut up [in the
House of the Dead] by day, but at night go wandering, and that
they eat a certain fruit *guayaba* (*guabazza*, in Italian) . . . and at night
they turn into fruit and they go partying and mingle with the living.
And to know them, they observe this rule, that they put their hand
to their bellies and if they do not find the navel, they say that he is

operito, which means, dead, since the dead do not have a navel . . . [still] they are sometimes tricked . . . and think they have [a woman] in their arms, [when] they have nothing . . . these [spirits] they say, appear often in the form of men, and of women, likewise . . . and they all commonly believe this, the young and old alike, and that they appear in the form of father, or mother or brothers or relatives or other forms. The fruit, which they say the dead eat, is the size of a quince.'[67]

One of the most common metaphorical substitutions in myth involves sexual acts and eating fruit, as alluded to earlier—it sits at the heart of the story of the Fall, after all, as well as the cause of Persephone's sentence in the underworld, after she is abducted by Pluto and fatally eats seven seeds of a pomegranate. Christina Rossetti elaborated this curse in the sustained nightmare of her ballad 'Goblin Market', where Lizzie falls into the clutches of the queer little men after eating their proffered fruits.

The species the Taino dead eat, the fruit the size of a quince, has been identified as guava, and indeed their Lord of the House of the Dead shares the same name.[68] Most importantly of all, the polymorphous, different, multiple modes of germination and propagation, of berries and drupes and all kinds of fruits, falling from the bough, spreading through runners, growing as tubers and rhizomes, pack the painting with symbolic fertility and vitality.

Could something of these stories have clung to Bosch's mind? The bathing pools, the fruit groves, the varieties of bean and gourd and bud from which human-shaped creatures are sprouting, wriggling, being born, the sharp-beaked birds, including a green woodpecker, could they be echoes of a story he had heard about sexless fruit that are pierced by a wood-boring bird to become women? Is it possible the fish in the foreground, near the gourd-shaped vessel, alludes to the creation story with which this chapter began?

And again, could the miniature scale of the figures, or, alternatively, the giant dimensions of the flora and fauna, link them to souls and spirits or beings from another world? Does this perhaps catch at fragments of the Indians' reported belief in spirits who take any form and lie with humans? Does Bosch annex alternative realities discovered in the Other World of America to enflesh the vision of a lost age of innocence and bliss? Is he combining two mythic traditions, the Hesiodic and Ovidian vision of the Golden Age with Caribbean myths of women made from something that falls from trees and of ghosts who survive on fruit and even return in the shape of fruits to lie with humans?

Pané was a Hieronymite monk; in other words he belonged to the Order of Saint Jerome (Jerome is also of course Hieronymus Bosch's first name and his patron saint). It is not impossible that the Hieronymite account of the Indians' cosmology could have reached the Spanish Netherlands, and the circle of Spanish nobility who were Bosch's patrons, if not in manuscript form, at least by word of mouth, and its contents passed on to the artist.[69] Bosch's advocate at court later on in the sixteenth century, his staunch interpreter and supporter at Philip II's side, was Fray José de Sigüenza, the distinguished historian of that monastic order which lived and looked after the royal palace of El Escorial, where the painting was hung.[70] It is improbable that Sigüenza would not have known the document Pané wrote. Nor is it beyond the bounds of plausible conjecture that the order would have talked of Pané's report and adventures during his lifetime. And it is Sigüenza who makes the earliest reference to the *Garden of Earthly Delights*, in a letter consigning the painting to the Escorial of 8 July 1593, in which he calls it 'La Pintura del Madrono' (The Painting of the Strawberry [Tree]). With this designation, Sigüenza is specifying arbutus, the tree or shrub common in the Mediterranean which mimics the soft fruit, and which features, alongside the wild edible variety, in Ovid's paean to the Golden Age (see above).[71]

It is revealing that Sigüenza referred to the painting in this way, because either it shows that he was following reports on its contents and writing about it before he had seen it, since as a Spaniard, he could not have mistaken Bosch's giant strawberries on which his revellers are feasting for the unpalatable arbutus; or the wording demonstrates the pervasive aesthetic preference for textual over visual reference, and his understanding of the painting as an interpretation of the famous Ovidian passage on the Golden Age.

The scheme of the *Garden* required that the artist imagine a time out of time, in a nowhere place out of the known, familiar world: an adynaton, or impossibility. These are the principles that underpin the idea of a Golden Age and an earthly paradise. When stories started floating back about the discoveries the Spanish were making in the Americas, their particulars furnished a new, literally outlandish vocabulary of adynata. 'Alternative realities . . . are those that do not know alternative realities,' Joseph Koerner has written:[72] in order to express these at all, images and stories were borrowed and new 'realities' meshed with pre-existing fantasies, both Christian and classical, as I have said. Pagan ways of being and doing, in the eyes of observers from Europe, converged with the deeply ingrained conceptions of sin. George Sandys, in his commentary on Ovid, drew attention to the devil's influence on 'the salvages . . . [who] solemnize . . . their principall times of devotion with drunkennesse (procured insteed of wine, by certaine intoxicating roots and berries) accompanied with all kinde of impudency . . .'[73] In the eighteenth century, the description of a sensual false paradise was commonplace: 'They [Indians] look upon this soul as a sensual being, which is necessitated to eat, drink and divert itself in the next world . . . the soul will go to certain fortunate islands, where their enemies will be their slaves . . . it will be plunged up to the neck in a flood of pleasure.'[74]

The Indians' own stories combined with narratives about them to shape a metaphorical alternative reality, an imaginary primordial state. In the earliest phase of encounter, the mythology exhibited quite remarkable variety, originality, and strangeness; only a decade later as the Taino themselves grew weaker, the stories about Indians fell under the long twin shadows of mythemes about cannibals and gold, which dominate the storytelling in the later sixteenth and seventeenth centuries.

I am not suggesting that the *Garden illustrates* the Taino stories. This would be too strong a claim; I am offering another document, and the successive screens superimposed in its reception, as a way of looking afresh at the imagery of the painting. But if it were the case that the literature of first encounter infuses the *Garden*, what meanings would then develop?

On the left wing of the *Garden*, the Creator is presenting the newly created Eve to Adam, and although Bosch does not paint the eating of the forbidden fruit, he includes a tree—the tropical Dragon Palm, as well as the strange grilli and hybrids crawling out of the ponds of Eden.[75] So his image of the creation of woman portends the coming disaster. In classical mythology, the arrival of women similarly brings about the end of the first, golden generation. Hesiod describes the making of Pandora and follows it with the laconic line, 'And then,' writes this poet, 'this race was hidden in the ground.'[76]

Just as the Hesiodic evocation of the lost age is framed by the misogynist moral, that woman is the cause of grief, so Bosch's vision might depict the coming/invention of women, by annexing and conflating the belief system of a people (a 'race') who were being identified with the primordial predecessors of the human species, and who were, in the conflict with the Spanish, being superseded by a new generation of metalworkers and users (the second, accursed Age of Silver in Hesiod's scheme).

The male figure in the bottom right-hand corner, who is either hairy all over or wearing a suit of skins, points with a knowing, almost gleeful look at the woman who is indeed half buried in the ground; she too is hairy, and pale as death, and so is the fruit she carries in her hand (Pl. III). It looks like an apple, or a quince, in which case it is the only such among the many species of fruit in the painting. Could she represent a kind of death? Could her companion be the painter, wearing the sackcloth of a tertiary brother? Bosch belonged, either as a wealthy citizen, or a cleric in minor orders, to a confraternity, the Brotherhood of Our Lady. Is this figure facing us indicating, with that finger, the woe that brought about the end of this Golden Age of happy, vital (colourful), vegetarian innocence? Is this pair the same pair, at a later stage in the story, of the couple standing to their right, also hairy like wild folk? If this could be so, then the wings would be commenting on the story of the central panel, and illustrating first the cause and then the consequences of sin: the whole triptych would dramatize from three angles the theme of woman as the 'devil's gateway', she who brought sin, death, punishment—and biological, animal procreation—sex and viviparous birth (and body hair??)—into the world.[77]

Reading *The Garden of Earthly Delights* through the reports of Indian myths in Pané, or perhaps through garbled, oral digests of Pané, brushes in a possible moral schema which would have been familiar—and congenial—to any number of the artist's contemporaries. *The Garden of Earthly Delights* might be communicating a very familiar Christian message: a lesson in the perils consequent on the creation of woman. This approved theme would tie together the pictures on the inside of the triptych in a manner that corresponds to the convention of such works of art and sets them within a Christian narrative of salvation and damnation. It would also conform to Bosch's general apocalyptic pessimism.[78]

Yet, underlying the whole wondrous, carnival-like invention beats the longing to return to a prelapsarian time in an Other world, another time of innocence. As Jonathan Bate has commented, this yearning to regain the Golden Age suffuses literature—since Hesiod and Ovid.[79]

The age of conquest at first recognized the Indians as magically blessed, unselfconscious ancestors—but only for a very short period. But this idealizing approach conflicted with the strong current of fear, censure, and demonization in the imperial imagination, while in history and actuality the indigenous population was decimated. By the time the painting reached the court of Philip II, in the summer of 1593, the Indians whom Pané had listened to were ruined by disease, slavery, and plunder and seizure of their lands.

So it appears that, yes, Bosch *is* a profound moralist, but not perhaps about sexual pleasures. Or not at least in a spirit of whole-hearted opprobrium—but with nostalgia, with a sense of loss, with remorse. Yet context changes meanings; the picture's reception began to shift in import; until, read from the vantage point of a different time in the history of empires in collision, it conveys to us now innocence that had been lost, not when God created Eve, but when the kindness of strangers was abused in the race for gold and territory in the Americas. Bate urges us to bear in mind the myth of the lost paradise, as a warning: 'Myths are necessary imaginings,' he writes, 'exemplary stories which help our species make sense of its place in the world. Myths endure so long as they perform helpful work. The myth of the natural life which exposes the ills of our own condition is as old as Eden and Arcadia. Perhaps we need to remember what is "going, going" as a survival mechanism, as a check upon our instinct for self-advancement.'[80]

Metamorphosis as divine fantasy, as vital principle of nature, as punishment, as reprieve, as miracle, as cultural dynamic, as effect of historical meetings and clashes, as the difference that lures, as the lost idyll, as time out of time, as a producer of stories and meanings: reading the poor hermit Ramón Pané together with Ovid at the end of the fifteenth century, taking one set of vivid stories written during the Roman empire as they impinge on the narratives written down during the expansion of a new power—all this has thrown light, I hope, on the other world that Hieronymus Bosch so dazzlingly created in his mysterious and fantastic triptych.

In the next chapter I shall pick up on the imagery of hatching, with special regard to the imagery of the butterfly, and of Leda and the swan.

2

Hatching

MONSTERS

The dramatic metamorphoses that Ovid so vigorously describes in his great poem embody a perpetual conflict: between due organic change on the one hand and incongruous and disruptive mutation on the other. In this structural contradiction at the very core of the poem, the term 'metamorphosis' itself remains ceaselessly in play; how the weight falls and how the values are ascribed between these two poles can offer key insights into ideas about consistency and integrity, and their problematic vulnerability. In this second chapter, I propose that at the end of the seventeenth century a new way of looking at and assessing naturally occurring metamorphosis, especially in insects, began in contact with the newly encountered habitats of the Americas; the strangeness of it awakened perceptions and altered ways of thinking about change and character over time which gradually, with a certain time lag, influenced the characterization of human identity in literature, and foreshadowed contemporary themes: it contributed to stirring ideas about consistency within inconsistency, contradiction within integration, fragmentation, difference, and plurality within the self—states of being familiar, even natural, in twentieth-century fiction.

Hatching forms a potent subset in the transformational imagery of alchemy and of witchcraft—eggs offer witches all kinds of sympathetic possibilities, including transport. (Pliny pointed out how important it is to crack the shell after eating a boiled egg for breakfast in case witches will set sail in it.[1]) Hatching generates a double valency; it implies the sudden emergence of a new being and this moves in contrary motion: airborne (bird) or earthbound (reptile) or ambiguous (amphibian), between winged creatures whose habitat encompasses the heavens, and those condemned like the serpent to crawl on their bellies—snakes, lizards, and other oviparous reptilian and amphibian creatures (toads) required for the witch's cauldron. It figures richly in the imagery of the supernatural: from fairies such as Moth in *A Midsummer Night's Dream* to the relation between bug meaning devil, and bug meaning insect.[2]

The metaphor activates, as discussed in the last chapter, the perverse generativity in the visions of Bosch; Bosch populated his visions of hell and temptation with hatchlings of various orders, proportions, and assorted limbs.

On the right inner wing of *The Garden of Earthly Delights*, the colossal, spectral, bone-white tree-man in hell seems to be both egg and hollow trunk at once (Fig. 18). In some instances, the artist's fantastical semi-comic, semi-horrific inventions are still wearing their shells, as snails do, or crabs. As Bosch's imagery reveals, the physiology of birds, the marvel of eggs and of hatching, in short the processes of avian generation, were adopted into the repertory of medieval and Renaissance depictions of hell's instability, flux, and mayhem; they were perceived to share some hellish affinity with the metamorphosis of insects and the self-renewal of reptiles and serpents. In Bosch's nightmares, grown men walk on all fours inside cracked shells; lovers mate inside eggs, and witches and hobgoblins ride in half-cups. In the later sixteenth century, the motif spread beyond the Netherlands to contribute to the pleasures of horror, reaching Venice and Prague and, of course, Spain.[3] More widely —and obviously—the egg symbolized origin and potentiality.

Horace coined two key phrases about storytelling techniques when he cited the case of Leda: *ab ovo*—out of the egg—means beginning at the beginning, in contrast to *in medias res*, coming in in the middle.[4] Creation myths dramatized the egg as origin: the Orphic cult still flickers in the tradition of the Easter egg in spring. Eggs figure virtuality: they hold the promise of life with a symbolic intensity that shaped scientific observation: Pliny for example writes that an egg contains a seed, or germ—from which the being sprouts.[5] In alchemy, the primordial egg of origin was even identified specifically with a swan's.[6] Incubation offered a more appropriate metaphor than parturition for the particular transformation of matter at which they aimed: alchemical texts reverberate with encomia to yolks and albumen and their potentiality. The eggshell itself becomes the metonymic vehicle of the alchemical process, the gourd-shaped vessel in which the raw matter is cooked and changed. 'The philosopher's egg . . . is Nature's vessel . . . and even during putrefaction . . .'[7] This viewpoint engages with metamorphosis as part of the cycle of nature, an inherent energy directing growth in all things and in all directions, from emergence to decay; change here is not sudden, extreme, or willed, but a material and organic cause and effect. In alchemical imagery, the egg-shaped vessel in which phenomena are quickened into life is frequently represented as if it were the inner sac, not the outer shell, so that Mercury, or the Sun and Moon, can be seen inside it *in potentia*;[8] similarly, the engraving of *Leda and the Swan* by Cornelis Bos after Michelangelo, which I will be coming back to, includes one unbroken shell, transparently revealing Helen curled up within, foetus-like, while behind this first egg a second has hatched a second pair of twins—perhaps Castor and Pollux (Fig. 25).

   This concept of ovulation as the most fundamental and overarching process of generation included even *stones*: no less a rational empiricist than Sir Hans Sloane, Jamaican tycoon, physician, explorer, collector, and founder of the British Museum, whose portrait hangs in the Examination Schools in Oxford, wrote of some corals he picked up in Jamaica (he left for Jamaica in 1687): 'These Stones are most certainly bred from a Seed; for in the places where they are most to be found in shallow Sea-Water, I have seen what one may call their Seed or Spawn very frequently, viz. a mucilaginous, crystalline, clear Body, of the same shape and with the same spots on their Surface, only no Striae going from the center of the holes, which when taken up in the heat, does out of the Water corrugate and contract itself into narrower dimensions, turn Opaque, and of an Ash, or pale Yellow Colour, in which notwithstanding may plainly be seen the rudiments of the Stone . . .'[9] He then reports its excellent medical properties, and concludes in a rare, indeed unique flight of fancy, 'The Stone was pretended to come from the East, and that there it was generated in the Head of a Dragon . . .'[10] So Sir Hans Sloane, who otherwise shows hearty scepticism throughout his great work on West Indian flora and fauna, also yielded to the fantastic, mythopoeic potency of the hatching metaphor and even imagines, in 1725, *stones spawning* in the Wide Sargasso Sea.[11]

While hatching offered a potent metaphor in the language of abomination and monstrosity, it also helped install metamorphosis at the heart of ideas of *appropriate*, rather than aberrant development of forms. Highly productive relations exist between natural hatching and magical metamorphosis, which have themselves helped to change ideas about human identity and psychological development. After the earliest close scrutiny and detailed representations of insects at the turn of the seventeenth century, creepy-crawlies took on another character, and their ordinary life cycles could no longer be so easily annexed to express diabolical ugliness. As I explore the processes of hatching and of its counterpart, pupating, and the relation of these vital processes to telling stories about persons, I shall unfold the metaphor—unravel the cocoon—in relation to two of the most productive stories of transformation from the ancient world: first, the ancient novel by Lucius Apuleius, with the significant alternative titles, *The Metamorphoses of Lucius, or*

The Golden Ass,[12] and second, the rich, fascinating myth of Leda and the swan, which has come down through a variety of artefacts and texts—and iconotexts. On the way we will encounter other tales and stories of hatching and pupating—these related metaphors are so mythologically rich that I am afraid they threaten to rip any silk threads in which I try and wind them. And at the end of this chapter, I shall look briefly at Franz Kafka's famous story of 1915, 'Metamorphosis' and at Vladimir Nabokov's butterfly imagery: both writers who reconfigure the transformation romance plot through insect life cycles in order to follow the unmaking of their protagonists, not their making.[13] But first, to one of the great entomologists and artists, Maria Merian, who changed the understanding of butterflies, moths, and other bugs through her sumptuous scientific illustrations.[14]

MARIA MERIAN: *Of the Metamorphoses of the Insects of Suriname* (1699–1701)

'It has happened to me more than once,' the naturalist and artist Maria Sibylla Merian writes, 'that the most beautiful caterpillars have transformed themselves into very ugly butterflies, and that there have emerged very beautiful ones from the ugliest caterpillars.'[15] Her comments on the outcome of her cocoons convey the force of her surprise, for, according to the prevailing teleological view of natural development, the future should be deducible from the seed and the outcome appropriate. Aristotle had laid down the principle that 'To be generative of another like itself, this is the function of every animal and plant perfect in nature . . .'[16] Close observation of the phases in the butterfly cycle, as Merian undertook, uncomfortably introduces permutations of dissimilarity, not of similarity, into the development of an entity.

Merian was working in the Dutch Caribbean colony of Suriname. She had taken the extraordinary step for the times of sailing there, at the age of 52, in 1699, with her daughter Dorothea, to continue her lifelong studies of butterflies, plants, and other natural wonders (her word). In tune with the times and in the enterprising Dutch spirit of her adopted domicile, her underlying ambition was mercantile: she wanted to discover another kind of spinner, a second *Bombyx mori* or silkworm, and thus make possible a new insect textile, to substitute or even rival silk.[17] She was to fail in this aim, since—until recently—nobody had harvested that comparable natural wonder, the spider's web. Only now is spiders' silk, which is stronger than steel, being synthesized for industrial use.[18]

Merian had been observing and drawing the 'wonderful metamorphosis' of caterpillars, since she was a child, and had already published her observations and illustrations of European species.[19] The folio edition that resulted from her two-year-long stay is called *Of the Metamorphoses of the Insects of Suriname*, and was published in 1705.[20] The first English use of the word 'metamorphosis', in connection with the life cycle of butterflies, moths, and other insects, is given by Dr Johnson to William Harvey; its earliest instance in connection with butterflies is dated 1665 by the *OED*. The concept was explored by another English contemporary of Merian, the naturalist John Ray, in his pioneering studies of insects from the beginning of the eighteenth century.[21] It turns out that you *could* explore the wonders of insect transformation in nearby Essex: it was not completely obligatory to travel far afield, although cross-cultural spaces do seem to sharpen powers of observation. (Essex man John Ray's name will turn up again, in another context.)

Maria Merian's father, Mathias Merian, was the prolific and imaginative printer-engraver who had collaborated with Theodor de Bry, his father-in-law, on an influential series of magnificent folio volumes of propaganda engravings and travel writings on the Americas (1594–1634).[22] Although Mathias died when Maria was only 5, she would have thus been aware, from the formative years of her imagination, of the Americas as a land of wonders, magic, monsters, and—metamorphoses. One of the maps that appears in their volumes shows the Suriname coast, inhabited apparently by one of the wonderful men called blemyae, whose heads are seated in their chest, and who are also mentioned by Gonzalo, clearly a well-read man, in *The Tempest* (III. iii. 46–7). It is striking, too, that before Merian travelled to the Caribbean, she used the word *Dattelkern*—date stone—for the pupa of European insects.[23] This is a kind of nursery parlance, but one that places even domestic specimens in a distant, exotic, perhaps tropical landscape, an invitation to a voyage, and even particularly to Dutch colonial possessions, where date trees would be growing.

The part of fantasy in the 'positive shadowplay' projected onto the chronicles and records of the newfoundlands cannot be excised from the historical picture: even at their most empirical, as in Merian's studies of insects, imagination constitutes the very stuff of history.

Merian's Suriname volumes enjoyed a huge success, several editions and wide dissemination, which brought her fame all over Europe, including Russia. She is one of history's little-considered links between many worlds. It was in Russia, in the attic of his family's country house, that Vladimir Nabokov, aged 8, came across 'Maria Merian's lovely plates of Surinam insects' as he writes in *Speak, Memory*, his memoir.[24]

Hers was the first generation of scientists to understand that insects *lay eggs*: these are so tiny that even Aristotle's keen powers of observation missed this stage, and he had situated the metaphor of hatching at the later stage of insect metamorphosis, writing that 'the chrysalis is in effect an egg'.[25] He also held that flies and so forth generated, spontaneously it was imagined, from decaying matter. Pliny, following Aristotle, reports that flies give birth to worms.[26] Unlike her predecessors in entomological illustration, Maria Merian did not single out a single specimen for attention,[27] but dramatized instead the small eco-system of laying, hatching, feeding, pupation, and final emergence in the whole transformational process, in symbiosis with the specific plants on which a particular butterfly or insect species was dependent (Pl. VI). Nor does she compare one species with another, or attempt to order and classify by similarity of appearance or behaviour as her predecessors and her contemporaries did.[28]

Maria Merian did not incline to allegory either: she has a literal directness that sets aside the previous emblem book uses of the butterfly and its life cycle. With the freshness of an autodidact, she looked and looked hard.[29] She tells a story, compressing time in her plates, so that creatures and plants are seen in consecutive stages at one and the same moment: the emergence of the glorious blossom or butterfly, or of the reptile or serpent happens coterminously with the egg, or larva. This compression grants each stage of the butterfly's existence almost equal value with every other, possessing intrinsic importance to the metamorphosis; without the grub, however unsightly, without the cocoon, however inert, there would be no butterfly.

Her vision of metamorphic hatching is also a vision of mutual interdependence, even of a form of determinism. She represents the individual specimen of the species in a mesh of relations with other life forms, some of which are its own earlier embodiments, but others are different species altogether, without which it could not grow and reach its final flowering. Indeed, the richly layered colouring techniques she developed confirm the impression that the insects are somehow produced by the plants they devour: the butterfly as emanation, as itself the bloom of the flower, nourished on buds, leaflets, and leaves and petals.

She consistently presents herself as a witness of the transformations, even as their *metteur-en-scène*: using the first person, she tells of collecting the larvae and pupae in the jungle, the way hacked clear before her by her slaves, of waiting for the chrysalis to hatch, of watching the butterfly unfold its surprise. Frequently, she expresses her frustration that her fellow Europeans will not participate in this natural cycle and learn from the local people to harness its economy profitably—as medicine, as textile, as nourishment. In the metamorphic zone where the maritime culture of the Dutch clashed with the indigenous peoples of Guiana, where the colonial powers struggled to maintain their control with abominable cruelties, a fresh way of reading natural transformations happened; Merian expresses her repugnance for the methods of the colonists, the planters, the slave task masters, and the mercenaries.

Her close scrutiny of ecological interdependency does often appear seethed in a mood of morbid melancholy as she watches insect devastation, intraspecies massacres (a spider eating a humming bird), and general savagery. She also gathered, she declares in her preface, 'some things from the account which the Indians gave me' and she sets down local uses, for body paints and poisons, for abortion, and even for light: some nocturnal moths so bright that she could read the *Holland Gazette* by their glow.

Merian's keen curiosity, which turns her into a participant not an observer, can lead to a way of reading stories that relate the twists and turns of an individual life, the surprises that can spring from a subject's life. Changes in the understanding of hatching as a principle were produced, not merely reproduced, by changes in the imagery that narrated its occurrence, as here in Merian's magnificent images.

Such a vision emblematically marks another contemporaneous break, between one kind of narrative and another. It reveals how a challenge was developing to long established ideals about the essence of an individual being. Merian's investigation of continuity within formal change upsets the settled idea of development as an unfolding of personality, as the psyche moves towards epiphany, fulfilment, and closure (the butterfly as *telos*, or finality)—Aristotle uses the concept of *perfecting* the form. It suggests instead a more accidental, adventitious, discontinuous kind of narrative in which each stage, from the start, however incongruous, communicates the person (the sequential metamorphoses become the subject *in extenso*)—think of Laurence Sterne's *Tristram Shandy*, first published between 1759 and 1767, a novel which stays with its protagonist for pages before he is even born; and of Jean-Jacques Rousseau's *Confessions*, written from 1764 to 1770, and his exceptional examination of his childhood self. This is not to say that Maria Merian herself instigated the change; she is rather a symptom of its beginnings, when the psyche's warps and inconsistencies over the subject's lifetime enter the whole picture. Merian's insect pictures in fact coincide in time with the earliest extant journal kept, in the Netherlands, by a father about the development of his children.[30]

Before this natural scientific readjustment of metamorphosis, as changes of identity in a continuous existence, the animal process was rather perceived within the categories of regeneration and renewal and their analogue, repentance, and conversion: as a variation on shedding, on sloughing, on changing one's skin and one's spots, and leaving the shed skins behind. For example, a striking boss in the choir vaults of Iffley church, near Oxford, shows a dragon 'scraping off its skin of evil', as the leaflet for visitors puts it. Such a morality is entirely characteristic of medieval thinking about change: change is progression, not cumulative process. (Dante contrasts the worm's imperfections in its primitive, undeveloped state with the 'angelica farfalla' (the angelic butterfly' which it so often fails to become (*Purgatory* X: 121–6)). The butterfly offered an image of the etherealized self, it communicated the idea that the fleshly, inferior integument would be shucked off to release the essence, soul: self shuffling off this mortal coil.

APULEIUS, THE TRANSFORMATIONS OF LUCIUS, AND THE TALE OF CUPID AND PSYCHE

Pupation, the weaving of the cocoon, followed by the sudden, wondrous emergence of the imago—the butterfly—from the chrysalis, offered, in the classical repertory of symbols, a correlative of hatching, with the significant difference that while hatching produces like from like, as does viviparous birthing, pupating produces something almost entirely unpredictable: the parent in this case does not ensure any recognizable feature in the offspring. Many metamorphic tales, classical or classical by emulation, follow this pattern of arriving at anagnorisis or recognition through a series of concealments, or even disfigurements, of revealing true, inner character through a series of outer changes of shape. The traditional storytelling of a hero or heroine who journeys through numerous ordeals, through misprisions and neglect, finally to arrive at selfhood, follows this model of metamorphosis: the protagonist's true self generates itself in its proper character after undergoing several transformations; the larger transformation of their circumstances and the appearance of the person's fullness of being unfolded through several smaller transformations. Apuleius' *The Metamorphoses of Lucius, or The Golden Ass*, offers a richly layered example of this type of storytelling, and one in which many much loved fairy tales have their origin.

In this initiatory romance, written in the second century, the unlucky first person narrator and hero, Lucius, peeps on the witch Pamphile and sees her rub on a magic ointment and then turn into a bird; he longs to do the same, and suborns her slave, Fotis, to steal the ointment for him. But there is some mistake, and the salve Lucius enthusiastically applies has the unfortunate effect of changing him into a donkey. Lucius in his donkey shape then suffers through many adventures, some ribald, some terrifying, erotic, and painful, until he reaches at last the antidote—roses—and gratefully munches through a bunch of them and is turned back into human form (Fig. 19).

In his extraordinary proto-novel, Apuleius nests one metamorphosis inside another, before unwinding them at the end to reveal the proven and tested protagonist, restored to his appropriate outer form, but also radically transformed by his ordeal. *Before* his own metamorphosis into an ass, Lucius moves through a frenzied and shifting Thessaly, 'a province notorious for magic and sorcery';

Fig. 19 The unfortunate Lucius, who was transformed into an ass, at last reaches the antidote—a bunch of roses—and begins to turn back into a man (from Apuleius, *The Golden Ass*).

driven by his own over-stimulated hunger for adventure, he plunges into a labyrinth of delusion and nightmares, much influenced by Ovid: 'I wondered', he writes, 'whether the stones I kicked against were really, perhaps, petrified men, and whether the birds I heard singing were people in feathered disguises . . . and I began to entertain doubts about the trees around the house, and even about the faucets through which the fountains played.' In this Ovidian setting of ambiguous metamorphosis and leaking identities, Lucius is hailed familiarly by a woman he does not know, a rich widow called Byrrhaena who claims to be a relation of his, and warns him in lurid language against the dangers he is running; but the risks of sorcery, seduction, and metamorphosis only inflame Lucius further: 'I had an irresistible impulse to study magic,' he says, 'however much money it might cost me.' Apuleius does not draw back from insisting further on the threatened loss of self Lucius faces: crossing Byrrhaena's courtyard, he sees a many-figured sculpture showing the fate of Actaeon, the young hunter who unwittingly came across the goddess Diana bathing and was punished for this involuntary blasphemy. The sculptures are so vividly dramatized that the hounds 'looked so menacing with their fierce eyes, pricked ears, dilated nostrils and snarling jaws, that if any other dogs near by had suddenly barked you would have thought for the moment that the sound came from their white marble throats.' As in Ovid's poem, which Apuleius has already invoked elsewhere, this complex art installation depicts Actaeon 'already half-transformed into a stag' as 'his punishment for spying on the Goddess'. The extended, stylish ekphrasis tells the story with such dynamism that it reads more like a filmed episode than the description of an immobile group of statues. 'All this is yours', declares the widow, passionately, with prophetic irony. So the passage imbricates, deliberately, Lucius' misadventures when he looks when he should not, and sees what should not be seen: though he will escape the full fatality of Actaeon's punishment.[31]

This remarkable passage of classical storytelling, from Apuleius not Ovid, inspires, I would suggest, the enigmatic frescoes that the young Parmigianino painted of the transformation of Actaeon into a stag in the castle of Fontanellato near Parma. Several other sources, some of them far more recondite than *The Golden Ass*, have been offered, but this rather obvious (but overlooked) candidate fits most eloquently with this most beautiful of domestic, painted rooms (Fig. 6).[32]

After his own unfortunate, grotesque transmogrification into the donkey, Lucius remains himself inside throughout his later afflictions; only, like Actaeon in his beast form, he cannot talk. He brays instead—one of several features of his plight that

Shakespeare adapted when Bottom is 'translated' into an ass in *A Midsummer Night's Dream*. Another is Lucius' charms for women: his ass state provokes many lovestruck advances, as with Titania. And at the conclusion, Apuleius lifts his funny, sexy, odd book on to another register altogether, and utters an impassioned, religious orison to the polymorphous Great Goddess, who then announces herself to be every goddess, but Isis, above all. At last he reaches the coveted roses:

He [the priest] stood still and held out the rose garland to the level of my mouth. I trembled and my heart pounded as I ate those roses with loving relish; and no sooner had I swallowed them than I found that the promise had been no deceit. My bestial features faded away, the rough hair fell from my body, my sagging paunch tightened, my hind hooves separated into feet and toes, my fore hooves now no longer served only for walking upon, but were restored, as hands, to my human uses. Then my neck shrank, my face and head rounded, my great hard teeth shrank to their proper size, my long ears shortened, and my tail which had been my worst shame vanished altogether.

A gasp of wonder went up and the priests, aware that the miracle corresponded with the High Priest's vision of the Great Goddess, lifted their hands to Heaven and with one voice applauded the blessing which she had vouchsafed me: this swift restoration to my proper shape.[33]

This offers a deliberate reverse spin on Ovid's animal metamorphoses; Pythagoras is invoked by name. Lucius' further transformations then follow a sequence of prophetic dreams calling him to become an 'illuminate' in the rites of Osiris; he robes himself in 'twelve different stoles' and is revealed to the crowd 'as when a statue is unveiled, dressed like the sun. That day was the happiest of my initiation, and I celebrated it as my birthday . . .'[34] He has come back from the dead, and been reborn into a new existence, but in his 'proper shape'.

The serene, exalted, and mystical conclusion implies that he has been proved until he has come into his true self—which is the ultimate goal of such a concept of metamorphosis. The stories Apuleius has told have worked towards Lucius' recognition: both to others of what his true worth is, and to himself, of his true vocation.

His translated shape can be cured by eating roses: this remedy might be connected, in the logic of the imaginary, across the borders of species to the emergence of a butterfly, which develops in symbiosis by eating leaves and flowers. (This suggestion has not been made before, as far as I can see in the literature on Apuleius, though the many entomological associations of his imagery have been discussed.[35])

Lucius' successive misadventures fall into a rattle bag of bawdy, raunchy, hilarious, and horrific stories—of spells and savagery, witches and murder—but chief among the interpolated tales remains the famous romance of Cupid and Psyche, which originates here.[36] It mirrors in *mise-en-abyme* the structure of its frame narrative illuminatingly, for Psyche is also dropped into an abyss of shame and degradation through her own fault, when she disobeys her lover Cupid and lifts a lamp to look at him where he lies sleeping beside her.

This haunting and influential fairy tale, the source of many later stories in the Beauty and the Beast tradition, then describes how the whole enchanted castle of love, with its invisible attendants, supernatural music, conjured pastimes and banquets, vanishes into thin air; Psyche finds herself alone, and subjected to terrible ordeals, beatings, and betrayals, just like Lucius in his asinine form, before she is restored to her health and happiness, reunited with Cupid, and gives birth to their daughter, called Voluptas, Pleasure, in the final, joyous opening of the story's happy end. She is then numbered among the immortals.

Psyche does not work a transformation on herself: her fate simply picks her up and drops her and picks her up again, and again; like many a heroine of *erotika pathemata*, or stories of love in suffering, or Hellenic romance, she weeps piteously through her ordeals.

But Psyche is central to my inquiry into hatching, because Psyche's name in Greek means Soul—which has of course given us the English Freudian term, the psyche. Apuleius knew Greek, though he wrote in Latin—he was a North African in the late antique world and consequently a man who moved between cultures. He chose his heroine's name to a purpose, to figure her life as exemplary of the human odyssey; so the medieval Christian allegorists, Boccaccio, and, after him, later Neoplatonist interpreters in fifteenth-century Florence understood, when they descried within Apuleius' mischievous ironic commentary on a mortal life a poetic allegory of the soul's journey towards fulfilment.[37] But what is crucial here in relation to hatching is that 'psyche' is also Greek for butterfly and moth, as first attested in Aristotle's *Historia Animalium*;[38] this double meaning underpins the correspondence between the frame story about Lucius' troubled metamorphosis and ultimate resolution, and Psyche's destiny in the fable.

Butterflies figured soul in ancient Egypt, and Plato spoke of the winged soul, in a famous passage of the *Phaedrus*; Greco-Roman antique cameo portraits of the deceased (Fig. 21) and memorials on sarcophagi frequently show the deceased with a butterfly. In Latin, too, animula can be used of both soul and butterflies or moths, and the image occurs in early Christian imagery of God creating Adam and Eve, as in the mosaics of San Marco, Venice.[39]

But the reasons for the identification of psyche and butterfly go further, I think, than a simple analogy within the logic of the imaginary to a visual concept of winged spirits, insubstantial, aspiring to rise above earthbound matter;[40] it operates at a deeper level within the syntax of metaphor, in models of a generative process, which figures the emergent butterfly as the vital essence which is inherent within the cocoon and other metamorphic stages. In ancient classical medical thought, the butterfly did not figure a feminine flitting thing but the male generative power (as depicted on a Greek vase painting of an ithyphallic satyr of the sixth century BC).[41] A Roman

Fig. 20 The soul or psyche was figured as a butterfly, and was associated with male semen, the active principle of life in classical biology; from a Roman gem-carving.

gem also shows a butterfly taking wing towards a herm with an erect and flowing phallus (Fig. 20).[42]

These images may depend on Aristotle's model of generation, that the male provides the active life principle, while the woman provides the material mass. He wrote, 'the semen ensouls the menstrual fluid—the matter—largely by fabricating the embryonic heart, which in turn "makes" the rest of the animal.'[43] Elsewhere he offers a vivid biological analogy: the process resembles, he writes, the way rennet is used to set milk for the making of cheese (often itself still called after words for form, *fromage, formaggio*). This dairy imagery may even resonate, softly, in the mysterious English word

Fig. 21 The butterfly soul flies free of the mortal body on classical memorials of the dead, as on this Roman cameo portrait.

butterfly itself, whose origins are not established, as well as in other words, such as the German *Molkendieb* (whey-thief) while *phalène*, French for moth, possibly combines psyche and phallos, making a feminine phallos—the flying psyche—as has been suggested by entirely respectable scholars.[44]

According to this concept the vital principle then leaves the body at death, exiting from matter to regain the ethereal realm. The Ancient Egyptians figured the body as the chrysalis from which the winged soul is set free, and the Greek word for the pupa, *nekydallos*, means little corpse; *pupa* itself means doll in Latin, suggesting an inanimate, unconscious state. The spooky features of several cocoons later excited much wonder at nature's spontaneous artistry; the uncanny mimicry of a human face on the mask of the pupa was remarked on by several observers.[45]

Since both Lucius and Psyche, his storybook female double, are restored, renewed, and perfected at the end of their respective stories, their metamorphoses reflect the reassuring principle of some inalienable essential character that they both retain undiminished through thick and thin, and eventually lifts them from the earthbound realm: Lucius achieves spirituality as an initiate, Psyche becomes a goddess, at one with the Olympians.

This consistent truth-to-self underlying the metamorphoses is what will be changed itself when the entomology itself changes; this is the shift that Merian's illustrations unsettle.

LEDA AND THE SWAN

Apuleius' comic romance directly shaped the construction and coloured the conflicted tone of one of the most mysterious late classical texts ever composed, Francesco Colonna's *The Strife of Love in a Dream*, or *Hypnerotomachia Poliphili*, published in 1499, in very Italianate, almost made-up late Latin, another very curious and highly aestheticized mingling of eroticism and metaphysics.[46] (For example, the lovers kiss 'each other more tightly and mordantly than the sucklers of an octopus's tentacles . . . They kissed with juicy and tremulous tongues nourished with fragrant musk, playfully penetrating each other's wet and laughing lips and making painless marks on the white throats with their little teeth.'[47]) With nearly 200 extraordinary vignettes, *The Dream of Poliphilo*, as it is commonly called, remains one of the most seductively designed volumes in the history of early bookmaking, by the great Venetian printer Aldus Manutius.[48]

The story begins in the first person, telling of the stricken narrator's dream quest for his true love, the lady Polia. Then, after he has regained her, and sailed with her to Venus' island of Cytharea, she takes up the story, and winds the reader into more recursive loops of time past, and more fantasies intricately set one inside the other, until, after several more partings and reunions, and even Poliphilo's death, her testimony is revealed as all part of his dream and he wakes up—alone.

The author intricately reweaves several antecedents: Apuleius' work suffuses this belated myth of pagan transformation (and is often invoked by name); Colonna also gives a heady and profane twist to Dante's visionary journey through the heavens with Beatrice at his side. Poliphilo, a male Psyche and the author's alter ego, suffering agonies of erotic longings, submits to punishing trials of his strength, his fidelity, his passion, in a fairy-tale sequence of enchanted castles and gardens and temples, and after many vicissitudes which include initiation into the cult of Priapus, he attains his heart's desire, but only to lose his beloved in the end. The book was written, it is now thought, by a disaffected monk called Francesco Colonna, who was attached to the church hospital of San Zanipolo, SS. Giovanni e Paolo in Venice; the enigmatic, poetic, often explicit illustrations have been attributed to Mantegna but remain anonymous for the present.

This fantastical fiction can take us further into the permutations of hatching. The lover must struggle, in a heightened, hallucinatory atmosphere of dream and inner torment, towards the desired transformation and release of self. He submits to ordeals to achieve fullness of being, and not incidentally, in the course of his mystical journey, the protagonist Poliphilo encounters several myths of metamorphosis, including the loves of Zeus. He becomes the privileged spectator at a series of four triumphs: the chariots, encrusted with gems and intaglios and arrayed in rich marbles with magical properties, are fabulously and extensively described, the author giving happy rein to his very particular combination of sybarite relish and accumulative pedantry. As the very fine engraved illustrations show, the first triumphal car is pulled by 'six lusty centaurs' ridden by musician nymphs; the centrepiece features Europa, carried off by Zeus in the shape of a bull. On the second triumphal chariot, the side panels show a nativity scene, set in a contemporary bedroom, with midwives and helpers gathered around. In this case, the mother has laid two eggs: 'there issued from one egg a little flame, and from the other two bright stars'.[49] On the corresponding panel on the car's other side, the attendants are depicted carrying off the eggs to a temple of Apollo and praying to the oracle for the meaning of this portent.[50] This depicts the birth of the two pairs of twins, Helen and Clytemnestra, Castor and Pollux, to Leda after Zeus took the form of a swan to seduce her.

On the next double page, the second triumphal chariot is depicted, drawn by six bejewelled and betasselled white elephants, and crowned by a *tableau vivant* of Leda and the swan at the moment of their union: 'The swan was kissing her with its divine beak; its wings were down, covering the bare parts of the noble lady, as with divine and voluptuous pleasure the two of them united in their delectable sport . . . Nothing was lacking to contribute to the increase of delight.' This erotic performance, the author continues, 'gave especial pleasure to the onlookers, who responded with praise and applause' (Fig. 22).[51]

Colonna here picks up Ovid's description, from the passage in which he evokes Arachne's tapestry, showing the rapes of the Olympians:

Fecit olorinis Ledam recubare sub alis . . .

(She [Arachne] made Leda lie back under the swan's wings . . .)[52]

As in Ovid, further amours of Zeus follow the pageant of Leda: the triumphal procession Poliphilo beholds then continues with Danae, the mother of Perseus, and Semele, the mother of Dionysus, narrated in equally excited prose. Regarding the band of youths dancing and singing near the pageant, the author exclaims, 'I

Fig. 22 In *The Strife of Love in a Dream*, an early printed book and one of the most unusual erotic adventures ever written, a triumphal procession unfolds before the dreamer's eyes, showing the loves of the gods; it inspires wonder and envy in all the beholders (*Leda and the Swan*, engraving, Venice, 1499).

might even have dared to propose, in jest, that the infernal spirits suffer no torment except that of envying these [here] . . .'[53] In the same way as the Neoplatonists overlooked the caprices of the gods, and the arbitrary afflictions of poor Psyche in their allegorization of her story, a Venetian humanist sets aside the mordant critique that Ovid conveys through his protagonist Arachne in order to exult in mystical erotica.

The reinvention of paganism by the Florentine humanists here casts a positive shadow across Christian ambitions to control women, in a way that is not altogether acceptable to contemporary taste, and Ovidian irony is set aside in a flagrantly voluptuous encomium to sexuality and procreation. Towards the end of the book, the lovers are eventually united in the temple of Venus of Living Nature, Venus *Physizoa*, and, as Edgar Wind noted, the story of Leda in Colonna's romance occurs in a sequence of theogamies allegorizing the elements 'subject to the *physizoa Venere*: namely, Europa, Earth, Leda, Water, Danae, Air and Semele, Fire'.[54] Wind also pointed out that the comparatively rare epithet, *physizoos* (life-producing, life-giving), is used of the fertile earth in connection to the Dioscuri in both the *Iliad* (III, 243) and the *Odyssey* (XI, 301). The Dioscuri are the boy twins Leda bore, who hatched from the shell; Homer's adjective suggests that the twins are somehow doubly made of living natural matter, combining *physis* and *zoon*; they are, in today's imagery, authentic, guaranteed organic material.

If we look more closely at the most famous interpretations of Leda's story, and the fate of the paintings in question, we can appreciate the extent of the sacrilege for Christian believers presented by this myth, with its celebration of nature, flesh, rapture, aberration (and even bestiality).

In the story of Leda, a mortal woman, after the visit from the god in the shape of a swan, gives birth to two sets of twins—to the future Helen of Troy, and her sister Clytemnestra, and to the Dioscuri, the twin heroes Castor and Pollux.[55]

Mythographers worried about the outlandishness of the story, and tried to sidestep its literal-mindedness with ingenious twists.[56] In Euripides' play, Helen herself casts doubt on the tale of her paternity, declaring airily, 'There is, you know, a legend which says that Zeus took the feathered form of a swan, and that being pursued by an eagle and flying for refuge to the bosom of my mother Leda, he used this deceit to accomplish his desire upon her. That is the story of my origin—if it is true.'[57] The anxiety about the status of the story is revealing; it shows how the myth's incongruity persisted and that the idea of a human woman laying eggs after mating with a swan could not settle into a fixed form. The mythographers continued to worry at it ('we shall leave the matter undecided', writes Hyginus)[58] because it displays those fantastic and uncouth features that Plato despised in 'old wives' tales'; it also disobeys the congruity of analogous, animal metamorphoses.

However, as a victim of divine lust comments in the *Odyssey*, apparently without irony, 'a god's embrace is never fruitless',[59] and many such episodes of rape and insemination lie at the foundation of cultures and nations in Greek and Roman history and of divine dynasties—hence Io, Danae, Europa.[60]

The trope of the triumphal pageant is related to ekphrasis, and indeed, while Colonna/Poliphilo is clear that the side panels of the chariots are images, the narrative does more than imply that the figures on top are acting and moving: only the most ingenious of automata could return the swan's caresses. Yet the lovers' lifelikeness could remain an impression made on the beholders through the dazzling *enargeia* of the images, as vivid and highly wrought as the caparisons and trappings of the vehicles. The indeterminacy is important: it helps to communicate the dream state of the teller, and of all the people and things he sees. But as ambiguous ekphrasis, suspended in the oneiric state beyond both the reality of artefacts and the actuality of experience, Poliphilo's vision interestingly echoes two earlier, comparable sequences about Jupiter's dalliance, in which Leda appears: first, the procession of shades of dead lovers whom Odysseus encounters in the underworld, and second the scenes of the gods' 'heavenly crimes' woven into the defamatory tapestry of Arachne in the *Metamorphoses* of Ovid before she is turned into a spider by the enraged goddess Minerva.

In these ekphrases, the bizarre metamorphoses of the god are arrayed in 'picture-flesh'—Maurice Merleau-Ponty's illuminating phrase for the status of the living likeness.[61] These tableaux on the chariot partake of their poetic predecessors' insubstantial character; the phantoms whom Odysseus cannot touch, cannot feel, as he discovers when he tries to embrace his mother, exist in an analogous, imaginary, immaterial dimension as Poliphilo's dream pageants and Arachne's embroideries: they appear to be alive, but it is a mere semblance: they are become insubstantial. The images are figments, the shades similar illusions of presence.

However, according to many representations and tellings of the myth, Leda literally hatches out her offspring: this is no figure of speech. The temple of the Leucippidae in Sparta even displayed shards of a gigantic eggshell, which was said to be the very one she laid. A delightful sculpture dated to the fifth century BC, now in Potenza, Italy, counts as the earliest extant to depict the theme (Fig. 2.5); a spirited fourth century BC southern Italian vase, inspired by a clearly highly comic play, shows Helen springing out of a large, white, upright egg, in the manner of a soubrette from a cake; the episode also parodies the birth of Athena from the head of Zeus, since Hephaistos is wielding an immense double axe.[62]

Leda's union with the swan and the subsequent entry of fatal beauty into the world, in the shape of Helen of Troy, connects to my earlier theme about metamorphosis, with butterflies and their life cycle, because the swan is doing duty in this myth as an active, animating, inspiriting agent. Metamorphosis here begins to represent vitality itself. The Ovidian vision that all is change raised the question about the agency of change. Even if spontaneous generation is posited, what is the quickening principle, the animator? Within the phenomenon of fertility what kicks flesh into being?

Fig. 23 The future Helen of Troy is hatched from one of the
two eggs Leda lays after her union with Zeus in the shape of a
swan (Greek, fifth century BC).

The morphic rhymes between these changing types of vital
agency, between human and divine (animal) origins, between spirits and butterflies, are glossed in a very fine, and unusually tender
sixteenth-century engraving of Leda and her children, now given to
G.-B. Palumba (Fig. 24).[63] For the vigorous baby on the right is
holding up a butterfly to his mother, as if the artist were alluding,
through a kind of blithe child's play, to the natural possibility of

Fig. 24 One of Leda's children vigorously draws his mother's attention to the butterfly he holds in his hand, as if to stress the natural energy of metamorphosis, while in the background the ruined temple of Minerva Medica in Rome itself resembles a cracked eggshell. *Leda and the Swan*, attributed Master I.B. with the Bird (Giovanni Battista Palumba), 1500–25.

producing unalike from unalike, as opposed to the mammalian facsimile of human reproduction. 'Hey, Mum,' the child might be saying, 'it's not so weird that we came out of those eggs. This—this butterfly, this creature—it comes from something even less like itself—a caterpillar!'

Butterflies, as the embodiment of the ensouling virtual power, act analogously to the phenomena which the Gods assume in order to bring about those ever fruitful unions. The question tying together the metaphors of swans and butterflies, hatching of children and transformation of caterpillars, addresses quite simply the continuing problem about the origin of life. The divine bird-lover suggests quickening, and belongs in a cluster of metaphors, again with roots in that Aristotelian biology about the imprinting of form onto matter and the activity of spirit in generation: this is metamorphosis as *making*, as materialization, and it correspondingly inhabits rhetorical and narrative modes—the extended word-pictures of Apuleius' romance, of Ovid's poem (Arachne's tapestry), and of Colonna's dream book (the series of four triumphs) where language is doing the work of making the real, of making it up, and drawing attention to the powers of words, and by extension, of images, to bring things into being. (This theme will be coming up again in my final chapter, about the reproductive effect of new media: the magic animating power of representation itself.)

The god Zeus/Jupiter, generating life, operates as a *fictive* agent, and in performing these acts of procreation, he demonstrates this power and refashions himself into an animal, or a cloud, or a shower of gold—into figments of himself. It is suggestive that the scenes of these transformations are so frequently celebrated in the form of artefacts, not real events, as if the poets and writers intuited the correspondence between metaphor's work of metamorphosis and the gods' changes of shape (Pl. VII).[64]

If the rapes committed by Zeus/Jupiter with women such as Io and Leda are not aligned with metamorphosis as violent translation between species, but more with metamorphosis as ongoing vital principle of creation, as in the butterfly life cycle, these stories can be interpreted differently, and their elemental character linked to different manifestations of the life force, and thence, to different theories of generation. The whirling white swan, alongside the shower of gold for Danae and the dewy cloud for Io, presents one of Zeus' poetic biological permutations as impregnating agent.

For there is a further corresponding step taken in the myth of Leda: she is not *herself* brought to life by the airy creature, as is Adam by the infusion of his soul, or Pandora after she is 'moulded from earth' and 'breathed' on—animated—by the gods;[65] Leda is *fertilized*; here, the myth seems to me attentive to the biology of hatching and imaginatively cogent, for the male does indeed quicken otherwise sterile eggs that, in contradistinction from the mammalian mode of reproduction, can be birthed—laid—but do not then hatch.

Nevertheless, such supernatural transformations, contrary to anything found in nature, which the gods can accomplish to wreak their will—Zeus as a swan mating with a human woman—only intensify the difficulty of distinguishing natural metamorphosis, the gestation of a creature, animal or human from the anomalous irruption of life, as in a woman laying eggs. The confusion is not helped by language's failure to discriminate between categories of wonders; it lies deep within the mystery of change itself.

LEONARDO ET AL.

The engraving in the *Hypnerotomachia Poliphili* precedes the dates suggested both for the beginning of Leonardo's interest in Leda (1504) and Michelangelo's painting (1529–30), also lost, as is Leonardo's; although Michelangelo's reclining nude, covered by the swan who is billing her lips with his beak, bears more than a little resemblance to the Poliphilo illustration.[66] The earliest market in pornographic prints took cover under learned allusion. In the case of Leda and the swan, the artists were prompted less by the extant literature than by survivals of sculpture from 500 years of antiquity.[67] Some of these examples are bizarrely anatomical, revealing the sculptors working out how such a union could have taken place physically. One solution, represented on several surviving classical carvings, depicts Leda standing, bowed under the bird whose bill grips her neck while he 'treads her'. The composition, even to contemporary eyes, has a literal quality that edges it into pornography's forensic domain: something about the way Leda's knees bend turns the scene into an experiment in sexual positions rather than a meta-physical myth.[68] Yeats saw one of these antique reliefs in the Doge's Palace, in Venice, before writing his famous poem—of which more later. Renaissance artists also had access to gem carvings and sar-cophagi; Michelangelo, for example, could have known an onyx cameo, which was in Lorenzo de' Medici's cabinet.[69] Michelangelo clearly succumbed to the story, with rather unaccustomed sensual-ity, and caught its fantastical dream quality. His Leda does not fend off her assailant, but lies sleeping, as if conjuring the bird in her mind's eye.

The Cornelis Bos engraving after Michelangelo reveals his Leda to be a powerfully muscled androgyne, in her heavy recumbency very close to the monumental figure of *Night* on the Medici tombs (Fig. 25); she lies in an arc, tightly intertwined with the bird's wings (wonderfully conveyed by Bos's draughtsmanship—every feather aquiver), her head fallen forwards in slumber, and her left arm falling languidly, as if she were dreaming the swan's presence, not assaulted by him. The arc of the swan's neck responds to the curves and bows of her limbs and her braided hair and the flighty topknot in a marvellously rhythmic series of points and counterpoints, which Bos picks up with the line of both his burin on the plate and the touches of drypoint drawing on the print. This Leda is mas-sively built, as Michelangelo's figures are, with anachronistically mature female breasts added to imposing male physique, but her

Fig. 25 One pair of twins, perhaps Castor and Pollux, with the tracings of shells' craquelure on their heads, have emerged; another baby appears inside a transparent egg as Leda lies dreamily intertwined with the swan. (Cornelis Bos, engraving after Michelangelo, sixteenth century).

heft adds, in Bos's sensitive engraving, to the intoxicated languor of the unlikely but enraptured union. Unlike the classical reliefs which show the pair grappling for a fit, like lock and key, Michelangelo's composition lingers on the harmonious sinuosity of their made-up lines, not the anatomical match of their limbs. Behind her, the hatched children have a slight craquelure drawn on their skulls, as if eggshells were still stuck to their crowns.

Leonardo da Vinci made some of his most exquisite drawings towards a composition of Leda and the swan before Michelangelo adopted the theme: the mystery of this myth belongs to his continuous explorations into the origins and manifestations of life. His interest in the theme developed into two compositions, both known only from drawings and copies of his followers. One pose shows Leda on one knee in the position of a classical Venus *anadyomene*, as in a lovely warm brush sketch from Parma, possibly a head for the Leda. Another, exquisite pencil drawing from the Chatsworth collection for the second composition on which Leonardo seems to have worked, depicts a naked Leda standing, beguilingly musing with downcast eyes at the sight of her babies, who have hatched at her feet (Fig. 26). The swan extends a wing to cradle her and she twists her body into his downy serpentine curves. The painting or paintings are both lost—if the artist ever painted one at all,[70] but several epigones interpreted the drawings, and the naked Leda is accompanied in these strange pictures by her hatchlings, one pair of twins or, sometimes, two pairs of twins on the flowery meadow under her feet. The Leonardo scholar Martin Kemp comments, 'The *Leda* and the *Lady* [a portrait on which Leonardo was also working in 1507] express two sides of the macrocosmic coin: the procreative powers of all living things; and the circulatory processes of "vivification" which arise from natural flux.'[71] Although the painting of Leda is missing, as I say, both Raphael and Correggio worked in the light of Leonardo's composition, so its imagery is celebrated.[72] Several copies after Leonardo also survive: Cesare da Sesto's version, in Wilton House,

Fig. 26 Leonardo da Vinci imagined Leda as an unfallen Eve, tenderly enfolded by the wing of Jupiter in swan form, kneeling naked in a natural paradise, with a double pair of twins hatching at her feet.

Hampshire, is considered by Martin Kemp to come closest to Leonardo's lost picture.[73]

The fecundity of these female nudes, materializing in paint within the new paganism of northern Italy, appears to promise goodness from sexual union and natural processes such as fertilization and division; the imagery defies Christian concepts of sin, inherent in the very idea of the god's rape in animal form. It reconciles contraries, announces bounty, praises beauty and its effects. The blossoming earth, the moist, fertile ground, the gambolling pairs of hatchlings out of their eggshells, the docile and still lovestruck swan in Leda's encircling arm of Leonardo's vision communicate a dream of unstained plenitude, embodied by a Living Venus—a Venus *Physizoa* at harmony in natural creation. Yet this naked woman is not unadorned: Leonardo explicitly resists the equation of female with nature, by crowning his Leda with elaborate braids and curls betokening cosmetic self-fashioning. From sexual encounter to blessed, fertile, and aesthetic physical harmony, Leda, the swan, and her children, including Helen of Troy, offer a poetic theophany of beauty triumphant in the earthly paradise.

This vision is however thoroughly profane; it opposes the foundations of Judaeo-Christian thought about species integrity, sexual decorum, and the divine resemblance of the human image. Leda's paradise is grounded, her bare feet in the damp, fertile greensward, her babies gambolling on the earth. It is a place where creatures live in harmony and fertility, an earthly paradise continuing after the Fall, and in apparent ignorance of its consequences, an Eden without grace, or God, or any transcendent dimension at all. She is an anti-Virgin, an anti-Mary, an unfallen Eve, mother of the living, innocent of—or is it indifferent to?—the knowledge of good and evil.

The identification of Leda with fruitfulness, lasciviousness, and female carnality constituted a scandal—against the proper condition of women and the restraint of sexuality. It discloses the ambiguity within metamorphosis itself. For a human woman to give birth in this way monstrously opens a breach in due natural process: a mother who laid, it was widely reported, a prodigious clutch of eggs, featured in sixteenth-century scandal sheets incubating her multiple brood (Fig. 27).[74]

Aristotle had laid down the principle, as quoted before, that 'To be generative of another like itself, this is the function of every

Fig. 27 Books of natural wonders reported, among monstrous births and fiery meteors, the prodigious laying of a clutch of eggs by a human mother (from Conrad Lycosthenes, *Prodigiorum . . . Chronicon*, sixteenth century).

animal and plant perfect in nature . . .'[75] It was for this reason that he pronounced the female to be a deformity in nature, because she did not conform fully to the imprint of the male vital agent. Leda's progeny in this perspective are matrilineal, made in their mother's image, not their swan father's. Here mythical biology became *ipso facto* perverted, into a traducing of divine order itself.

It is sobering that both the Leonardo and Michelangelo paintings mysteriously vanished, while Correggio's characteristically charming, playful, affectionate variation on the theme (Pl. VII), painted in 1531, was savagely defaced—Leda was literally hacked out—in the eighteenth century: the picture is heavily restored by Antoine Coypel, among other hands.[76]

As a female embodiment of pleasure, as a Venus *Physizoa* presiding over a postlapsarian state of bliss, this Leda stirred one viewer's righteous frenzy. It is possible that the vanished *Leda*s of Leonardo and Michelangelo may also have been erotic figments too powerful to bear. Poliphilo was perhaps more acute than he knew when he exclaimed, as we have seen, at the sight of the lovers' pleasure, 'I might even have dared to propose, in jest, that the infernal spirits suffer no torment except that of envying these [here] . . .'[77] Correggio was certainly successful in creating, from the unlikely figment of a swan's caresses, an image of serene and unalloyed joy, and it excited a terrible torment of envy in one iconoclast at least.

W. B. YEATS: PROFANE ANNUNCIATION

Did the audiences of these pictures perceive the scandalous inversions of classical and Christian theories of parturition? Did they catch, in Leda's prodigious maternity, an echo of the miracle of the Holy Spirit, when, in the shape of a bird, he quickened Mary's womb according to the central tenet of the Incarnation?

Noting the popularity of Leda and the swan in the sculpture and painting of Christian Egypt, Hellenistic scholars have suggested that the analogy with the Holy Ghost probably helped the pagan myth's survival.[78] However, even if the resemblance was serenely accepted and enjoyed by Christian Copts in Alexandria, it was certainly rejected by Christian authorities. Medieval images of the Annunciation vary in their representation of the beam emitted by the dove, and its point of contact with Mary's virgin body. Any number of images picture the bird hovering as he irradiates the Virgin, and occasionally he acts as a hyphen between the mother of God and the very lips of the Trinity, to infuse her with the life force.[79] In the Ashmolean Museum, Oxford, a Nottingham alabaster represents the holy dove swooping down and actually billing the Virgin Annunciate with his long beak.

But it would be a mistake to see Leonardo's and Michelangelo's potent erotic visions as anything but profound, even scandalous challenges to the Christian doctrine of the virgin birth. W. B. Yeats, in his sonnet of 1923, seizes on the analogy with deliberately provocative intent. When he was working as a copyist in the 1880s, Yeats transcribed the Elizabethan translation of Colonna's erotic pilgrimage, *The Strife of Love in a Dream*, for the edition edited by Andrew Lang in 1889.[80] So he knew Colonna's description of Leda's union as well as the antique reliefs.[81] It is Yeats who, picking up the myth from classical and Italian culture, forced it open to reveal its deepest and most dangerous profanity: that the story of Leda and the Swan mimicked the virgin birth of Jesus.

In the poem 'A Vision', Yeats calls Leda's two eggs 'Love and War'; later, he expands this imagery to violent dramatic effect in the famous, rhetorically overwrought sonnet 'Leda and the Swan' (1923). The poem opens with the assault, the bird's action reproduced in the heavy spondaic stresses of the first line:

> A sudden blow: the great wings beating still
> Above the staggering girl, her thighs caressed
> By the dark webs, her nape caught in his bill,
> He holds her helpless breast upon his breast.

Yeats then foresees the tragedy of Troy, brought about by Helen, offspring of the union, and breaks off with a dramatic caesura, itself imitating the cutting down of the King:

> A shudder in the loins engenders there
> The broken wall, the burning roof and tower
> And Agamemnon dead.[82]

In the middle of the poem, Yeats expands on the swan's 'white rush':

> How can those terrified vague fingers push
> The feathered glory from her loosening thighs?

The metonymic phrase ('feathered glory') casts the swan as a light-ringed angelic radiance, glory here invoking the halo of light which envelops divine agents, such as the Holy Ghost. Furthermore, in a poem written several years after 'Leda and the Swan', Yeats openly, even swaggeringly, strikes the profane resonance even more explicitly and evokes 'The Mother of God' in person suffering a violent assault from a bird. Three times he uses the word 'terror' to express the conception of the saviour:

> The threefold terror of love; a fallen flare
> Through the hollow of an ear;
> Wings beating about the room;
> The terror of all terrors that I bore
> The Heavens in my womb.[83]

The contradiction between natural development, as in meta-morphosis, and counter-natural prodigy, as in the assault of the swan and the miracle of virgin birth, blazes in Yeats's fierce lines.

But while Yeats's powerful fantasy reveals symbolic principles at work in both myths, it has the effect of obscuring differences to which earlier, Catholic interpreters were certainly alive. The earthly paradise is strictly earthly, and Leda, as a type of Venus or anti-Mary also represents the fallen world of unredeemed creature-liness, where virginity is lost and grace other than the physical set aside. As Elizabeth Butler Cullingford has analysed in her book on Yeats, he wrote the Leda poem as a challenge to the newly victor-ious Young Irelanders and a protest against their Catholic conserv-ative politics with regard to sex and women.[84] Such a blazingly rapturous account of a rape reads uneasily however in the sexual politics of today. As she perceptively comments, 'Yeats's personal empathy with two female rape victims who were closely associated in his mythological imagination does not, however, entirely dispel the doubts of a feminist reader. 'Leda and the Swan' demonstrates what happens when a writer cares more about using explicitly sexual situations as a strategy for challenging censorship than

I. The vision of Hieronymus Bosch has made him an honorary Surrealist, but classical myths and the earliest reports of New World legends may have shaped his fantasies of a false paradise (*The Garden of Earthly Delights, c.* 1504, central panel).

II. Giant birds, or tiny humans? Such a variety of species—including a kingfisher, a hoopoe, and a woodpecker—figure vividly in stories of metamorphosis and the migration of souls, in both Ovid and early American-Caribbean literature (detail, Bosch, *Garden of Earthly Delights*).

III. The revellers in the Garden eat, carry, flourish, and play with all kinds of fruits; they also emerge from berries and gourds, and even appear to be turning into strawberries and plums (detail, Bosch, *Garden of Earthly Delights*).

[about] the implications of that strategy for women, who are both the subjects of and subject to the power of his imagination.'[85]

The myth of Leda and the swan has inspired numerous male interpretations, often lubricious in character, but it has also appealed to women artists, from Arachne onwards, and Angela Carter, in one of her early novels, *The Magic Toyshop*, consciously revisited the Yeatsian foundation myth of catastrophe when she staged the crisis in her heroine Melanie's coming-of-age at a live puppet show of Leda and the Swan devised in the book by the wicked Uncle Philip, master toymaker and puppeteer.[86] In 1967, Angela Carter, who was then seismically acute in her feminist analysis, can still melt all the confusions and tumult of this terrifying metamorphosis into the catalyst of Melanie's selfhood—of her emergence into elected sexuality directed at another, so that, while Melanie's uncle remains wicked, tyrannical, and lewd in his role as diabolical master of ceremonies, the effect of the experience on the young girl is explosively liberating. Carter is shadowing Yeats in her adoption of shock tactics to spark new life in her subject.[87]

GRUBS AND NYMPHS

When Kafka chose the title, *Die Vervandlung*, the word used in German translations of Ovid's *Metamorphoses*, was he replying, obliquely, to the storytelling of his great Latin predecessors Ovid and Apuleius? Certainly there are resonances, far beyond the direct echo in the title, however startling and incongruous this may seem; both writers take us into the process of transformation so closely that even while they concentrate on its physical effects on the victim's body, the reader experiences the change viscerally, from the inside, as it were.

The story opens with the famous scene:

When Gregor Samsa woke up one morning from unsettling dreams, he found himself changed in his bed into a monstrous vermin. He was lying on his back as hard as armour plate, and when he lifted his head a little, he saw his vaulted brown belly, sectioned by arch-shaped ribs, to whose dome the cover, about to slide off completely, could barely cling. His many legs, pitifully thin compared with the size of the rest of him, were waving helplessly before his eyes.

'What's happened to me?' he thought. It was no dream.[88]

Kafka communicates his protagonist's plight with such convincing particularity and intense identification that it is difficult, in thinking about the story, to remember that, unlike Apuleius, it is not written in the first person. But it cannot be, because it ends with Gregor's extinction. However we, the readers, experience his fate from within his mind and feelings, from his point of view, and share his anguish at his lost form, as we partake of Lucius' grim predicament too. But unlike Ovid, in a move that indeed turns its back on the optimism of the Pythagorean creation myth, we follow the fate of the bug *after* the change, as if Ovid had remained with Arachne, attentive to her mental state after Minerva had spellbound her in the shape of a spider. The loss of identity that a change of shape implies in the Judaeo-Christian thinking about human body–soul relations effectively heightens the horror and despair in Kafka's story. Variously seen by his several antagonists as a cockroach, a dung beetle, and a monstrous vermin ('ungeheueres Ungerziefer'), Gregor has lost his humanity and, with it, his human appetites and habits: he is UN-done, and several of the words used in the German begin with this prefix, UN-, to denote his passage into an uncanny state of non-being.[89] While Gregor eats filth and dung and prefers to scuttle under the sofa, he is racked by the hostility of his father, the disgust of his mother, and the pity of his sister for his beastly form. The paean of a Leonardo to the flux and fertile variety of creation, itself swelling with ancient philosophy's excitement, withers in the grip of twentieth-century despair; and a Judaeo-Christian hierarchy of being, with unclean beasts (especially carapaced invertebrate bugs) at the very bottom, replaces the Heraclitean vortex.

Transmogrification into a bug, with its diabolical overtones, precedes the reinvigoration and restoration of the Samsa family, in a cruel irony that intensifies poor Gregor's fate. His disposability, literally swept up and thrown away, circulates energy through the organism of his immediate family. But as he himself does not migrate to another form, the Pythagorean resemblances could end there. Kafka's story also opens up the question, who is the agent of the metamorphosis? Gregor feels deep shame that he has somehow merited it, that, like the fates of so many beings in myth, his beetle shape suits him, expresses an essence of Samsa that was concealed hitherto by his decorous and upright external appearance as a young man. But if one considers that Gregor's father might be the implied perpetrator of his transformation, then Kafka is ringing an interesting and characteristic change on arbitary divine power, exercised throughout classical myths on hapless humans who attract gods—in the case of raped girls. His change of shape invites further humiliation at the hands of his father, and physical assaults.

Vladimir Nabokov, uniquely both distinguished lepidopterist and fabulist, wanted to establish exactly which species of insect Kafka is evoking—a difficult, perhaps impossible task, and not entirely appropriate either, since Kakfa's realism serves to make his stories leap to life in the mind's eye, not to map their elements on to actual, observable situations outside the frame of the stories. Nabokov concludes that the bug is simply 'a big beetle', indeed, as he can reach the door knob with his feelers, one that is three feet high. Nabokov points out that Gregor should have realized that as a beetle he had a pair of wings hidden under 'the hard covering of his back', which could have carried him for miles and miles in a blundering flight.'[90]

But Kafka is another kind of allegorist, and a myth-maker, offering fables and metaphors to penetrate the feeling of what happens; metamorphosis becomes a means of communicating a profoundly altered concept of the self, in which the emerging being does not express self-knowledge but destroys the possibility of self-recognition; when you become unlike yourself, give birth as it were to another self unbeknownst to you. Gregor is himself at the grub stage; his ultimate development alienates him from his family, his world, and, mostly, from himself.

In 1949 Nabokov was planning a study of butterflies in art, starting with the Egyptian wall fresco in the British Museum.[91] His interests ranged far beyond the lepidopterological scientific into the symbolic. It is a little glib to map his rare butterfly-hunting on the chase of Humbert Humbert and Quilty across America in pursuit and capture of Lolita; it has been remarked often enough. But one small detail perhaps has not been pointed out: the celebrated litany of pet names which opens Humbert Humbert's deposition tells us Lolita was a diminutive of Dolores, including 'Dolly at school'.[92]

She is a doll, Humbert Humbert calls her later,[93] as is a pupa, as mentioned before—it is the word for doll in Latin. And with this writer, wordplay is never less than studied. *The Annotated Lolita* makes something of the lepidopteral thematics of the novel: the doctor in the frame story, who presents Humbert Humbert's sad case, is even called John Ray, Jr., as if he were the belated progeny of Maria Merian's English contemporary and theorist of insect metamorphosis.[94] In lepidoptery, the nymph is not the blossom but the bud, if you like, and in many ways, the grubby knees and other blemishes on the nymphet Lolita capture the proper state of zoological nymph, while the drab pathos of the heroine in the final desolating glimpse given at the end of the book matches that disillusion that Maria Merian expresses so spontaneously at the specimens she sometimes hatched.

In a more comic mode, Nabokov elsewhere gives a vivid account of the extraordinary process of metamorphosis. Here is the caterpillar:

It is a tight feeling—here about the neck and elsewhere, and then an unbearable itch. Of course he has moulted a few times before, but *that* is nothing in comparison to the tickle and urge he feels now. He must shed that tight dry skin, or die. As you have guessed, under that skin, the armor of a pupa—and how uncomfortable to wear one's skin over one's armor—is already forming . . .

One wriggle, another wriggle—and zip, the skin bursts down the back, and he gradually gets out of it, working with shoulders and hips like a person getting out of a sausage dress.

Nabokov, in this *jeu d'esprit*, purposely anthropomorphizes the protracted development, drawing attention to the pupa's papoose-like appearance:

The pupa splits as the caterpillar had split—it is really a last glorified moult, and the butterfly creeps out . . . She is not handsome at first. She is very damp and bedraggled . . . You have noticed that the caterpillar is a *he*, the pupa an *it*, and the butterfly a *she*. You will ask—what is the feeling of hatching? Oh, no doubt, there is a rush of panic to the head, a thrill of breathlessness and strange sensation, but then the eyes see, in a flow of sunshine, the butterfly sees the world, the large and awful face of the gaping entomologist.[95]

He offers no explanation for the dramatic shifts in gender from it to he to she for the final butterfly, beyond drawing attention to this unsettling aspect of a single organism's continuing existence. But in this, as you know, he is following the Greek feminine of the word butterfly, Psyche, soul.

Nabokov had far more subtle recourse to the metaphor of hatching in 'Christmas', a perfectly shaped, eerie, subtle fragment of a story written in 1924.[96] He conveys here the unpredictable psychology that lies at the basis of modern concepts of self explicitly through the image of a cocoon. After a deep snowfall in the country, a landowner called Sleptsov, who has lost his child, a boy who collected butterflies, enters the manor house where they spent idyllic summers. He breaks down in grief in his child's room. There he finds 'a large, exotic cocoon . . .' which the child had bought for three roubles. 'It was papery to the touch and seemed made of a brown folded leaf. His son had remembered it during his sickness, regretting that he had left it behind, but consoling himself with the thought that the crysalid inside was probably dead.' Sleptsov brings it back with him, with the child's diary of summer days; and as he weeps, suicidally, over the death of this beloved child, he hears 'a sudden snap—a thin sound like that of an overstretched rubber band breaking. Sleptsov opened his eyes. The cocoon in the biscuit tin had burst at its tip, and a black, wrinkled creature the size of a mouse was crawling up the wall above the table. . . . having broken out, it was slowly and miraculously expanding . . . and its wings— still feeble, still moist—kept growing and unfolding . . .'

The delicacy of contrasting moods, as the streak of hope slants across the texture of the story's unutterable sadness, works through a series of densely evoked images, the muffling weight of the new snow, the shuttered, swathed, curtained, shut-up house expressing the mutedness, inertia of mourning; when the chrysalis suddenly, unexpectedly hatches from its long torpid simulation of death, it is as if the soul of the child has sloughed off mortal weight and in its new lightness has interrupted the father's mourning with a promise. The last, finely balanced words of the story are 'tender, ravishing, almost human happiness'.

This process does however present a problem; it even perpetrates the scandal that lies at the core of metamorphosis itself: the same spirit/soul/essence appears to occupy different forms and yet remain itself. This discomfiture can be avoided by narrative unity of viewpoint, the storyteller's skill of linking the disparate pieces, if the successive stages are not seen as different, fully developed forms at all, but as aspects of the single creature which is the being in question.

Nabokov introduced his lectures on the modern literature of transformation with his account of butterfly metamorphosis. I am going to borrow from him: in the next chapter the topic will be 'Splitting', and I will be giving a genealogy of the zombie, as found in the writings of Coleridge, among others.

3

Splitting

The word 'zombie' first appears in English, according to the *OED*, in Robert Southey's three-volume *History of Brazil* published between 1810 and 1819; the British Library copy was presented by Southey to his friend and brother-in-law Samuel Taylor Coleridge, who annotated it, but sparsely, and left many pages uncut. Coleridge did however gloss the footnote Southey provides on the meaning and origin of the word zombie, in ways that throw a thoughtful light on the concept of the living dead in circulation today, as I shall discuss later. Southey is recounting the terrible revenge taken by the Spanish in 1694 on the maroons, or escaped slaves who had established their own stable society and were continuing to revolt against their masters. For sixty years, he relates, they had 'acquired strength and audacity [and] . . . acted upon the offensive . . . Their numbers were continually increased by slaves who sought for freedom, and men of colour who fled from justice . . .'[1] This community was ruled, Southey continues, by an elected chief, 'chosen for his justice as well as his valour . . . it is said that no conspiracies or struggles for power had ever been known among them. Perhaps a feeling for religion contributed to this obedience; for Zombi, the title whereby he was called, is the name for the Deity, in the Angolan tongue . . .' Southey goes on to evoke the fortified 'palace of the Zombi' in awed terms, and grieves for the cruel suppression of their revolt and the mass suicide that followed: in its consequences for the vanquished, this conquest resembles 'the inhuman wars of antiquity', he concludes.[2]

Southey then appends a revealing footnote, where he writes that his source for the story, the Portuguese historian Sebastiam da Rocha Pitta, says 'the word means Devil in their language'. Finding this 'unlikely', Southey researched it, and then affirms that 'Nzambi is the word for Deity'.[3] Still showing traces here of the poets in their youth, and their revolutionary sympathies, he thereby inverts the colonist's prejudicial gloss, and rejects his equivalence of another's deity or lord with the devil. But, in this inaugural passage, the contemporary meaning of zombie has not yet come into view.

Gradually, imperceptibly, and at the start, anonymously, the zombie becomes a new way of thinking about a person, from the turn of the eighteenth century onwards, until the concept was naturalized in mainstream orthodoxy of the supernatural. The zombie's increasing salience since the nineteenth century results from the collision of forces in mercantile imperialism still clashing so turbulently in the present day. The classical idea of soul migration, which underpins Ovid's *Metamorphoses*, was rediscovered and reconfigured in the growing imperial possessions, and became, in the fallout from slavery, a vehicle to express a new, psychological state of personal alienation, moral incoherence, and emptiness. I am using here the term 'splitting' to describe, above all, one type of metamorphosis: the severance of the spirit from its bodily envelope. The split selves resulting from this magical operation— the mortal husk on the one hand and the disembodied, roaming spirit on the other—lead into a bewildering, uncanny world of the night, thronged with spectres and unsettled by false appearances. Amid the undone crowd of ghosts and revenants, ghouls and phantoms, zombies emerge as the dominant and most fascinating terror in the literature—and entertainment—that the African diaspora has influenced. Doubles, who will figure in the next chapter, depend for their existence on the possibility of mind–body scission, or splitting; and from them arises the hosts of replicants and doppel-gängers, victims of scooping by aliens, and clones that teem in the popular and literary culture of Victorian and contemporary Gothic. So splitting here does not refer to the prehistory of schizo-phrenia as a diagnosis, or the common idea of 'split personality', nor does it invoke the psychological strategy, analysed especially in Melanie Klein, of splitting good and bad objects. The zombie, and its counterpart, the double, thrive in the 'positive shadow' of his-torical fusion. Certain particular twists of the supernatural in the fiction, drama, and poetry of the late eighteenth century and after-wards happened in contact with the spirit beliefs of colonized subjects, as a direct influence; while many sources have been offered for Gothic's characteristic spectres, the empire has not, in my view, figured significantly.

The word has changed in value today from a living god, a nature spirit or divine power, as in Southey, to a vacant person, a husk, a shell, the living dead, and this passage of comment, in which it is first embedded in English, offers an almost too neat and cogent context for such a fall from grace in its meaning. The word zombie appears here as the prototype liberation martyr-hero: an early exemplar of elected ruler, the chieftain of a free band of rebels who dies heroically rather than resume a life in chains, who is instantly demonized by the colonial historian, and then converted, once again, into a spirit of inspiration, an inner, vital force or soul. I shall discuss later how Coleridge reveals dramatically in his poetry the draining of meaning from the word 'zombie', as it was transferred from one in whom daemonic power has been legitimately invested, to the victim of internal demons. Just as Zombi the Brazilian hero gives his name to the living dead in nineteenth-century culture, so the dream of enfranchisement of mankind, male and female, such as the young poets had proclaimed at the end of the eighteenth century was itself emptied of hope—for a complex set of historical, political, and personal reasons.[4]

THE NATURE OF ZOMBIES

What is a zombie? The ghosts in most eschatological belief systems walk abroad as *disembodied spirits*: death has split the soul from the body and the deceased only *appears* to have personal, bodily form. The Judaeo-Christian tradition agrees with Indian, Japanese, and Chinese religion and storytelling in this respect: a ghost is an illusion. Dante is the only being in hell who casts a shadow, because only material bodies displace light; the dead who appear to him in their persons are phantom images, formed, Virgil explains to him, as light makes itself manifest as rainbows in vapour or fire takes shape in flames.

But the zombie reverses this phantom state; a zombie is a living body without a soul. The concept gives a local habitation and a name to the terrifying possibility of a living person who has been vacated of all the faculties and qualities that make up personhood: of memory, of will, of thought, of sensation and emotion, in short of consciousness. The concept of the zombie runs the timeline on mind–body, life–death separation backwards and postulates a living thing evacuated of soul *before* dying, a husk inhabited by a non-being that mimics being automatically but with eerie emptiness. This type of the living dead revolves the axiomatic mind–body divide, to come out with a different equation. If you take Soul as a working expression for inner self and add it to Body you get the whole Person (P), so Soul (P − body) = ghost; Body (P − soul) = zombie. Zombies have come to typify a modern personality, to convey a danger to self in figurative terms.

Put in zombie on the web and you will hit thousands of entries, 130,061 on Alta Vista alone, many of them enthusiastically expressed, in words and pictures. For example, the classic *I Walked with a Zombie*, but also websites called *I Love Zombies!* and *A Field Guide to Zombie Behaviour* and *Survival Guide for a Zombie World*. The word is now adopted into many languages besides English, most likely carried far and wide via American entertainment.

The zombie's currency thrives today, because a zombie exemplifies, it seems to me (and to the many merry fans of zombiedom), a twentieth-century anxiety that is not being allayed in this new era, but increasingly revisited as an alarming, ever present possibility that can be dwelt in. In common parlance, work turns people into zombies; other people turn people into zombies; life does it (so do committees).

A philosopher interested in zombiedom, David Chalmers, has distinguished different varieties of zombies abroad today:

First, 'Hollywood zombies': they infest video nasties now and used to be confined to B movies (then made in Pittsburgh); this kind eat carrion human flesh—on film—drip with slime and gore and gloop, and are close cousins to Hollywood vampires. With their counterparts from the kitsch voodoo of role-playing games, they feature pervasively in comic horror culture. Secondly, there now circulates the case of 'the philosopher's zombie', a device for thinking about consciousness. Such zombies 'differ from humans in not having conscious (or, at least, qualitatively conscious) mental states . . . they are not conscious because they do not have sensations, or *qualia*.'[5] The philosopher Simon Blackburn distinguishes, in his recent introduction to philosophy, called *Think*, the test cases of the Zombie and the Mutant as defining the possibilities and limits of the human. Both 'look like you and me, have inside stuff like you and me', but in his scheme, the Mutant, who has a 'ghost within' behaves differently, unpredictably, divergently, whereas the Zombie eerily duplicates human behaviour, only has no ghost within. Blackburn adduces zombies in a very contemporary way, to press against complacent assumptions about personhood. 'Because Zombies look and behave just like you and me, there is no way of telling which of us are Zombies and which are conscious in the way that you and I are. Or at any rate, in the way that I am. For now that I have raised the Zombie possibility, I see that I cannot really be sure about you or anyone else. Perhaps consciousness is an extremely rare correlate of a complex system of brain and body. Perhaps I am the only example of it: perhaps the rest of you are all Zombies.'[6]

This scary proposition, for all its skirmishing wit, adumbrates fundamental questions that have run through literary explorations of identity since modern fictions of haunting and possession began in the eighteenth century. The philosophical zombie does however restrict the concept to a being without consciousness altogether, and this state exceeds the labile, storytelling metamorphoses of zombies who often function consciously, but without power over their behaviour; their consciousness has been taken over. They are annulled; another works their will through them.[7] A certain dim awareness that they have been voided of personhood exacerbates the anguish of their condition, as we shall see in the case of the kind of spellbound husks or shells that emerge in nineteenth-century literature. Nevertheless, 'absent qualia' seems to me a good way of describing what used to be called spirit possession or soul theft, when the bundle of faculties that make a person recognizable—mind, volition, expressiveness, feelings— have been reduced, if not extinguished.

The zombie originates in African and West Indian beliefs and stories, and was disseminated from its birthplaces into Europe through the geography of empire. The ancient philosophical idea of soul migration returned in the growing imperial possessions and became a vehicle to express a new, psychological state of personal alienation, moral incoherence, and emptiness. The theme threads melancholy through the merriment of the sly, ironical, posturing oriental fairy tales of the eighteenth century, and reaches its full expression in the zombification of twentieth-century melancholic protagonists, crystallizing in the creole outsider, Antoinette Cosway in Jean Rhys's novel, *Wide Sargasso Sea* (1966).

But how does this change take place, and what does it reveal?

There are forerunners of the zombie in medieval literature. Dante, for example, meets in the frozen depths of Cocytus the shade of Fra Alberigo, who explains that traitors like him can predecease their bodies, and fall into the lowest circle of hell to start their eternity of torments—eyes sealed shut by the ice, wholly entombed in permafrost, a kind of cryogenesis—while they are still in the world. Dante exclaims in horror, for he has seen one of the sinners around and about in the world above, recently, eating and drinking and wearing clothes. The friar then explains that this sinner was so wicked that before even his murder victims had arrived in the afterlife, the devil had taken possession of him; Dante had effectively beheld a zombie, and the idea repels him so profoundly that he refuses the man's plea to melt his frozen eyes with his touch.[8]

Dante imagined the possibility, but he did not have a word for the soul-less, hollow man left in the world above; his traitors remain exceptional cases in medieval thought, and the suggestion Dante makes even heretical.

Early, literary examples of the use of the word zombie only really begin to enter English storytelling towards the end of the nineteenth century; the writings of the Irish-Greek fantasist Lafcadio Hearn offer a peculiar and often charming source. Hearn was a migrant between several worlds: born to a Greek mother and an Irish father in 1850 in the Ionian Islands, of a mixed Orthodox and Protestant background, he was raised and educated in Dublin and then emigrated to America as a young man, to work as a journalist and sketch-writer, first in Cincinnati, then in New Orleans, where he married a woman of mixed race who had allegedly been born a slave; he was an early, influential translator from the French of the Symbolists and the Decadents, of Flaubert's *The Temptation of Saint Anthony*, Théophile Gautier's *One of Cleopatra's Nights and Other Fantastic Fancies*, and of Villiers de L'Isle Adam, among many.[9] Hearn's final metamorphosis took him to Japan, where he died in 1904, considered a national treasure (a reciprocal mutation); his works pioneered knowledge of Japanese culture abroad.

In his own life and character, Lafcadio Hearn presents a unique case of mediation between different *mentalités*: he himself invoked excitedly the episode in Ovid's *Metamorphoses* when Salmacis, in her passionate embrace of Hermaphroditus, fuses with him altogether to become a new, androgynous being. As a writer, he is a curiosity, but socially and historically he is an interesting and strong example of an active 'congener'. He has been persuasively placed in the Irish-Victorian Gothic tradition, and his attraction to 'hosts of fantastic heterodoxies' throughout his peripatetic life certainly gave rise to some shivery ghost stories, recognizably kin to Sheridan Lefanu (who was even a relation by marriage), and his work in turn recombined with Yeats's supernatural fantasies.[10] But there is a crucial transition in Hearn's formative years as a storyteller, which has been overlooked, and which can offer a different, compelling source for the Gothic obsession with soul theft and soul wandering. Between his far better known American and Japanese incarnations, the polymorphous fantasist Hearn became for a brief spell a creole writer, when he spent time in the French West Indies.

In 1888, inspired by the creole culture he had already encountered in the southern United States,[11] Lafcadio Hearn arrived in Martinique, where he stayed for two years and became a pioneer recorder of local stories, jokes, songs, beliefs, recipes, proverbs. Compiling a creole dictionary of proverbs, called *Gombo Zhèbes*, which means a Spiced Gumbo or stew with herbs,[12] writing many animated sketches, and above all transcribing for the first time, in his ground-breaking book *Trois fois bel conte . . .* , the islands' oral storytellers with vibrant phonetic vitality, and capturing the sound of the creole voices with infectious precision.[13] Though Hearn often shows the racist discrimination of his times—especially in his magazine pieces in the USA[14]—and displays a dubious, sensualist's taste for the racial nomenclature of colonial societies, proclaiming his preference for 'fruit-coloured populations' over 'universal blackness',[15] he has been embraced by the grand old men of *négritude*—the poet Aimé Césaire most warmly. More recently, in a new introduction to the collected essays and pieces of 1890, entitled *Two Years in the French West Indies*, the Martiniquais writer Raphaël Confiant calls Hearn 'this magnificent traveller' and praises him as 'a modern pagan (or pantheist), a man who had an instinctive relationship with the various lands he visited . . . [with] an unusually fine ear for language and natural sounds. His unconscious mind had probably captured the Romany, Italian and Greek melodies his mother used to sing him when a small child. He may have remembered, too, the Gaelic and English ballads his father, a military man, sang when he longed for his native land . . .'[16]

Lafcadio Hearn developed a theory of the place of the supernatural in experience that avoids lip-smacking Gothic sensationalism, and shows an unusual humility in the face of common fears. He is neither defensive nor contemptuous about the irrational, nor does he relegate superstitions to the savage mind. Exceptionally, he recognizes creole credulity, accepting that he suffered from nightmares as a child, and that the fear had not altogether faded. He wrote, 'The impossible is much more closely related to reality than the greater part of what we designate true and ordinary. The impossible isn't perhaps the naked truth, but I believe that it is often the truth, undoubtedly masked and veiled, but eternal. He who claims he does not believe in ghosts lies in his own heart.'[17]

Like the Symbolist poets whom Lafcadio Hearn admired, he was compelled by the uncanny, and in Martinique he found, as he put it, The Land of Spectres, 'Le Pays de Revenants' (The Country of Those Who Come Back). His maid, Cyrillia, a valuable informant, develops the cast of characters in the island's phantom crew, including zombies. Popular belief held that flying creatures, especially nocturnal ones—bats, moths, fireflies—could be 'engagés', sent by those with power to transform themselves, or even zombies on a mission from witches to do harm. She also tells him the zombie deludes, taking the form of anything you might meet after dark, 'a stray horse, a cow, even a dog . . .'.

'But, Cyrillia,' I asked one day, 'did you ever see any zombis?'
'How? I often see them! . . . They walk about the room at night;—they walk like people. They sit in the rocking-chairs and rock themselves very softly, and look at me. I say to them:—'What do you want here?'— . . .
'What do they look like?'
'Like people,—sometimes like beautiful people . . . I am afraid of them.'[18]

The term zombie here has widened out, to enfold ghosts and spectres of all kinds in its grasp, and the wider the arms of the term, the more spooky the effect and the more pervasive the menace.

Hearn's oral transcriptions in *Trois fois bel conte* . . . preserve several sulphurously fierce and funny-scary stories about zombies, including 'Pe-La-Man-Lou', a cautionary tale about a little dumbling, a naughty boy with a flute who wanders into the woods and meets, first, Le Cheval, who lets him go, then le Zombi who would have eaten him, and sniffs him with his great white teeth, but is also charmed by his songs, and then La Bête—the beast with seven heads, which, 'Flouam! Swallowed him up.'[19] The best story, 'Nanie Rozette', also circles round the issue of hunger, and the dangers of gluttony, through the misadventures of the greedy protagonist, who gets her deserts. Nanie Rozette steals away into the forest in order to eat her fill in peace without anyone begging food from her while she guzzles. But she sits down on an accursed rock, La Roche du Diable, and finds herself stuck fast to it. Her mother finds her, builds a magic shelter to keep her safe there that night, and tells her not to admit anyone, unless they sing her the special pass song. But this turns out to be the rock where the Sabbaths take place, and there the Devil gathers his followers—Zombi, Soucouyan, Loup-Garou, Agoulou. 'It was the table where the Devil smeared them with grease and snakes, of the oil of the departed, of phosphorus and a thousand ingredients, which, in the night, give

Zombie his brightness.'[20] When this gang of fiends find access to the rock barred by the mother's spell, the devil promises them their rock will be returned to them on the morrow; he tries to storm it, without success. The devil mimicks Nanie Rozette's mother in order to gain entrance to the cabin in which she's been enclosed. He has his tongue filed—by the blacksmith—in order to speak more sweetly, more like her mother. He pays him well, to make it 'as fine as a piece of paper . . . as the tender leaf of the banana plant'.[21] And Nanie Rozette is tricked, and she opens to him, and 'the Devil gobbled her up like a baby goat'.[22]

The imagery of devouring, a form of metamorphosis encountered in Hell, as discussed in connection with Bosch, here mirrors the themes of consuming, using up, hollowing out in the imperial adventure. This economy of bodies and souls runs through the stories of possession; the competition for ownership, for self-possession, for mastery underlies the whole development of the zombie. The zombie emerges, however, in its more familiar, current meaning in ethnography, not fiction, and one of the earliest and important places it occurs is in the work of Zora Neale Hurston (1891–1960), writer and anthropologist, author of the novel *Their Eyes Were Watching God* (1937), the most chic female presence in the Harlem Renaissance of the Twenties (she even called herself 'Queen of the Niggerati'), and a controversial figure in the history of black America.[23] Hurston investigated voodoo in Haiti and Jamaica and describes her findings in her classic of travel-cum-anthropological writing, *Tell My Horse*, published in 1938. 'What is the whole truth and nothing else but the truth about Zombies?' she asks in the opening sentence of a chapter in which she visits a hospital. 'I do not know,' she goes on, 'but I know that I saw the broken remnant, relic, or refuse of Felicia Felix-Mentor in a hospital yard . . . We have the quick and the dead. But in Haiti there is the quick, the dead, and then there are Zombies.'[24]

Hurston stresses the reality of the terror this kind of spirit possession exercises on believers, and describes the way the sorcerers suck out victims' souls. After this operation, 'a Zombie . . . will work ferociously and tirelessly without consciousness of his surroundings and conditions'.[25] In a spirit of urban scepticism, tempered with grim fellow-feeling, she attended many ceremonies in what is the first modern outsider's description of such rituals. She reports a bewildering profusion of terrors, exorcisms, and other attempts to allay the malice of sorcerers. Her zombies have several counterparts, including the duppy. '"One day you see a man walking the road,"' one of her informants tells her, '"The next day you come to his yard and find him dead. . . . He is still and silent and does none of the things that he used to do. But you look upon him and you see that he has all the parts that the living have. Why is it that he cannot do what the living do? It is because the thing that gave power to these parts is no longer there. That is the duppy, and that is the most powerful part of any man."' Once the duppy has been taken, it turns evil: '"Everybody has evil in them,"' the old man goes on, '". . . when the duppy leaves the body, it no longer has anything to restrain it and it will do more terrible things than any man ever dreamed of . . ."'[26] The throng of the undead also includes soucouyants and revenants, and other permutations on the vampire/zombie pattern thriving in the prevailing atmosphere of anxiety.

Hurston took photographs, and the book publishes an image of the Haitian patient Felicia in her hospital shift (Fig. 28); it conveys the harshness of Hurston's acceptance of the zombie label: Felicia looms into the lens, her body tilting, her arms lifted, her gaze blind, her face blurred in shadow. The loss of self that Hurston describes is re-enacted by the image itself: it only allows its subject a desolate and tormented vacancy. In this case of mental illness, she shows little sympathy, but rather goes along with the fears excited by her subject's supposed spellbound state. The observations of the anthropologist are never straightforward documents.[27]

In the case of this Caribbean zombie, the body from whom the spirit has been extracted then works for the sorcerer and is subject to his (or her) will; it has become enslaved, a *souciant*, otherwise

Fig. 28 A zombie, or 'the broken remnant, relic, or refuse of Felicia Felix-Mentor in a hospital yard', as Zora Neale Hurston harshly described her subject (from her book *Tell My Horse* (1938)).

known in creole as a *soucouyant*, a term with vampiric associations. The entranced body becomes an 'empty skin'.[28] The existence of this kind of zombie depends on ideas of soul theft deriving from beliefs in spirits existing independently of bodies and hence able to leave and wander; this fundamental premiss colours many of the accounts given by early visitors to the Americas, as described by Pané in his *Account* of metempsychosis in Hispaniola (as discussed in my first chapter). The influential Scottish scholar of fairy tales and related literature, Andrew Lang, considered the idea of soul travel a 'singular theory' of what he called 'savage metaphysics'.[29]

Regarding zombies, soul travel does not take place at will, but undoes the victim's will: within the field of liberty, zombies lie at the opposite pole from shamans, spirit travellers who can leave their bodies when they put their mind to it.

Zemis AND *obeah*

Obi or *obeah* is the earliest word used to describe the cluster of rituals and spells in Jamaica, first attested in the second half of the eighteenth century.[30] The now far more familiar word, voodoo or vodun (or hoodoo) took root in the practice of the Caribbean later; it is thought that *obeah* and voodoo originated among different West African peoples. But both *obeah* and voodoo are established as concepts in circulation in European literature after the diaspora of slaves; the aboriginal islanders, such as the Taino and the Caribs, had their own spirit cults, which combined and recombined and are thriving today in their latest metamorphoses from Brazil to Puerto Rico under a variety of names, including Santeria and Macomblé.

The various forms of religious rituals, involving trance, possession, and narcotics, are extensively chronicled in the early ethnographical writing about the Caribbean, and consistently excited ambiguous responses. Often explained in terms of known practices and principles—Roman soothsayers and augurs and medieval imagery of witchcraft and the supernatural—the authors nevertheless drew attention to extraordinary psychological possibilities. Of course, it would distort the history of psychology to attribute split selves, living dead, and soul theft exclusively to the Caribbean, however aware one remains of the multiple cross-currents that flowed and clashed there to combine into Creolité. But metamorphosis induced by local produce excites interest throughout chroniclers from Ramón Pané onwards: powders and herbs, pastes and unguents, are smoked, inhaled, eaten, swallowed, and vomited, and used for body decoration. The pharmacopoeia of local fruits and herbs and shrubs—of vegetation—figures chiefly as mind-altering substances, not food, and the use of tobacco and other drugs inspired much fascinated discussion, and, eventually emulation.[31] Pané himself describes the way the Taino inhaled, with a long tube from their elbow to their nostril, administering purges and intoxicants, as well as medicine during certain healing rituals; his account profoundly influenced concepts of soul–body union and disunity, and consequent tales about soul-travel, multiple personality, animal metamorphosis. These notions, comparable to beliefs found among the commonly despised agricultural labourers and other homegrown social inferiors, gained a new exotic, compelling patina when entertained by 'savages', noble or otherwise, monstrous or not.

Territorial expansion marched alongside epistemological ambition: the mission to know the minds of other, subjugated peoples, became as overwhelming as the mission to own and subdue them; the *magnum opus* of Bernard Picart, for example, called in its English translation of 1733–9 *The Ceremonies and Religious Customs of the World*, is a multi-volume encyclopedia that examines different cultures in turn but aims at a supreme, all encompassing, and authoritative overview; it is a true precursor of the Victorians' enterprises such as *The Golden Bough* by J. G. Frazer.[32] Picart was typical in synthesizing early encounter literature, in which the empire-makers are much exercised about the idols which the local people worship: in the Caribbean, these are called *zemis* (sometimes, *çemis*) and the word *zemi* is related, etymologists have suggested, to zombie.

Zemis were divine powers, embodied in cult statues made of wood or stone and of cotton cloth, with metallic shining eyes (Fig. 29), and were the subject of rituals involving hallucinogens, sacrifice, and ventriloquism.[33] Ramón Pané's description of a healing trance, for example, is picked up and rehearsed over and over again; the passage becomes a *locus classicus* of this literature, impressing itself on all the authorities coming after and through them disseminating a model of mind–body relation involving a multiplicity of

Fig. 29 A few examples of statues called *zemis*, which were used to mobilize powers of prophecy, healing, and fertility, survived the iconoclasm of the missionaries (*zemi*, from Jamaica, 1200–1500).

souls, transmigration, and a priestly or spiritual command of metamorphosis or physical transformations—all concepts now entirely familiar, but which were then recognizable through their perceived kinship with classical thinking about eternal flux, the migration of souls, and metamorphosis, as I reviewed in my first chapter.

Pané describes how doctors use the *zemis* to assure a harvest, call up a wind, make it rain—and heal the sick. He relates how the 'behique' or priest-doctors visit the sick, and how they both then purge themselves by sniffing a hallucinogenic called *cohoba* (which has not been identified for sure); it induces trance, in which state the priest-doctor contacts the *zemis* for a diagnosis. 'Then he pulls hard on him [the sick man], as if he wished to pull something out . . . From there he goes to the exit of the house and closes the door, and he speaks, saying "Go away to the forest, or to the sea, or wherever you wish." And . . . he sucks on the sick man's neck . . . "look how I have taken it [the cause] out of your body . . ."' With great relish, Pané then goes on to relate in detail the vicious punishments meted out by the family to *behiques* who, after these sympathetic magical operations, failed to assure their patient's survival.

Richard Eden, translating Peter Martyr, added a vivid simile to the account of the priest-doctor's falling into trance: 'he begynneth his inchauntment, and calleth the spirite with loude voyice by certayne names, whiche no man understandeth but hee and his disciples . . . '. He then slashes himself, Eden continues, 'with a thorne' and drinks a potion which makes him 'waxeth hotte and furious . . . marvellously turmoylyng him selfe, as wee reade of the furious Sybilles, not ceassyng until the spirit be come: who at his comming entreth into him, and overthroweth him, *as it were a greyhound should overturne a Squerell*, then for a space, hee seemeth to lye as though hee were in a great payne, or in a rapte, woonderfully tormentyng him selfe . . .' He continues, linking spirit possession with prophecy: 'They [vegetarian cultists] gave them selves to the knowledge of naturall thinges, and used certain secrete magicall operations and superstitions, whereby they had familiaritie with spirites, which they allured into theyr owne bodyes at such tymes as they would take uppon them to tell of thinges to come . . .'[34] The priest-doctors seem mostly to be male, however; in Suriname, on the Latin American coast, the mercenary John Gabriel Stedman did however describe ceremonies and serpent cults which had been outlawed, he writes: 'these people have also amongst them a kind of Sibyls, who deal in oracles; these sage matrons dancing and whirling round in the middle of an assembly, with amazing rapidity, until they foam at the mouth, and drop down as convulsed . . . It is here called the *winty-play*, or the dance of the mermaid, and has existed from time immemorial . . .'[35] Stedman then compares these prophetesses, he says, with Virgil's sibyl.

But Peter Martyr, echoing Pané, set a trend when he ignored the healing intentions (and occasional efficacy) of the ceremonies and emphasized instead the dangers of attempting to handle *Zemis*: they 'represent night time spectres, the most cruel devourers of our souls by demons'.[36] Detailed engravings presented as historical records frequently focus on rituals involving trance and spirit possession, sometimes, as in an engraving illustrating Bernard Picart's *magnum opus*, in front of hideous and monstrous metamorphic gods, who are hybrid concoctions in the European diabolical tradition, and entirely imaginary (Fig. 30).[37]

Another first-hand witness, the French Dominican Jean-Baptiste Du Tertre, writing around half a century later, clarifies the psychology: everyone has three souls 'one in their heads; and another in their arm. That of the heart . . . goes to heaven, but those in the arm and the head which manifest themselves in the beating of the pulse and the movement of the arteries become Maboyas, that is to say, evil spirits . . .'[38] Bernard Picart, gleaning all he could from such travellers' tales, sums up the position when, in his third volume, *Concerning the Ceremonies of the Idolatrous Nations*, he turns from North America to the 'Caribbee Islands': here, he declares, 'The human Body is inhabited by a variety of Souls . . . The first is immortal, which after its leaving this world, goes and inhabits another young, beautiful, newly-created body in the next. The other Souls continue upon Earth, and transmigrate into the Bodies of Beasts, or are changed into evil Genii . . .'[39]

The writer often reaches for analogies with European witchcraft. Du Tertre, for example, puts the matter simply: 'To talk

Fig. 30 Fantasies of savage rites depend heavily on medieval ideas of devil-worship and monsters, as in this image of a Caribbean ritual (eighteenth-century engraving from Bernard Picart).

sensibly, all the duties that the Icheiris [evil spirits], as well as the Maboyas, exact from them through their [Boyez—priest-doctors] are rather lively imitations of what happens at the sorcerers' Sabbath.'[40] Embodied in cult sculptures, the *zemis* acquired the materiality that is one of the properties of the pagan idol and of the fetish; they were also, travellers reported, intimately bound up in individual identity: the *zemi* was a personal, specific vital energumen; the removal or destruction of a *zemi* could produce the zombie, but they also thereby took their place in an undefined and troubling psychological area of consciousness, where the imaginary became a part of experience. They were inanimate objects, but inhabited by a demon, who could be summoned to life and agency by the priest-mediator.

This material is not however representational, but constitutive: the practices and beliefs it relates do not so much record past events as conjure thought, and project onto the future life influential models for application in political, social, and psychological contexts.

Very few of the original statues have survived the iconoclasm of the missionaries, but three wooden sculptures with gilded eyes were brought to London after they were discovered hidden in a cave in Jamaica in 1792 by a surveyor, and formed part of the founding collection of the British Museum.[41] They are dated to AD 1200–1500, and are now mutilated, however, since they were ithyphallic (Fig. 29). Another seated *zemi*, which has received the same treatment, was found in former Hispaniola, where Pané collected his information, and is now in the Metropolitan Museum, New York.

In his memoirs, the Dominican Jean-Baptiste Labat, a French Dominican missionary, describes his efforts at eradicating superstitions among the slaves; he describes the backsliding of Christian converts into their former beliefs in spirits and ritual practices, and recalls with furious energy the action he took against the 'nègres sorciers' (negro sorcerers) and their 'idols'.[42] Labat spent twelve years in Martinique, at the turn of the seventeenth century, from 1693 to 1705 (thus spanning the period when Maria Merian was making her studies of butterflies in Suriname). But on the whole, Labat was less interested in Catholic missions than in light engineering, at which he excelled, and he spent his time on the island designing and building waterwheels, mills, and irrigation systems for sugar plantations and indigo farms. He remains one of the most articulate and truculent of the early colonial representatives in the Caribbean (Fig. 31).[43]

In his hatred of the English, France's belligerent rivals for power in the region, Labat also patronized the local filibustering ventures, professing himself very pleased with some booty he picked up

Ecrivain curieux des païs et des mœurs,
Il orne ses Ecrits des graces de son ſtile ;
Corrige en amusant, l'homme de ses erreurs ;
Et ſaiẗ mêler par tout, l'Agréable et l'utile.

Fig. 31 The French missionary Jean-Baptiste Labat designed sugar mills and waterworks in the slave plantations of Martinique; in the islanders' memories, he lived on as a spook to frighten children (engraving from his memoirs, published in 1724).

cheap from the sale of a foundered British ship, courtesy of the famous pirate Captain Kidd.[44]

In 1698, Père Labat discovered a slave conducting a ceremony by the bedside of a dying woman with a terracotta 'marmouzet ' (the disparaging word in use for such an 'idol', derived from Mahomet and meaning hobgoblin). In his memoirs, he recounts his reprisals with some pride. He ordered the slave to be flogged with 'around three hundred lashes that flayed him from his shoulders to his knees . . .' and then describes how his other slaves trembled at his actions 'and told me that the devil would cause me to die, and they were so overtaken by these crazy notions, that I could not make them come back . . . Finally, to make them see that I was not afraid of the devil or of sorcerers, I spat on the face [of the idol] and kicked it to pieces, even though I would like to have kept it . . . and [I] had all the rags of the sorcerer burned; I had the pieces of the statue heaped up, and the ashes and dust thrown into the river. . . . I had the sorcerer put in irons after having him washed with a "pimentade" . . . brine in which pimentos and little lemons have been crushed. This causes horrible pain . . . but is a sure remedy against gangrene . . .'[45] Lafcadio Hearn, relating this episode, adds, 'The legal extreme punishment was twenty-nine lashes.'[46]

Not all observers were so hostile, or sceptical. Lionel Wafer, a buccaneer who had sailed with William Dampier on his voyages, remained on land in Central America in 1681 with a nasty gunpowder wound to his knee; he wrote in his memoir, 'they are very expert and skilfull in their *Sort of* Diabolical Conjurations . . .' (emphasis added), after he was nursed, and cured, by the local Indians; for a time he turned native, as the saying goes, and set down their belief in maternal impression and other psychological fantasies.[47]

In this admittedly unusual example, the tension between the conventional view—that the tribespeople were devil-worshippers and sorcerers—and the personal experience can be clearly felt.

In all these various reports, the animist crowd of spirits and souls do not, at this point, include zombies as such, in the current sense of the term; the trances and rituals described aim at healing, prophecy, or power of one kind or another; they involve summoning spirits and then releasing them; even the most pejorative commentators do not describe *permanent* entrancement or maiming of personality—that is, as far as I can tell, until the later ethnography of Hearne and Hurston. It seems that it would take the full development of imperial economics for the zombie proper to emerge.

'I AM THE SLAVE OF THE LAMP'

Such accounts of others' beliefs had many historical effects, but one repercussion that has perhaps not been sufficiently discussed involves literary genre: themes that had hitherto been deemed proper to fantastic entertainments and imaginary realms or to belong to a classical past of pagan superstition, were now actively reclassified as fact, and moreover, fact taking place now. Such rubrics as 'true account', 'true history', 'true relation' recur insistently to fend off the reader's incredulity at the prodigies and marvels and horrors recounted. The narrative category of truth-telling, not fabrication, opens on unbelievable and fantastical magic. Shakespeare in *The Tempest*, dramatizing the wonder of the survivors of the shipwreck when they begin to explore Prospero's isle, captures the excitable perceptions of contemporary travel writers, whom he was mining for his themes and images. And the early eighteenth century saw productions of the play, in its whimsical refashioning by John Dryden and William Davenant, which stressed its relations to other worlds and fantastic magic arts, to spells and enchantments.

Creolization—the combining and recombining of different influences in the Caribbean as the strata of different cultures composted in the region, further complicates the question of disentangling the elements now; but it is worth stressing the reality effect such ambitious monuments as Picart's tomes strived to achieve: this type of overview was presented as a historical document. The effacing of boundaries between the imaginary and the documentary, between fantasy and history, achieved a new kind of spectacular and sensational entertainment genre: Imperial Gothic. This genre of writing, presented as true relations, had its own metamorphic effect—on poets, storytellers, and even popular entertainers.

In London, in 1785, the real interfused the imaginary in a dramatic form when a tremendously elaborate spectacle—a masque cum opera cum political pageant cum travel extravaganza—was produced at Covent Garden just before Christmas. This theatrical event was called after Omai, the South Sea islander and so-called 'prince' whom Sir Joseph Banks brought to England, to show off around society in 1774–6.[48]

Omai, or A Trip around the World presents a syncretic farrago of exotic tourism and patriotic omnipotence. The author of this spectacle, the Irish playwright and pantomime specialist John O'Keeffe, is chiefly remembered today for the comedy *Wild Oats*, but he was a prolific hack in and around Drury Lane. His dramatization of Omai's story depends on Banks's and Captain Cook's explorations of Micronesia and Polynesia, and illustrates vividly late eighteenth-century wishfulness about imperial dominions and native religions. But the pantomime was above all the creation of the brilliantly versatile designer and inventor Philippe de Loutherbourg; De Loutherbourg was a favourite collaborator of William Beckford, the *richissime* Jamaican sugar millionaire and Gothic cultist, author of the pseudo-Arabian night *Vathek*.[49] *Vathek*, first written in French, was published in 1786, the year after *Omai*. Only five years before, in 1781, De Loutherbourg had worked on Beckford's notoriously sybaritical Christmas revels; *Omai* was his last production, and his greatest extravaganza.[50]

The play opens in 'the burning cave of the devil spirit' where Omai's father Otoo, 'a Priest and a Magician', is performing a sacrifice, and it concludes after a tremendous series of pageants and tableaux dramatizing peoples and scenes from all over the Pacific, with the apotheosis of Cook, invoked here as 'the great Orono' (as it were Panjandrum) accompanied by a 'Chorus of Indians' united in mourning his death but acclaiming his assumption into heaven. It is a highly uneven work, even risible, veering between grand drama and low comic business, between opera and *commedia dell'arte* buffoonery. But there are aspects worth singling out with regard to the argument about cross-cultural influence and Imperial Gothic.[51]

For example, the wicked witch who attempts to destroy Omai is called Oberea, which was the name of a celebrated Tahitian queen whose favours Sir Joseph Banks was rumoured to have enjoyed.[52] However her name neatly (and conveniently) combined a hint of *obeah* magic with a feminized Oberon, king of the Fairies in Shakespearian lore. But above all, De Loutherbourg bought at auction costumes and other items from Captain Cook's collections to feature them as props in scenes based on picturesque drawings of Cook's voyages, such as fans and stools and weapons and cloaks, and he was helped with the scenery by none other than John Webber, who had travelled with Cook as the third voyage's official painter.[53] Thus straightforward, practical objects became theatrical curiosities, and other, sacred instruments tools of the magic and stagecraft that excited so much admiration. A newspaper enthused: 'To the rational mind what can be more entertaining than . . . to bring into living action, the customs and manners of distant nations! To see the exact representations of their buildings, marine vessels, arms, manufactures, sacrifices, and dresses?'[54] In a recognizable fashion in our times, the distinctive orders of reality and representation become utterly confused.

In the play, the devil god appears and gives Omai 'a potent talisman': as in the accounts of *zemi* ritual, this object causes sneezing, yawning, whistling, laughing, crying . . . The Chorus cries, 'These feathers contain sure some magical spell'.[55] The play neutralized the threat presented by native drug applications and spirit cults by casting them as sport: Beckford undertook a similar manoeuvre of aestheticizing the unfamiliar in the Arabian learning of his hyperbolic and bloodthirsty novel.

Three years after *Omai*, at the Theatre Royal Covent Garden, another pantomime by John O'Keeffe was staged as a rather more familiar Christmas show. That most frivolous and amusing of fancies, the fairy tale *Aladdin* flagrantly flourishes the panoply of orientalism. Just as the '*Trip around the World*' of *Omai's* subtitle collapses the horizons of empire into one huge glorious tableau, so the imaginary China of Aladdin extends to embrace other worlds with catholic expansiveness.

This much-loved and much-replayed story had appeared in print for the first time in the French collection of *A Thousand and One Nights*—*Les mille et une nuits* in the translation by the brilliant orientalist Antoine Galland, in Paris in 1702.[56] Arabists are now agreed that no prior text of 'Aladdin'—or for that matter of 'Ali Baba and the Forty Thieves', manuscript or print, exists in Arabic; it follows that it is likely that Galland was spiritedly making up his own fictions in the manner of the bazaar.[57] And with his Arabian Nights, Galland ignited the fad for *contes orientales*, which burned brightly throughout the eighteenth century, catching up many of the Enlightenment luminaries in its light: Montesquieu and Voltaire no less.

In the story, as in the pantomime, the hero rubs the magic lamp, and a genie appears: 'I am the slave of the lamp,' he says, 'and I and all the other slaves of the lamp are here to do thy bidding.' As every child knows, these genies can do anything. They conjure a whole palace for Aladdin out of thin air, they transport it—and anything else—fabulous distances. They are the agents of a Master—one of the first dark lords of popular fiction—who never appears in the story, but they channel his all-powerful magic. Later, in the muddled denouement of the written tale, the dread and all-powerful Master who has enslaved the genies of the Lamp and of the Ring turns out to live inside the egg of the magic bird the Roc (Rukh), 'a giant fowl which carrieth off camels and elephants in her pounces

IV. 'Nothing was left to Picus | Except his name' writes Ovid, after Circe takes her revenge on the youthful king for rejecting her advances, turning him into a woodpecker (here a devil-like monster). *La Bible des poètes* (Paris, 1493).

V. The pursuit of Apollo terrifies Daphne, daughter of a river, who calls on her father for help, and then, 'her limbs grew numb and heavy, her soft breasts | Were closed with delicate bark, her hair was leaves, | Her arms were branches . . .' (Antonio Pollaiuolo, late fifteenth century.)

VI. The naturalist artist Maria Merian, working in Dutch Suriname, observed carefully the successive transformations of snakes and butterflies, here in the dramatically compressed image of the colony battened on a manioc plant (early eighteenth century).

VII. Correggio's *Leda and the Swan* unfolds the story sequentially with uncommon tenderness, but an outraged viewer attacked the picture and hacked out Leda's face. This is a copy made from the original before the damage, by the seventeenth century Spanish painter Eugenio Cajes.

and flieth away with them, such is her stature and strength'.⁵⁸ The Lord of the Lamp, fabulous progenitor of Mordor and Voldemort, actually begins life as a hatchling; this curious outcome is rarely attempted on stage.

Aladdin knows all about these captives' husk-like condition: when he loses the princess, he cries out, 'I do command thee, *slave without a soul!*— | Bring back my love, my life, my Nourmahal!'⁵⁹

The slaves are confined in the talismans of the ring and the lamp: interestingly Greek equivalents of such magical instruments, such as the ring of Gyges in Plato's *Republic*, which renders its wearer invisible, or the cap and winged sandals of Hermes and the invisible hood of Hades, Lord of the Dead, are not activated by indwelling daemons or genies, but potent in themselves. The trapped condition of the slaves in *Aladdin* both reflects definitions of slavery by its proponents, and returns us to the theme of the zombie. For it contributes to the changing psychological profile of a person robbed of will and feeling, a being who no longer enjoys choice, mobility, and all the other freedoms that the era of revolutions invested in the individual, the citizen. As has happened before with the materials of metamorphosis, words and images are borrowed from the host culture by the incomers; Galland here, masquerading as an Arab storyteller, annexes concepts from other worlds to talk of something close to home (as of course do Voltaire and Montesquieu); the ideas are then exchanged back and forth in a rippling interplay of reflections, echoes, and vibrations, themselves shaping other forms of expression, rather as the genie of the lamp fluctuates and dissolves and reassembles again as he rises to the summons.

It is possible to see, through the lens of Galland's authorship, how mischievously he is guying the improbabilities and outlandishness of fabulous conventions, not least the far-flung exoticism of its magical cosmos. The tale, 'Aladdin', opens in 'one of the large and rich kingdoms of China, whose name I do not recollect', the first sentence informs us; Aladdin's father is a tailor called

Mustafa, so we are in Chinese Islam, somewhere in central Asia. But this is an Arabian Night, a fairy story, and when the enchanter appears, as he soon does, he presents himself to the feckless youth as a long lost brother of his dead father, notwithstanding his origins in Africa. He is introduced, in the eighteenth-century versions, with the sentence, 'Now this stranger was a famous African magician', and remains referred to throughout the story's peregrinations from book to stage and back again, as 'the African magician'.[60] Galland was no doubt having fun with this vulgar motif, which works in this kind of story as a simple passkey to magical devices and incredible flights of fancy. 'It is true he came from Africa,' the story relates, 'where he was born, and since Africa is a part of the world where people are more dedicated to magic than anywhere else, he had applied himself to it from his youth; and after about forty years' experience in magic, geomancy and fumigations, and reading of magic books, he had found out that there was somewhere in the world a magic lamp . . .'[61]

When the story was adapted for the London stage by O'Keeffe, the motifs of treasure caves, exotic wizards, captive genies, enchanted rings and lamps would have situated the action in an imaginary Moorish empire, more Old Cairo than far Cathay; but, given the date of the pantomime's first staging, 1788, its themes of imprisoned spirits, of immobilized and zombie-like psyches, touch with unexpected directness the fundamental question of slavery, not inside the Ottoman empire, however foregrounded, but closer to home.

In the popular illustrated retellings of the tale in the eighteenth and nineteenth centuries, the superimposition of descendants of transported Africans on to the figure of the slave of the lamp takes place unconsciously. The genies are often huge, savage, monstrous but indeterminate creatures—in the tale, one is evoked as 'a genie, of an enormous size and frightful look, [who] rose out of the earth'.[62] Illustrators show their prejudices however, and colour him in—blue-black—and give him exaggerated African racial

Fig. 32 The wicked wizard of the traditional pantomime, *Aladdin*, inspired by *The Arabian Nights*, often appears as 'the African magician'; here he cries his wares, 'New lamps for old' (from Walter Crane, *Aladdin*, 1883).

physiognomy, as popularly conceived at the time. In this the spirits that work their master's will reflect his imagined origins. Walter Crane, in his luscious and hyperbolic full-colour engraved picture book, portrays the 'wicked magician' crying his wares as a kind of pantomime dame crossed with a black minstrel (Fig. 32), while Aladdin and his Princess trail entourages of dozens of slaves, black and white, in settings of spectacular luxury.

The second and only surviving edition of the song sheets by John O' Keeffe was published in 1788, the year that the abolition of the slave trade was first moved in parliament.[63] It was that year too that Edward Long, author of a virulent *History of Jamaica* in 1774, gave evidence to the Privy Council during their investigations on the possible injuries and deaths brought about by magic on that island.[64] The captive genie in the fairy tale or pantomime was the slave, throughout aeons of time, of the master who rubbed the talisman—ring or lamp; the concept of a volitionless but all powerful spirit communicated the soulless, dehumanized condition of enslavement, as decried by the abolitionists.

The next generation, living between the British declaring an end to the trade in 1807 and the abolition of slavery in the British empire in 1833 (but of course not in the United States) saw popular staging in London of several romantic liberation melodramas in the Imperial Gothic mode.[65] But one of the most in demand within this spectrum of abolitionist musical dramatic spectaculars remained *Aladdin, or, The Wonderful Lamp*. The exotic locations gave opportunities for terrific, new stage effects, the genies supporting the Flying Palace en route to Africa where the African Magician whisks it.[66]

Significantly, these spectacles all close with the freeing of the genies when the lamp is shattered and the spell of the wicked magician is broken. The pantomime which was performed at Drury Lane in 1826, for example, during an intense phase of the abolition campaign, climaxes with a rousing—and abysmally written— chorus of praise from the three genies:

'We are free!'

Then one, named Astra, sings,

'Thy hand has rent the spell
That made us slaves

Roll away like waves
To the cave . . .'[67]

The association—even the clumsy echo of 'Rule Britannia!'—
must have been picked up by the audience at that time.[68]

As with *Omai*, this extravaganza made a claim that Britannia was
the champion of light and liberty; it flattered the Regency crowd
that the horrors of enslavement were practised chiefly by wicked
other people, and could be lifted by a British performance of a
magic reversal, a counter-spell. The play helped the English to feel
aligned with the side of enlightenment, who would not use the
lamp for evil ends, by shutting up prisoners inside it and denying
them humanity and liberty. The blame for this wicked perversion
of the lamp's true purpose falls on the invisible Master, and his
rival, the 'African magician', both of them distanced, strange, ultimately alien figures (whom children in the audience still boo with
great gusto).

However, at the very same time, during the agitation for and
against slavery, the pantomime participants might have unconsciously needed this kind of persuasion, since it might not be all
that fanciful to think that the wonderful lamp itself bitterly summons up the ideals of civilization, or culture, of enlightenment,
with the slave trapped within?

As the outrage of slavery receded from public interest in the
course of the Victorian age, productions of *Aladdin* towards the end
of the reign recast the genies in a changed language of power: at the
Grand Theatre, Islington, the Christmas panto of 1889–90 featured
'Steam, Gas, Mechanical, and Limelight Effects' and the genies
were called Fiz-Fiz, Paraffin, Benzoline, and Colza. Not a mention
of freedom anywhere: the genies remain at their energy posts, at the
final curtain, working the wonders of new industrial fuels.[69]

Magic and metamorphosis had entered the repertory, even of
pantomime; it is against this background, of pantomimes about

Captain Cook and about Aladdin, in the turbulence around slavery, that Coleridge's potent imaginings of spellbound personality can perhaps be placed, ready to stalk many shadowy and shivery corners in later narratives.

SPELLBINDING COLERIDGE

What Coleridge writes in the margin at the bottom of the page when he glosses the word Zambi in his friend Robert Southey's *History of Brazil*, shows him grappling with the religious beliefs of Southey's subjects from the ground of his own far-ranging reading:

R. Pitta syllogized. Zambi is the name of the Angolan God. But the Angolan God is the Devil. Ergo, Zambi is the name of the Devil.— The logic limps in the article 'the', instead of 'a'.[70]

Coleridge is arguing here that the Angolan God and the devil could be identified with each other only from the point of view of Christian monotheism, which holds all other gods to be diabolical. But Zambi could be freed from his perceived evil character by recourse to the indefinite article—*a* devil instead of *the* devil; then Coleridge could bring about his own coup of transformation and replace the devil with a daemon, an energumen, within his plural, Neoplatonist polytheism, neither exclusively earthbound nor celestial, moral nor immoral, intrinsically malign nor benign. Zambi takes on the character of a Platonic daemon, a vital spirit. But Coleridge's poetry exhibits the inversion, with regard to the idea of soul-death, and he makes the first declared link between the West Indies and a new psychology of the supernatural.[71]

One of Coleridge's uncanny ballads, 'The Three Graves', is subtitled 'A Fragment of a Sexton's Tale', and in its hyperbolic accumulation of horrid and wonderful features it verges on the absurd: a churchyard, mysterious graves (one unmarked), grisly unexplained portentous happenings: this enigmatic, even muddled tale of horror strikes early notes of Coleridge's persistent imaginative conflicts.[72] It deals with spellbinding powers, with frenzy, with violent hauntings, with the Janus-doors of perception which can be opened to let the outside in, and take possession, and vice versa.

Coleridge began the poem in 1796–7 during the time he was collaborating with Wordsworth, from an idea supplied by Wordsworth, a *fait divers* about a widow who falls in love with her daughter's suitor and attempts to seduce him. The older poet relinquished the poem because 'he [Coleridge] made it too shocking and painful, and not sufficiently sweetened by any healing views . . . *he took to the supernatural*, and hence his Ancient Mariner and Christabel, in which he shows great poetical power . . .'[73] In his later, prefatory note of 1818, Coleridge becomes highly defensive, even self-destructive, characterizing his work as 'a fragment, not of a Poem, but of a common Ballad-tale' and going on to say, 'At all events it is not presented as poetry, and it is in no way connected with the Author's judgment concerning poetic diction. *Its merits, if any, are exclusively psychological*' (emphasis added).

The poem is indeed rough in execution, harsh music with full rhymes that teeter on the lip of doggerel, but its theme makes it more than a curiosity, for it describes the knot of relationships between the widow, her daughter Mary, her lover Edward, and Mary's friend Ellen, with a compelling starkness of tone and novelty of conception. When Wordsworth said that Coleridge 'took to the supernatural' he missed his friend's drift. There is no supernatural, there are no devils, only imaginative trouble. The widow's curse of her daughter spreads necrotically through the group, turning its three victims 'melancholy', emaciated, 'wild and weary', infusing them with 'bad thoughts', 'horror and huge pain', and making them stare 'like one who is struck blind'; the mother's

terrible and implacable curse eventually extinguishes all their joy
and, it is implied by the title, their existence:

> 'O God forgive me!' (he exclaimed)
>   'I have torn out her heart.'
>
> Then Ellen shrieked, and forthwith burst
>   Into ungentle laughter;
> And Mary shivered, where she sat,
>   And never she smiled after.[74]

Coleridge comments, 'I was not led to choose this story from any
partiality to tragic, much less to monstrous events . . . but from
finding in it a striking proof of the possible effect on the imagination, from an Idea violently and suddenly impressed on it.' He then
gives his sources: 'Bryan Edwards' account of the *Oby* witchcraft on
the Negroes in the West Indies, and Hearne's deeply interesting
anecdotes of similar workings on the imagination of the Copper
Indians . . . I conceived the design of shewing that instances of this
kind are not peculiar to savage or barbarous tribes.'[75] Edwards was
a lobbyist for the sugar planters; he quotes Peter Martyr, Labat, and
others from the usual sources. Samuel Hearne is another matter:
a mining surveyor who travelled in northern Canada into the
Arctic Circle, he gives a harrowing account of his adventures, and
observed curing by charms and ceremonies, including the building
of 'conjuring houses' and sucking out diseases.[76]

In these comments on his poem, Coleridge here, as elsewhere,
disengages the supernatural from the divine and relocates it in the
psyche: a daemon, not the devil. He also rejects the habitual dis-
tancing from native beliefs of the chroniclers, in a manoeuvre that
embodies the inward turn of the uncanny. That such phenomena
are all in the mind does not in any way diminish their power to
affect reality.[77]

But when Coleridge began reading Bryan Edwards and Samuel
Hearne, he was drawn to them because he was looking for more
on altered states of being he already intimated, or even knew first

hand, politically and personally; the adjustment of Southey's formulation of zombie as devil-power derives from Coleridge's at least ten-year-long fascination with the theme, as evinced by his widely known and influential poems.

As Wordsworth noted, 'The Three Graves' bears a strong relation to the visionary poems, to the convulsive spellbindings of 'Kubla Khan', 'Christabel', and 'The Ancient Mariner'. Entrancement permeates all three strange feverish inventions: after the death of the albatross, the doomed ship moves, bewitched, laden with its 'ghastly crew', all of them living dead whose sounds and looks deepen the narrator's spellbound condition. Similarly, Christabel is wound in a terrible, wasting trance by the mysterious, serpentine Geraldine, the fair lady who

> . . . with low voice and doleful look
> These words did say:
> 'In the touch of this bosom there worketh a spell,
> Which is lord of thy utterance, Christabel!'[78]

In an impassioned meditation on Coleridge's supernatural, Ted Hughes casts the embrace of Geraldine as a rape of Christabel, but it is more like the asexual soul extraction practised by the *behique*, or priest-doctor, as influentially described by Ramón Pané.[79] The mysterious encounter between the two women, when Geraldine, the counterfeit damsel in distress, shows herself to her victim, revealing 'that bosom old . . . that bosom cold',[80] never comes into focus, but remains dreamlike, insoluble, more impenetrable than enigmatic, and this ambiguity produces Coleridge's especial power in these visions; the imagery of torpor, chill, snakiness, gradually builds the atmosphere of the weird poem until the reader feels the hex that has taken Christabel's spirit and voided her, of her consciousness, her utterance:

> For what she knew she could not tell,
> O'er-mastered by the mighty spell.[81]

Mental enchantment is a psychological state, wrought by human rather than divine powers to take control of another and bind him or her; sometimes, as in Coleridge's poems, the inward mind moves in unholy union with the charms cast upon it. This kind of affliction will become more and more familiar in Victorian literature, and return to vivid summation in its original context in Jean Rhys's last novel, set in her native West Indies, in which the figure of the zombie achieves a new, contemporary definition.

JEAN RHYS AND *Wide Sargasso Sea*

The phrase, 'Le pays de revenants', found in Labat and picked up by Hearn, was lovingly repeated and revolved by Jean Rhys: the working title for her masterpiece, *Wide Sargasso Sea* (1966) was 'Le Revenant'; the novel shows in several places that she was reading Lafcadio Hearn. The two writers' approach, ninety years apart, to 'le merveilleux créole' (the creole marvellous) is however starkly different: as a sceptical observer, Hearn takes pleasure in the uncanny and aestheticizes the spectral, while Rhys, who was born in Dominica (a former French colony), revisits the supernatural spells and spectres of her upbringing from a participant's—or even a victim's—point of view. She communicates its terrors while repudiating them in anger and despair. Her last books (the novel, and the autobiography *Smile Please*) exemplify the changes in the concept of the zombie, and its protean reversibility: how the power to hollow out changes origin and direction, perpetrator and victim. Like Hearn, Jean Rhys traces the body of magical lore back to a woman, her nurse; unlike Hearn, her supernatural informant was 'the terror of my life'. In *Smile Please*, she recalls, 'It was Meta who talked so much about zombies, soucriants and loups-garoux. Soucriants were always women, she said, who came at night and sucked your blood. During the day they looked like ordinary women but you could tell them by their red eyes. Zombies were black shapeless things. They could get through a locked door and you heard them walking up to your bed. You didn't see them, you felt their hairy hands round your throat. For a long time I never slept except right at the bottom of the bed with the sheet well over my head, listening for zombies.'[82]

The linkage between the two writers is forged however by that earlier chronicler of this territory, the missionary Père Labat, whom we saw so vengefully destroying idols. For it was Labat, to whom Hearn devotes a chapter in his book *Two Years in the French West Indies*, who first invented the phrase 'le pays de revenants'. Memories of the harsh treatment the Dominican meted out may indeed lie behind his own metamorphosis in the folklore of the island. For Père Labat, who stole men's souls—their lives—is now condemned to walk, an unquiet ghost, a revenant himself, a spectre and a bogey-man, brandished to scare bad children and bring them home after dark.

Hearn's informant, Thereza, one of many women he talked with, tells him 'He [Labat] was the first person to introduce slavery into Martinique; and it is thought that is why he comes back at night. It is his penance for having established slavery.' Of course, slavery was already flourishing when Labat arrived in 1693, but storytelling memories play tricks with time and history.[83] At the end of his chapter on Labat, Hearn writes, with frivolous, *fin-de-siècle* francophone floweriness:

. . . God's witchery still fills this land; and the heart of the stranger is even yet snared by the beauty of it; and the dreams of him that forsakes it will surely be haunted—even as were thine own, Père Labat—by memories of its Eden-summer: the sudden leap of the light over a thousand peaks in the glory of tropic dawn,—the perfumed peace of enormous azure noons,—and shapes of palm wind-rocked in the burning of colossal sunsets,—and the silent flickering of the great fire-flies through the lukewarm darkness, when mothers call their children home . . . '*Mi fanal Pè Labatt!—mi Pè Labatt ka vini pouend ou!*' (I see the lantern of Père Labat!—I see Père Labat coming to get you!)[84]

This encounter does indeed quiver with the genuine thrill of the uncanny, for these are the eerie spooks and ghosts who stalk the dark literature of Romanticism and nineteenth-century European fairy tales and folklore. Here, history stalks fantasy, and turns into stories for children, seeping into the imagination and seeding the ground of adult thought. But until imperial consciousness provided a screen on which these fantasies could be projected, and until encounters and exchanges provided a discursive framework for spirit visions of this sort, it seems to me this particular form of haunting had not been recognized, as it were, on home territory by the makers of literature and the recorders of fantasy.

Jean Rhys's use of 'Le Revenant' as a working title[85] stitches her fiction into another web of imagination, besides the salient connection with Charlotte Brontë and *Jane Eyre*. Her novel is set in the time of revolutionary upheavals in the French West Indies, and stages the burning down of the heroine's family plantation house by a violent uprising of the slaves. Left behind in the new, post-liberation world, Antoinette Cosway is hated by the people whom she and her kind once owned. In *Wide Sargasso Sea*, magic and countermagic propel the couple's ghastly union and conflict. Antoinette's undoing in her final fixed shape—her institutionalization as a deranged outsider—her metamorphosis into Bertha Mason of *Jane Eyre*—as in effect a zombie, comes about when the white fortune-hunter from England takes possession of a girl 'with the sun in her', as her nurse Christophine says. The novel dramatizes this encounter at a profoundly personal, inward level, through the juxtaposed first person accounts of Antoinette and the Rochester figure, but throughout, as I wrote in the preface, the predicament of Antoinette, a remnant of colonial power, expresses the legacy of imperial wealth-getting, the brokenness of culture and persons that it left in its wake even after history has changed. Through Antoinette, it is possible to see the figure of other, contemporary protagonists of Jean Rhys, who occupy the same suspended state of unbelonging and negation.

This novel crystallizes a new version of the self, through a metamorphosis of personality that was new and unfamiliar in literature of this kind at the time: the madness of the madwoman in the attic in *Wide Sargasso Sea* is more precisely delineated than that of a ghost or a spectre from the Gothic tradition: Antoinette is most particularly identified as a zombie. This novel, surprising as it may be, is the first great direct fictional treatment of a very modern subject that hooks it back into the weft where it was first woven: the Afro-Caribbean diaspora.

Looking back on her very recent childhood, Rhys's protagonist is taunted by one of the other children, her friend Tia, about her mother's 'craziness':

'She try to kill her husband and she try to kill you too that day you go to see her. She have eyes like zombie and you have eyes like zombie too. Why you won't look at me.'[86]

Earlier, during the slaves' revolt and the family's flight during the burning of the plantation house, Tia has thrown a jagged stone at her: Antoinette writes, 'We stared at each other, blood on my face, tears on hers. It was as if I saw myself. Like in a looking-glass.'[87]

This is the identification, however, that is now allowed: she, a Creole, is called a 'white cockroach', an anomalous horror, and she cannot become the black girl's twin, neither belong to Tia's world, nor to her English husband's. Caught in between opposing categories, she risks failing to keep her soul. Jean Rhys's Antoinette finds her only true ally and defender in her nurse, Christophine, originally a slave from Martinique who was gifted to her mother as a wedding present by her father; Christophine is an *obeah* woman, who knows charms and spells, and Antoinette begs her to make her a love spell, to win back her husband's love. But the charm only deepens his perception of his wife's queerness; so, while she fears her zombie taint, coming to her through her creole blood and her mother's derangement, the sex magic she tries plays her cruelly into his hands. Indeed, Rhys suggests with superb subtlety just how rough those hands are in bed and out of it.

Her husband accomplishes her destruction by playing to her terrors, Rhys suggests, wilfully and otherwise. He reads this definition of the word zombie in a travel book with the title *The Glittering Coronet of Isles*, in a chapter called 'Obeah'. The passage represents one of the first uses in English fiction of the word:

A zombie is a dead person who seems to be alive, or a living person who is dead. A zombie can also be the spirit of a place, usually malignant, but sometimes be propitiated with sacrifices or offerings of flowers and fruit. 'They cry out in the wind that is their voice, they rage in the sea that is their anger.'[88]

The title of the source catches Hearn's flowery tone, but could not be named as the events Rhys is relating are taking place at least fifty years earlier. But the genealogy that links Labat and Southey and Hearn catches up Rhys here into its mesh, for in the section narrated by Antoinette's husband, he describes how afraid he became in the tropical forest when he saw a voodoo offering laid under the orange trees at the end of a paved road, by a house in ruins; at the same time, the sight of him frightens a passing child, who screams and drops the baskets she is carrying on her head, and runs away. He loses the path, becomes entangled in 'the undergrowth and creepers': 'I was lost and afraid,' he recalls, 'among these enemy trees, [so] certain of danger . . .' Taken for a zombie himself, he has become lost and scared. The man who finds him denies that a house or paved road ever stood there.

The house in ruins in the forest belonged to a priest, a certain Père Lilievre, we learn later, and the whole passage hints that the Rochester figure has not only trodden on his shade but also somehow uncannily reincarnated him, or rather, reactivated him by repossessing his husk, and then become zombie himself. The chain of ghosts is now growing: Père Labat with his lantern troubles children, a restless spirit condemned for his cruelty; Lafcadio Hearn,

mediating the rich tales of the island, and reviving the lost history
of the missionary, resituates the Dominican's bobbing light among
'zombi-fires'; Jean Rhys recuperates the phantoms that haunt
the forest in *Wide Sargasso Sea*, and suffuses her entire vision of the
islands with a quality of unsettled, stifling uncanniness.

No wonder Raphael Confiant, speaking of Hearn, extols his
perceptiveness on this precise question of the haunted Caribbean,
and gives it a new twist: the spectre stalking this history is no longer
the malevolent missionary. 'Lafcadio Hearn', declares Confiant,
'had succeeded in penetrating one of the most jealously guarded
secrets of our ancient *quimboiseurs* (witch-doctors): that the secret
spirits of the countless thousands of Caribs and Africans who
perished under European colonization are still protecting us, the
Creole people. These spirits do not live in the skies like Christian
ones, but remain asleep during the day in the high branches of
sacred trees . . . Only once the last rays of the sun begin to glimmer,
do they start roaming in the darkness . . .'[89]

But one person's guardian angel is another's nightmare visitor.
The supernatural is difficult terrain; of its very nature, it resists
discourse; or, to put it more accurately, it is always in the process
of being described, conjured, made, and made up, without ascer-
tainable outside referents. The languages—and images—it uses
can only remain in flux, constituting the reality of what they claim
to describe or evoke, and are consequently shape-shifting themselves. Zombies are not within grasp, that is part of their allure—
and, now, of their retaliatory power. The concept does not only
describe a vacancy, it threatens it; in a recursive move characteristic
of postcolonial strategies, the zombie has been claimed as a figure
not of servitude, but of occult and diffuse potency for the very
regions where the concept arose in its reduced, subjugated, even
annihilated character.

The lineage of hauntings that animates *Wide Sargasso Sea* includes
younger revenants: Angela Carter was mindful of Jean Rhys's
inspiration and was planning a book about Adèle, the little girl

in *Jane Eyre*, whose governess Jane becomes when she enters Mr Rochester's house; but Angela Carter died before she could finish the novel.[90] These number some of the most recent metamorphoses of the zombie. Once, the zombie offered a mirror in which the annihilation of personhood was mirrored; the concept has now been reclaimed and is being reconfigured as hauntings of a different kind. The concept of person that such weirdly labile souls presume has attained stronger presence in contemporary storytelling, as the idea of the self comes under multiple strains; it is to the effects of these strains and their inspirational presence in literature that I shall turn next.

4

Doubling

Franz Schubert, in the year of his death, 1828, set to music a short intense lyric called 'Still ist die Nacht', (renaming it 'Der Doppelgänger'), by the German poet Heinrich Heine. The words' simplicity is however deceptive, for the image Heine conjures conceals seething complexities of psychological anguish:

> Still ist die Nacht, es ruhen die Gassen,
> In diesem Hause wohnte mein Schatz;
> Sie hat schon längst die Stadt verlassen,
> Doch steht noch das Haus auf demselben Platz.
>
> Da steht auch ein Mensch und starrt in die Höhe,
> Und ringt die Hände, vor Schmerzensgewalt;
> Mir graust es, wenn ich sein Antlitz sehe—
> Der Mond zeigt mir meine eigne Gestalt.
>
> Du Doppelgänger! du bleicher Geselle!
> Was äffst du nach mein Liebesleid,
> Das mich gequält auf dieser Stelle,
> So manche Nacht, in alter Zeit?
>
> (Still is the night. The streets are at rest.
> Here is the house where my loved-one lived;

Long it is, since she left the town,
Yet the house still stands where it did.

A man stands there too, staring up,
Wringing his hands in agony;
Horror grips me, as I see his face—
The moon shows me my own self.

Doppelgänger! Pale companion!
Why do you ape the torment of love
That I suffered here
So many a night in time past?)[1]

The three compressed verses set a scene as precisely contoured as a single nocturnal shot from a film, or a magic lantern slide: these similes, borrowed from optics and cinema, are to the point, as I hope to show. The lover remembers the house where his lost love used to live, and as he revisits it in the camera obscura or dark chamber of night-time thoughts, he finds himself still standing there, lit by the moon, this other self apparently mocking him with an imitation of the agony he felt in that same place before.

Many features of this morbid, terrifying scene recur in fantasy and fairy tales about hauntings by doubles or alter egos: the recollection he suffers brings back the feelings as intensely as he suffered in the past—time's flow is dammed and the past comes back; then the doppelgänger or copy springs on the original, the first person of the poem, by surprise, uncomfortably: while he 'apes' him he does not provide any narcissistic pleasure of recognition and kinship at all, but a horrific sense of alienation. Above all, the Schubert song partakes of the nature of doubles in modern imaginings, because it can be—and often is—heard as a recorded voice, issuing from a CD player, technologically communicated, but disincarnate, unhoused in human terms, an acoustic spectre. As another German poet, Rainer Maria Rilke wrote, remembering when he first heard recordings on a 'phonograph': 'We were confronting, as it were, a new and infinitely delicate point in the texture of reality, from which something far greater than ourselves ... seemed to be appealing to us as if seeking help.'²

The ubiquitous electronic voice has become domestic now, the everyday magic of hearing the voice of someone dead or faraway; likewise photography has established former selves and the presence of people as they were when they were alive in every corner of everyday experience. Visual and aural media of record and reproduction, which duplicate the indices of physical presence and, in so doing, cancel their reliability, profoundly affect the portrayal of characters, of consciousness, and of reality itself: they are the powerful recent agents of literary metamorphoses.

In the early decades of the nineteenth century, uneasy questions that body-hopping and soul theft had raised, about the location of identity and the stability of personhood, overcast the blithe wit and satire, the Enlightenment mockery of the orientalist fairy tales; in the spooky inventions of writers such as Adelbert von Chamisso and of E. T. A. Hoffmann, in several of the haunted short stories of Edgar Allen Poe, such as 'William Wilson', the doppelgänger breaks out into the conscious domain of artistic, popular entertainments. Doubling offers another disturbing and yet familiar set of personae in ways of telling the self; permutations of inner and outer selves catalyse uncanny plots about identity.³ The Double is a complex, even riddling concept: it can mean a second self, or a second existence, usually coexisting in time, but sometimes sequentially, as in soul migration plots, such as intricately executed in the Venetian Carlo Gozzi's *The King Stag* (1762).⁴ It can mean a lookalike who is a false twin, or, more commonly, someone who does not resemble oneself outwardly but embodies some inner truth. In this sense, the double, while wholly dissimilar, unnervingly embodies a true self. The combinations are bewildering, but many film plots today deal nimbly with them. To be doubled can entail, for example, that you are shadowed by another, and that someone else is living with your identity, and that that identity has been stolen; in this way the doppelgänger derives its being from the nexus of ideas about soul theft and multiple, wandering spirits that structure the living dead.

You can be changed, and concealed within another shape.

Or again, your double might be an alien creature inside you, a monster who claims to share your being, but who feels like a foreign body, a hideous stranger who might be impersonating you on the outside or taking possession of you and masquerading as you inside your own person. This may have happened, of course, without your knowing it.

Or, again, the metamorphic beings who issue from you, or whom you project or somehow generate, may be unruly, unbidden, disobedient selves inside you whom you do not know, do not own, and cannot keep in check. Emily Dickinson opens a poem of around 1863, 'One need not be a Chamber | To be haunted' and includes the line, 'Ourself behind ourself, concealed . . .':

> Far safer, through an Abbey gallop,
> The Stones a'chase—
> Than Unarmed, one's a'self encounter—
> In a lonesome Place—
>
> Ourself behind ourself, concealed—
> Should startle most—
> Assassin hid in our Apartment
> Be Horror's least.[5]

A predominant variation of doubling stages dissimilar pairs, a subject and an alter, or Other self. The most familiar narratives of this kind dramatize sinister, monstrous doppelgängers, as in Mary Shelley's *Frankenstein*, James Hogg's great novel, *The Private Memoirs and Confessions of a Justified Sinner*, Robert Louis Stevenson's *Dr Jekyll and Mr Hyde*, Freud's studies in unconscious promptings and concealed desires. These alters relate to your innermost, secret self, and act epiphanically to unveil you to the world—and to yourself.

The double also epitomizes by contrast the current state of metamorphosis: as a threat to personality on the one hand, of possession by another, and estrangement from self. But, tugging strongly and contradictorily against this at the same time, the double also solicits hopes and dreams for yourself, of a possible becoming different while remaining the same person, of escaping the bounds of self, of aspiring to the polymorphous perversity of infants, in Freud's phrase, which in some ways mimics the protean energies of the metamorphic gods. (Advertisements promise, 'Be whoever you want to be.'[6]) The uncanny double has expressed, since the late eighteenth century, modern intimations of inner demons, of being multiple rather than integrated. The shadow of the doppelgänger above all reveals that the threat to personhood comes from bodily manipulation and psychological multiplicity, the monstrous threat of the 'many-in-the one'.[7] The concept of self-possession—a word which enters English in the eighteenth century—diagnoses its antagonists in concepts such as acting 'out of character', 'not being yourself', but at the same time as the stories express the fear of loss of self, they entertain the possibility of metamorphoses and combinations of persons in one. The theme is intertwined with technologies of reproduction, first optical, then, increasingly, biological. Representation itself acts as a form of doubling; representation exists in magical relation to the apprehensible world, it can exercise the power to make something come alive, *apparently*. The figure of the other you inside you threatens to escape, not only in states of trance, as Lewis Carroll describes (see below), but in actuality, and become another, usurping your being as someone else: the idea of the clone is probably most frightening because even if it looks and acts like a copy, it cannot and will not be one.

Today—from the projected phantoms of eighteenth-century toys to the replicants of Philip K. Dick's *Do Androids Dream of Electric Sheep?*, the scooped victims of alien visitations, much featured in *The X-Files* and US folklore, the would-be flying shamans of New Age personal growth courses, who identify their power animals, the cyberbots promised by twenty-first-century futurists—all the products of waking dreams and of sleep, of hallucination and fantasy, find their predominant expression through apparatus and devices, especially the reproductions and duplications of projections and film.

In order to understand the ubiquity of the double and of doubling, it is helpful to take a short detour through the prehistory of the arts of illusion, in which mechanical duplication achieved magical substantiation of things beyond the reach of the senses.

AERY NOTHINGS AND PAINTED DEVILS

Demonology, ghosts, projections, and photographs are bound up in the figure of the double through the deep association of the devil with conjuring illusion; this connection underlies the very principle of doubling as a variety of metamorphosis. When the first Christians discovered the rituals of the peoples in America, they identified them with classical and medieval witchcraft and divination; they also, as Richard Eden describes, identified the images of their gods with 'the devyl, whom they paynt of the selfe same fourme and colour, as hee appeareth unto them in dyvers shapes and fourmes. They make also Images of golde, copper, and wood, to the same similitudes, in terrible shapes, and so variable, as the paynters are accustomed to paynt them at the feete of sainct Michaell tharchangell, or in any other place, where they paynte them of most horrible portriture.'[8] The devil's image is not stable, and the images of Catholic worship were themselves a source of horror for many writers in these islands: Lady Macbeth, for example, taunts her husband, saying, ' 'Tis the eye of childhood | That fears a painted devil' (II. ii).

In some senses, the painted quality of the devil revealed his fraudulence: he was master of deception and illusion, but also, as Lady Macbeth is saying, a manufactured bogey, a phantom of the sick brain. In one obvious sense, devils can only ever be 'painted devils', that is counterfeit, since they assume the forms they do in order to manifest themselves to humans. In the literature of doppelgängers, this question of the status of the double—is it real, or is it imagined?—and, if it is imagined, is it no less real for that?—returns insistently, and its undecideability, which gives many of its vehicles their narrative grip, finds expression through images of projections and images, artefacts and delusions and tries to decide their status with regard to the real.

Image magic frequently proceeds by mimesis and replication; verbal spells also use imitation and doubling to achieve their ends.[9] The spectres that conjuring raises are related to embodied doubles because magical operations allegedly raised ghosts, conjured apparitions, projected the shadow not the substance, the double not the original. 'Double double, toil and trouble,' chant the witches in Macbeth over their cauldron (*Macbeth*, IV. i) Elsewhere, Macbeth rails against, 'these juggling fiends . . . that palter with us in a double sense . . .' (V. vii).

Shakespeare knew his demonology. Thomas Aquinas, following Augustine, had determined that the devil could not be capable of actually performing metamorphoses, or of being in two or more places at once (the divine gift of ubiquity), or of knowing the future, since these were the unique prerogatives of God. But the devil was an ape, a mimic, a deceiver, who could create the illusion of such feats.[10] The condition of Shakespeare's many apparitions is uncanny: Banquo's ghost is both there and not there, visible but not palpable. In Scottish demonology, the devil could conjure a spirit double, a phantasm such as Helen of Troy, when she appears at the summoning of Mephistopheles in Christopher Marlowe's *Dr Faustus*.

The raising of spectral others develops in symbiosis with the development of media of representation, above all optical or, in the term the Jesuit experimenter Athanasius Kircher favours,

catoptrical, or worked through mirrors. The devil was the master of
raising spectres, but the illusions he created could only be seen in
the mind's eye—*until* the arts of illusion began to make them
present, call forth phantoms; the phantoms that appear by means
of new instruments of mimesis and replication provide the look
and limn the features of doubles and doppelgängers in fictions. As
early as the first literary version of 'La Belle et la Bête', by Madame
de Villeneuve, in 1740, enchantments use visual devices: Beauty in
the Beast's palace is given a magic glass in which she can see the
world, and she discovers there a charming youth who gives her
pleasurable intimations, but who will only be revealed to be the
Beast's true doppelgänger at the happy ending.[11]

By analogy with the painted devil and diabolical illusions, the
arts of simulation govern the successful performance of magic.
Making simulacra—puppets and figures—forms the chief basis
of casting spells, in medieval sorcery, as well as in the conjuror's
and healers' arts with figures and *zemis*, met with in the Americas.
Moreover, magic when not used to divine the future was above
all concerned with producing change, as harm or healing; it rules
over metamorphosis, especially when metamorphosis frequently
involves animating the inanimate, conjuring life out of stones,
turning rocks into bread, as the devil tempts Jesus to do, bringing statues and automata to life, as, in Ovid's *Metamorphoses*,
Pygmalion warms the marble Galatea by his ardour, and as the
New Pygmalion, Frankenstein, brings his monster to life. Through
such feats, the devil could imprint himself on the real. Magic
and art overlap over the practice of representations; the magician shades into the artist with the pictures of the future he
conjures.

As noted before in this book, metamorphoses are often narrated within word-pictures about artefacts: the reproductions of
art are the most potent sites of magical conjuration of lifelikeness.
In the web Arachne weaves, 'You would think him real, the crea-
ture, | Real as the waves he breasted', writes Ovid.[12] The tableau of

Leda and the Swan and the other shape-shiftings of Jupiter in *The Strife of Love in a Dream* persuade the onlookers that they are somehow really taking place. Poets and storytellers apply all their skills and give all their energy to make the works of art appear to come to life through the vividness of their language; their own texts, as Ovid above all exemplifies, realize this ambition. Figments absolve their own fictitiousness by an act of speech, as in magical operations; text brings impossible things into existence in the mutual exchange between readers' and writers' fantasy. Metamorphosis is typified by the work of art coming to life; it offers the test case of representation. Simply put, *figures of speech turn into figures of vitality.* Fantastic writing about doubling throws all the devices of representation at the task of forcing the unrepresentable into presence. One of the obvious characteristics of the most powerful of uncanny fictions is that they read like realism: Dr Jekyll actually turns into Mr Hyde, or at least Stevenson succeeds brilliantly in convincing us of this happening, in the lab, after he takes the potion.

'IF THIS BE MAGIC . . .'

In *The Winter's Tale*, Paulina, in the celebrated scene of Hermione's 'resurrection' play, acts bringing to life Hermione's eerie 'double'. This tremendous scene also develops the relationship between 'painted devils' and 'aery nothings' in Shakespeare's use of magic. For in order to bring Hermione back into the unfolding story, Paulina acts the priest-magician, turning to stagecraft, that is, pretence. The capacity of theatre to produce the illusion of real presence vexes Shakespeare, precisely because he is all too aware of its connections to diabolical illusion. The resulting ambiguity about the status of the image's picture-flesh enhances the hallucinatory atmosphere of the play's closing scene. Both Leontes and Hermione are poised between sleep and waking states; as the statue awakes, to Paulina's command, Leontes still thinks it might be an illusion, as in a dream. He exclaims,

> There is an air comes from her. What fine chisel
> Could ever yet cut breath?

(v. iii. 78–9)

And then, as he touches her—embraces her, 'O, she's warm!' here echoing Ovid's Pygmalion. 'If this be magic, let it be an art | Lawful as eating.'

The paradoxes of ekphrasis—its material immateriality—relate to the illusions of presence in spectral conjuring. Because the scene is not magic—in the play, it really *is* Hermione; but Shakespeare's art is, because he takes us to places in make-believe where we could not otherwise go.

The first performances of *Dr Faustus* and of *Macbeth* may have used early magic lantern effects, projections on to smoke and through glass, to summon painted devils.[13] When Prospero talks of his 'insubstantial pageant', it is hard not to imagine stagecraft of an optical variety. Indeed, in his famous speech, he says, 'We are such stuff as dreams are made *on*' (*The Tempest*, IV. i. 14 ff.)— could that 'on' suggest that dreams appear on something, on the screen of fantasy, the scrim on which shadow puppets play?[14] Theatrical illusion offers an analogy to the spectral conjurings of enchanters as well as to the phantasms of haunted minds, to Goya's nightmare of reason. In the *Dream* Theseus talks of 'shaping fantasies', 'aery nothing', to which 'the madman, the lover, and the poet | Give a local habitation and a name . . .' (v. i. 5–17). Reversing Prospero's metaphor, Theseus also says that actors themselves are 'shadows'; Puck repeats this in the play's envoi ('If we shadows have offended', v. i. 423 ff.). These shadows will gather as projections of the internal world of spectres; concepts of the mind's eye were reproduced in the devices of the magic lantern and the phantasmagoria or raree show.

But to Theseus' dismissals, Hippolita comes back, thoughtfully, challenging him for making too light of imagination's power to shape reality:

> But all the story of the night told over,
> And all their minds transfigur'd so together,
> More witnesseth than fancy's images,
> And grows to something of great constancy . . .'
>
> (*Dream*, v. i. 23–6)

The experience of this Dream has been more than mere fancifulness can bring about, she says, admiringly, thus opening the way to Coleridge's distinction between constitutive Imagination and playful Fancy.

THE EYE OF THE IMAGINATION

Just as the early photographic camera reproduced technically perspectival vision, based on a unified observer and a single vanishing point, so optical and other technical means were also developed to reproduce mental or eidetic images.[15] These put squarely the issue of the inner eye's reliability or unreliability, and the problem of the origin of visions; they sharpened the difficulty over the question of representation itself as a form of doubling.

The inner eye, or eye of the imagination, was conceived as a kind of projector, onto the screen of fantasy hovering somewhere beyond the back of the head. Robert Fludd, the Oxford philosopher, published his thoughts about human consciousness and its relationship to the macrocosm of divine creation in his book, *Utriusque Cosmi* (*Of the Other World*), in 1617–19, less than a decade after *The Tempest*. (The magnificent illustrations were engraved after designs by the author by the printer-publisher Theodor de Bry, Maria Merian's grandfather-in-law, as you might recall.) Fludd's

'Vision of the Triple Soul in the Body' shows the bodily faculties in haloes around the profile of a man with suitably enlarged and sensitive external organs: a luminous single eye, a prominent ear, a hand raised to display the fingertips, swollen sensual lips (Fig. 33). But Fludd is also interested in other souls, besides the world of the senses (*Mundus sensibilis*), including the imaginative soul which is linked to the world of the imagination (*Mundus imaginabilis*), where, in good Neoplatonist fashion, all is shadow—the rings of this system, the '*Umbra Terrae*', or shadow of the World, are all shadows of the elements. Fludd writes, '[this] soul [is] called the imaginative soul, or fantasy or imagination itself; since it beholds not the true pictures of corporeal or sensory things, but their likenesses and as it were, their shadows.' These shadows are doubles: not the thing itself, but its phantom: this is the natural habitat of the doppelgänger, who is itself a shade and inhabits a twilight realm, be it the gloomy wynds of Edinburgh, as in James Hogg's *Private Memoirs*, or the rain-soaked streets of *Dr Jekyll and Mr Hyde*.

One of the most remarkable illustrations places an eye over the exact position of the imaginative soul in the earlier diagram. The '*oculus imaginationis*' or 'eye of the imagination' radiates a tableau of images: a tower (of Babel?), a guardian angel showing the way—or perhaps Tobias and his guide, an obelisk, a two-masted ship on a high sea, and the Last Judgement with Christ in glory on a rainbow among trumpeting angels while the dead rise with supplicating hands (Fig. 34).

These images belong to various orders of representation, based on memory or imagination, but it is clear that the inner eye in Fludd's Neoplatonist conception does not receive images: it projects them into a space that does not exist except in fantasy.

Athanasius Kircher, a generation younger than Fludd, knew his work and its direct influence can be felt in *The Great Art of Light and Shadow*, his study of projections and optics, published in 1646. The illustrations of the magic lantern in the 1671 edition are the earliest extant of this device; Kircher was long credited with its

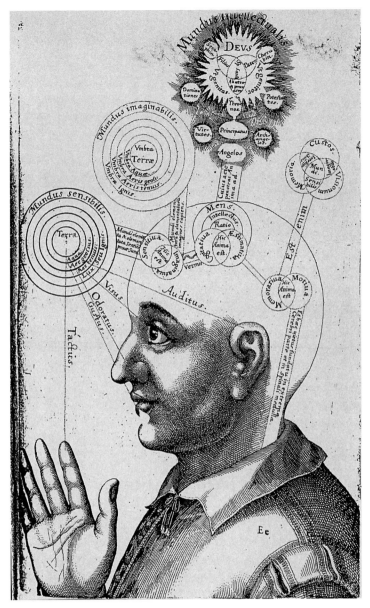

Fig. 33 The senses of the outer body are linked to 'souls' inside the brain, which include 'the imaginative soul, or fantasy', acconding to the Neoplatonist scheme of Robert Fludd ('Vision of the Triple Soul in the Body' from *Utriusque Cosmi*, 1617).

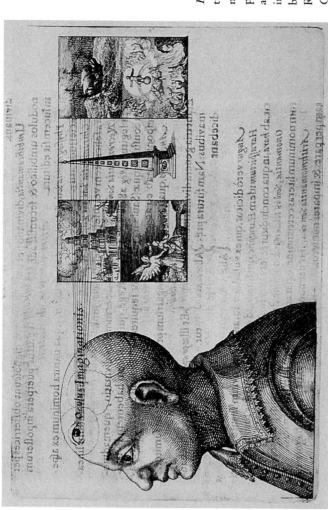

Fig. 34 The 'oculus imaginationis', or eye of the imagination, appears in the same place as the imaginative soul, and projects images onto an imaginary screen beyond the back of the head (from Robert Fludd, *Utriusque Cosmi*, 1617).

invention (Fig. 35). Kircher is a truly Faustian figure, who practised his catoptrical arts with smoking lamps, compound crystals, and various camera obscuras, equipped with lenses and slides of his own device.[16] This first movie theatre opened in the Jesuit college in Rome, where it was attended by cardinals and grandees who gathered to witness 'what was known, in jest,' writes a fellow Jesuit, 'as the enchantments of the reverend father'. But the later Jesuit's uneasiness is well grounded, for Kircher significantly chose to project supernatural images, and in this, he comes perilously close to the goety, or black magic, denounced by the Inquisition in his own day. One treatise published in 1641, i.e. during Kircher's heyday, gives a full inventory of the disruption and mayhem that the rebel angels create. In the midst of this terrifying and overheated litany of evil and catastrophe, the inquisitor instances metamorphoses of animal and human bodies. But these are not changed in their substance, 'sed aliam ex vaporibus extrinsecus circumponendo . . .' (but only by *investing them in another aspect, composed of extrinsic vapours . . .*).[17]

These illustrations of the magic lantern's prototypes have a significant feature in common: the subjects are fantastic, they depict hallucinations. They assume an intrinsic, unexamined equivalence between the technology of producing illusion through projecting shadows and doubles and supernatural phenomena: it is no accident that a naked soul in the flames of hell or purgatory appears burning on the slide projected onto the wall or that Death appears as an animated skeleton with the scythe of the reaper and the hourglass of Father Time. Similarly, an engraving, published in Leiden in 1720–1, illustrates another early slide projector, and despite the learned and scientific title of the mathematical treatise in which it appears, it shows a huge, magnificent devil leering on the wall. The device thus reproduces the mind's capacity to fabricate what the eyes of the body cannot see.

In his account of the phantasmic powers of imagination, Kircher explores the dominant metaphor of a screen, and then two dependent metaphors: first, the blackened surface of a mirror, and

Fig. 35 In Rome, the Jesuit Athanasius Kircher experimented with magic lantern slides; this early illustration shows a soul burning in the fires of hell (or purgatory) (from Kircher, *Ars Magna Lucis et Umbrae*, 1671 edition).

second, the smoky and boiling vapours in the brain of a person afflicted with melancholy. He borrowed the image of the mirror from optics, and the image of the inchoate and turbulent spirits from explanations of cosmic origin in hermetic physics, as represented in Fludd's work; it is not clear how metaphorically he intends their application to the mind.

The materials of the imaginative soul—the play of shadows, the opaque surface of a mirror and vaporous swirling clouds—these three media for producing and rendering fantasy—return as palpable, physical instruments of projection in the first cinematic public entertainments, the Phantasmagoria. Its subject matter was spectral illusion, morbid, frequently macabre, supernatural, fit to inspire terror and dread, those qualities of the sublime, and it enjoyed terrific popularity from the end of the eighteenth century, in Paris just after the Terror, until the invention of true moving cinema displaced it. The association between diabolical phantoms and spectral phenomena influenced the content and material of optical illusions, and shaped the characteristic uses and development of those varied and wonderful technological devices that have been used to represent the supernatural, to make present what eludes the senses and to make visible the invisible. Magic lantern shows sharpened the question that haunts the double: are such visitations phantoms conjured by external, diabolical forces, or are they ghosts within?

The Belgian-born showman, balloonist, and inventor Étienne-Gaspard Robertson was a brilliant innovator in this proto-cinema: it was Robertson who thought of blacking out the background, and coating the screen with wax to give it greater translucency, and pulling back the projector so that the apparition appeared to lunge at the audience (Fig. 36). The crowd accepted an unspoken, unexamined equivalence between the ghosts, skeletons, bleeding nuns, and ghouls that a burning lamp, flickering smoke, a series of mirrors and lenses, and a painted transparency can conjure and the invisible screen on which the mind casts its own envisionings, be

Fig. 36 In a Gothic convent in Paris, soon after the Revolution, the showman Étienne-Gaspard Robertson staged the first horror spectacles, with ghosts and bleeding nuns and other phantoms (the *Phantasmagoria*, engraving, nineteenth century).

they fantasized or recalled through memory. Also like the devil conjuring out of vapours, the galanty men, as phantasmagorists were called, discovered that you could project onto smoke and thereby produce an effect of wraith-like movement as the image came and went, shrank and grew in the beam of light. Soon after Danton was guillotined, Robertson projected his image, flickeringly, in smoke rising from a casket. This corresponds exactly to the metaphor that Virgil uses to Dante in the *Inferno*, as mentioned in Chapter 3, when Dante asks him about the spirits whom he meets—how can it be that he can see them and talk to them when they have no bodies or material substance?—and Virgil explains that souls take their form as rainbows in vapour, as flames in fire.

HALOES OF GLORY

The new optical means of conjuring up the spirit doubles of someone who was not there, but only appeared to be, informs the imagery of the haunted self in fiction that stages the drama of the doppelgänger, and struggles with its external or internal reality.

Coleridge, on a walking tour of Germany with some friends in 1799, made a pilgrimage to the Harz mountains to catch a glimpse of this famed conjunction between clouds, sky, and shadows that casts a huge phantom figure across the cloud floor. Coleridge's group were twice disappointed in their quest to see the spectre, though at the second attempt they were 'repayed by the sight of a Wild Boar with an immense Cluster of Glow-worms round his Tail & Rump'.[18]

In spite of this disappointment, Coleridge later explored the related meteorological phenomenon of the parhelion, or a spectral double sun, in the poem, 'Constancy to an Ideal Object'. As we saw in relation to the spellbound personality of the Ancient Mariner and of Christabel, Coleridge analysed his experience of the supernatural in psychological terms. In his poem, he transmutes the trick of the light into an extended metaphor for the split consciousness of the yearning lover, who transfigures the shadow double into the figure of his beloved.

The poet addresses his own thought, and questions its status: can a mental image have material presence?

'And *art* thou nothing?'

he asks. And then answers himself:

> 'Such thou art, as when
> The woodman winding westward up the glen
> At wintry dawn, where o'er the sheep-track's maze
> The viewless snow-mist weaves a glist'ning haze,
> Sees full before him, gliding without tread,
> *An image with a glory round its head;*
> The enamoured rustic worships its fair hues,
> Nor knows he makes the shadow, he pursues!'[19]

In this Orphic key, Coleridge summons a phantom Eurydice from the illusion. 'Constancy to an Ideal Object' ironizes, in its very title, the contrast between the attachment of the mind to its fantasies and the insubstantial character of their objects; Coleridge dramatizes, with rapt poignancy, the predicament of the lover who knows that he himself creates the love object he pursues, that she is not there.

Unlike James Hogg, who, as we shall see, leaves in doubt the source of his two protagonists' supernatural visions, Coleridge explicitly invokes the explicable, meteorological status of the shadow double, in both the halo of glory and the Brocken spectre, in order to communicate the happier condition of the ignorant rustic who does not know that the vision is illusion; the doppelgänger seals the loneliness of the Romantic lovelorn poet, who suffers because he is too self-aware not to realize that the boons his beloved's image summons for him—security and home, warmth and love—exist only as longings projected in air, as rainbows that have indeed been unwoven.

Coleridge felt he was 'a hive of selves', but mostly that there were two of him.[20] James Hogg, who read Coleridge deeply, distributed his protagonist's character, in *The Private Memoirs*, through two principal doubles, one of whom, the evil brother Robert Wringhim, himself is shadowed by an evil counsellor, a Mephistophelian double. Hogg consciously harks back to Marlowe's Mephistopheles, but he creates a chillier moral climate than *Doctor Faustus.* Throughout his 'confessions', Robert portrays himself as the puppet of his 'princely counsellor', his understanding clouded, his nature distorted by the unceasing shadowing and possession of his 'adviser'. This Mephistophelian evil genius has the necromantic capacity to change his shape: he either takes on the semblance of his victims, impersonating Robert in the execution of numerous further crimes, or he propels Robert to commit evil in a somnambulist state. Robert writes,

Either I had a second self, who transacted business in my likeness, or else my body was at times possessed by a spirit over which it had no controul [*sic*], and of whose actions my own soul was wholly unconscious. This was an anomaly not to be accounted for by any philosophy of mine . . . To be in a state of consciousness and unconsciousness, at the same time, in the same body and same spirit, was impossible.[21]

Hogg was aware of Coleridge's interest in weather portents and the spectre of the Brocken, and he reported on Scottish will-o'-the-wisps and such; furthermore, he had himself seen magic lantern shows in his native Scotland: Philidor, who was Robertson's chief rival, had toured in Edinburgh very successfully. Again, the cluster, phantoms, photography, and fantasy communicate a writer's psychological investigations. But *The Private Memoirs* does not share the rationalist stance of the galanty men, like Robertson, who liked to claim they spooked the public merely to show how vain such fears were.

The novel splits and doubles itself, its themes, and its characters. Two texts, one following the other, are written from two different points of view; narrating the same terrible story, they contradict each other here and there, forming an asymmetrical diptych, all the more compelling for its discordancy and conflicts. These two versions stage the fatal enmity of two brothers, George who is fair of face and sanguine of temper, and Robert, saturnine, fanatical, and malignant, brought up in a blazing, antinomian extreme conviction that the 'justified sinner' who has been saved can do no wrong. George finds himself continually accompanied by his brother:

'Yet he had never sat or stood many minutes till there was the self-same being, always in the same position with regard to himself, as regularly as the shadow is cast from the substance, or the ray of light from the opposing denser medium.'[22] Again, the optical imagery returns to communicate something mysterious, stalking him. The novel is set in eighteenth-century Edinburgh, a city of night and shadow, of lurking eavesdroppers and invisible pursuers, of gloomy wynds and crepuscular crannies, but Hogg stages one of the novel's climactic struggles between the two brothers in the open, elevated ground of Arthur's Seat, on a radiant morning. The scene, with its phantasmagoric epiphanies, its violent, near fatal encounter, and its hallucinatory multiplication of the doppelgänger figure, fuses modern dilemmas about the stability of the self with visual metaphors of meteorological wonders and optical illusion. It occurs early in the novel, and embodies the character of the book, for it is not possible to know what George experienced exactly, what he sees, who is possessed, who is haunted.

George has ascended onto the brilliant illuminated summit partly to evade the constant unwelcome attendance of his brother:

As he approached the swire at the head of the dell . . . he beheld, to his astonishment, a bright halo in the cloud of haze, that rose in a semi-circle over his head like a pale rainbow. He was struck motionless at the view of the lovely vision; for it so chanced that he had never seen the same appearance before, though common at early morn. But he soon perceived the cause of the phenomenon, and that it proceeded from the rays of the sun from a pure unclouded morning sky striking upon this dense vapour which refracted them . . .[23]

He continues to draw nearer, and the delicious morning vision changes all of a sudden:

Gracious Heaven! What an apparition was there presented to his view! He saw, delineated in the cloud, the shoulders, arms, and features of a human being of the most dreadful aspect. The face was the face of his brother, but dilated to twenty times the natural size. Its dark eyes gleamed on him through the mist . . .

At the sight of this cinematic close-up, a magnification we have now become accustomed to:

George conceived it to be a spirit. He could conceive it to be nothing else; and he took it for some horrid demon by which he was haunted, that had assumed the features of his brother in every lineament, but in taking on itself human form, had miscalculated dreadfully on the size, and presented itself thus to him in a blown-up, dilated frame of embodied air, exhaled from the caverns of death or the regions of devouring fire.

This overwrought language, compounded of Low Church liturgy and *Blackwood's Magazine* Gothic, gives the whole novel its violent complexion.

When it comes nearer, the protagonist flings himself upon it, only to find that it is 'a *real* body of flesh and blood', his fearsome brother Robert, who cries 'Murder! Murder!' Then George, 'being confounded between the shadow and the substance, [he] knew not what he was doing or what he had done . . .' He assaults the demon shape—an act that will land George a charge of attempted murder and precipitate the tortuous and terrible sequence of events that leads to his death and his evil brother's supplanting him.[24]

Hogg's 'halo of glory', fused in this vision with a shadow double, interestingly claims the phenomenon for a more profound psychological uncanny than Coleridge's use of it.

De Quincey, also engaging with Coleridge, in 'Suspiria de Profundis' quotes him when he in turn takes up the theme of the Spectre of the Brocken, to meditate in his turn with magnificent, brooding introspection on the figure whom he calls 'the Dark Interpreter . . . an intruder into my dreams . . .'[25] De Quincey, with expressive subtlety, shades Coleridge's certainty about the state of the illusion into a more troubling ambivalence. He is not as clear that he himself always knows that the figure is an illusion: 'He is originally', writes De Quincey, 'a mere reflex of my inner nature. But as the apparition of Brocken sometimes is disturbed by storms or by driving showers, . . . in like manner the Interpreter sometimes swerves out of my orbit, and mixes a little with alien natures. I do not always know him in these cases as my own parhelion . . . No man can account for all things that occur in dreams. Generally I believe this—that he is a faithful representative of myself; but he also is at times subject to the action of the god *Phantasus*, who rules in dreams . . . This dark being the reader will see again in a further stage of my opium experience; and I warn him that he will not always be found sitting inside my dreams, but at times outside, and in open daylight.'[26]

De Quincey never gets round to describing that further stage of his experiences with drugs, but it is worth recalling that narcotics were central to spirit travel in Caribbean rituals, and that tobacco and others were seen as noxious by early chroniclers not because they damaged your health, but because they produced diabolical hallucinations. 'The Devil', wrote one, 'who is a deceiver and knows the powers of herbs, has taught the Indians the virtue of tobacco: and leads them into deceit through visions and apparitions which the tobacco procures.'[27]

Significantly, in the phantasmagoric opening fugue of this marvellously complex essay, De Quincey, ravels up together even more tightly photography, ghosts, doppelgängers, and natural wonders, when he includes among the modern inventions that represent, in 1845, 'the new powers of heaven and powers of hell', the daguerreotype. He characterizes this new medium of duplication with the ominous phrase, 'light getting under harness as a slave for man'.[28]

Several characteristics of the daguerreotype deepened its affinities with spectral doubles: the pictures were often stereoscopic and therefore doubled; in portraits, the image comes and goes, phantom-like, as the polished silver surface is tilted towards the light; and the effects of pallor and immobility are so pronounced that subjects were tinted with pink cheeks and lips and their jewels pricked out with gilt so that they should not look like corpses. Their character as keepsakes and mementoes deepened the connection to memory and mortality, too, of course; and, now that the medium is no longer in use, it is suffused with nostalgia.[29]

Robert Louis Stevenson's tale, *The Strange Case of Dr Jekyll and Mr Hyde* (1885) owes a very large debt to James Hogg's *Private Memoirs*: it is a study in doubles, in the terrifying presence and power of evil, it is set in a city (London) of murky alleys and curling fog and looming lamplight, which recalls the writer's native Edinburgh more accurately than the English capital, and it grasps, but with a more decisive grip, the question of whether the evil is directed from outside or from inside. It also draws on the metaphor of the magic lantern to create its special, haunted, menacing atmosphere of corruption and gloom: when Mr Utterson, the lawyer with the storyteller's name, first hears of the horror that is 'Hydden' behind the familiar door, and when he learns of the child whom the ghastly apparition assaulted and battered in the street, the experience is evoked in the fugitive impressions of phantasmagoria and dreams: 'Mr Enfield's tale went by before his mind in a scroll of lighted pictures. . . . The figure . . . haunted the lawyer all night; and if at any time he dozed over, it was but to see it glide more stealthily through sleeping houses, or move the more swiftly . . . even in his dreams it had no face, or one that baffled him and melted before his eyes . . .'[30]

Both authors are writing from within the ambience of Scottish Calvinism, with its profound pessimism about human nature: evil lies ineradicably inside every body, we are all born in sin and condemned to live as sinners, unless reprieved by the inexplicable operations of divine election otherwise known as justification. This fateful perspective makes Hogg's protagonist accept the diabolical promptings of his evil genius, who urges him, as a justified sinner or one of the elect, to do as he pleases. Thus Hogg, writing sixty years before, casts his protagonist as the puppet victim of a devilish mastermind who can even change shape and appear and disappear at will. By contrast Stevenson does not rely on Calvinist extremism, and his story has found wider favour and readership partly because the 'strange case' he describes fits more commonly held fears of potential human evil. Stevenson brilliantly stirs scare stories about scientific experiment. His Dr Jekyll has placed his feet in the tread of Dr Faust who sold his soul to the devil for knowledge—and pleasure; and of Dr Frankenstein, who in Mary Shelley's new myth of our times, also creates a monster.

Mr Hyde is a monster, physically, although the full impact of his horrible appearance depends on his never being exactly described or even fully seen; he remains vague, shapeless, incoherent, and all the more unsavoury and disquieting for that. Stevenson steeps the modern drama of a split personality in the figures and images of Christian apocalypse. Words such as 'deformity', 'chill', 'savage', 'dwarfish' toss restlessly around his skulking figure as they did in medieval texts to evoke the devil or allegorical vices; he is likened to an ape in his fury, a monkey in his agility, both mockers of god, and provokes 'disgust, loathing and fear' in all who come near. Mr Utterson exclaims, 'O my poor old Harry Jekyll, if ever I read Satan's signature upon a face, it is on that of your new friend!'[31] Stevenson's Dr Jekyll, who does not look like a monster, but conceals the monstrous within him, has the honour of being the most famous inaugurator of this modern attitude to evil in fantastic stories—that you never can tell: 'He [Jekyll] was much in the open air, he did good; his face seemed to open and brighten . . .'[32] Appearances are disguises on the whole, and the devil's a master of masks and lies; Hyde is repellent, screened from view by the reassuring bulk of Dr Jekyll who knows himself to be 'a double dealer'.[33]

THE 'EERIE' STATE

The uncanny doppelgänger of Gothic and its followers continues to haunt twentieth-century literature, but grows less unfamiliar, and even, in some examples, inviting. As the media of communication begin to convey doubles in the form of recorded voices and photographed faces, ever more commonly and far and wide, the possibilities of soul travel or personal dispersal do not always terrify; they sometimes beckon, seductively. Again, natural magic, or scientific discovery, helps confer the pleasures of wonder, in contrast to the supernatural's power to excite fear but they continue to interact with models of persons and of subjectivity from a range of thought. This is most clearly the case in Victorian fiction for children, in which the realms of fairies above all offer fascination and consolation in equal measure, and a spirit voyage such as Alice undertakes—twice—does not disturb (at least not altogether)— even though the experiences remain, in Hippolita's words, 'strange and admirable'.

The acceptance of new dimensions to an individual's space-time coordinates appears most startlingly perhaps in the preface to *Sylvie and Bruno Concluded*, the last fantasy novel Lewis Carroll published, in 1893. He proposed here a theory of mind:

I have supposed a Human being to be capable of various psychic states, with varying degrees of consciousness, as follows:—

(a) the ordinary state, with no consciousness of the presence of the fairies

(b) the 'Eerie' [and he frequently puts the word in inverted commas and capitalizes it] in which, while conscious of actual surroundings, he is *also* conscious of the presence of Fairies;

(c) a form of trance, in which, while unconscious of actual surroundings, and apparently asleep, he (ie his immaterial essence)
migrates to other scenes, in the actual world, or in Fairyland, and is
conscious of the presence of Fairies.[34]

He terms these 'abnormal states' and goes on to discuss the
fairies' experience of the human dimension. Carroll, who hardly
left Christ Church, seems a strange locus for beliefs in shamanic
flight, out-of-body experiences, and the possibility of seeing
fairies; but he did leave Oxford, and his college, and not seldom
either, in order to take photographs. (His portable developing
equipment and slimline brass and zinc tank for preparing the plates
in situ can be seen in the Museum of Science, Oxford.) This practice, photography, proves central to the continuing engagement
with the supernatural in literature ever since its invention; when
Carroll imagined his young protagonists travelling to other realms
in their doubles, he is working with the grain of late Victorian
metamorphoses about bodies and their possibilities. The prolif-
eration of doubles develops with respect to ideas about haunted
consciousness, as in Proust's model of memory; this finds expression in the duplications and phantoms of the photographic presence, but is also sustained and intensified by the medium's character
and its offshoots, up to digitization and virtual imaging today.

Lewis Carroll's model of the three psychic states reconnects us
to the influence of encounters with other belief systems in the
Victorian empire. He also demonstrates the characteristic move
from outward to inward in stories about the status of the imaginary: the supernatural becomes located, not in an external realm, but
within, and can be reached through altered states of consciousness—trance, in his case. But Carroll, like many others, identified
in photography an intermediate state between the material and the
immaterial, which could seize evidence of the fairy world. He was
one of the collectors who was delighted with a purchase of a
photograph of fairies, from the famous Cottingley forgeries.
Another purchaser, even more unlikely on the face of it, was Arthur

Conan Doyle, originator of that master of deductive logic, Sherlock Holmes.[35]

Carroll combined a passion for new gadgets and devices, a fascination with children, with dream experiences, with magic and spirit voyaging, with doubles also known as alters, or other selves; he was preoccupied with images that duplicate persons, either in the looking-glass, as reflections, or in the lens at the end of the telescope. At the end of one telescope he owned, he glued a tiny picture of Alice Liddell, as if to fix the line which closes *Through the Looking Glass*:

> Still she haunts me, phantomwise,
> Alice moving under skies
> Never seen by waking eyes . . .
> Life, what is it, but a dream?[36]

The Revd Charles Dodgson took up photography in 1856 and grew adept at handling the tricky wet collodion process over a career lasting twenty-four years. The camera's intrinsic properties exactly matched Carroll's fantasy: the dissolving of the Cheshire Cat, and the inside out and upside down character of negatives and of images in a viewfinder.[37] In *Sylvie and Bruno* and its sequel of five years later, *Sylvie and Bruno Concluded*, Lewis Carroll plays with doublings of personae and dislocations of time as the children move between parallel realms, the Here and Now and two imaginary territories which he calls 'Outland' and 'Fairyland'. A short rhyming poem, in the same style as the Alice books, opens the story, asking the question again: 'Is all our Life, then, but a dream . . . ?' and, tellingly goes on to invoke a 'raree-show', or magic lantern performance. The protagonists continually slip into the parallel dream worlds of both Outland and Fairyland, leaving the Here and Now. The Here and Now stands still during the children's experiences elsewhere, so that when they re-enter it, nothing has changed; at one point a reversing watch even allows them to run time backwards, in order to prevent a traffic accident. Meanwhile the characters around them in the Here and Now, such as the Warden and the Sub-Warden, turn up as the King of Elfland and the Gardener respectively, recognizably the same and yet altogether changed.

Carroll's devices of moving between them even anticipate reverse spooling and slow motion and the rewind button on a video—this is one of the sharpest examples of the future development of a medium interacting with developments in thought. James Joyce read these books closely: perhaps as a movie buff, he responded to the jump cuts and flashbacks and dreamlike leaps in space that Carroll introduces, even more than to the contrary nonsense of Wonderland and the Looking Glass world.[38] But what is more germane is that Carroll invents these ways of telling (and by implication ways of seeing) because he needs them in order to communicate his ideas about persons: about out-of-body experiences, in Outland or Fairyland, about being in two bodies, or in two places at once, about intimations of being someone different at the same time as being yourself, about parallel time perspectives running at different speeds, about the possibility of extra dimensions and metamorphoses from one to another.

This echoes the handling of time in Alice's return from her other worlds, but differs in two respects, Carroll introducing new variations in relation to doubles. For Sylvie and Bruno are fey, in the Scottish sense that they have second sight and can enter those other 'eerie' states; so does the narrator, who can see them in their fairy roles. 'Eerie' implies doubling: as they move through the three space-time universes they meet their doppelgängers in adult shape, Lady Muriel Orme and, to complicate matters, Bruno's double doubles, Arthur Forester and Eric Lindon. (The sylvan references of their names may be attempts to suggest growth over time as well as the green and pleasant lands of Oxfordshire.) They thus encounter the promise of their future selves, equally enchanting and delightful as their childhood personae, and this juxtaposition achieves the effect of a cinematic dissolve of one child face into its adult charms, or, more to the point in this epoch, as if the pages of a photographic album were turned and the Revd Charles Dodgson were saying, twenty years later, 'You see I knew her when she was a little girl, and it was clear she would grow into the most charming young woman.'

Secondly, the suspension of time's flow in the Here and Now while the children enjoy their adventures in their doubled character in Outland and Fairyland still the real world into the frozen moment of a photograph. In Fairyland, the children become miniaturized, and uncanny, exhibiting no fear of death or large insects: Alice imperturbably (and tenderly) rights a beetle that has fallen on its back, while Bruno 'began arranging a dead mouse as a kind of sofa' (Fig. 37).[39]

In the story, their littleness does not seem to depend as much on Victorian visions of gnat-like elves and butterfly sprites as on the geometry of the camera, which can reduce its subjects and yet retains them complete, as if seen in the mind's eye.

As in *Alice*, Sylvie and Bruno dream, yet their adventures, comical, poignant, more romantic and diffuse than in the earlier books, are not the products of sleep, but of reverie, the waking dream state that much interested Carroll's contemporaries. The young hero and heroine adopt a variety of methods to transit out of their own time and space: they can effect it physically, through displacement, by opening a door or passing through a wall or through 'the gate of ivory', through which true dreams enter in Homer. But they also move between worlds in their minds, and Carroll specifies various states of daydreaming in these stories: including falling into a 'brown study' at the sight of the glowing coals. This phrase, no longer much in use, relates to the black bile, the melancholia and turbid dark spirits that are invoked in Kircher's theories of the imagination.

Before he wrote *Alice in Wonderland*, Carroll made many portraits of his friends—adults and children—in states of reverie: Christina Rossetti, who herself crossed into goblin realms in her poetry, was taken around 1863 with her head leaning on her

Fig. 37 The child protagonists in Lewis Carroll's novel have uncanny powers, and can time travel, change size, and move through parallel worlds (Harry Furniss, 'Bruno sitting on the dead mouse', from *Sylvie and Bruno*).

mother's lap, gazing distantly, through the pages of an open book, as if to the world beyond it.[40] His child-friends 'feigning sleep' was another favourite pose; on one occasion he even staged a tableau, 'The Dream', with double exposures suggesting the subjects appearing in the dreamer's mind.[41] It is interesting that he was one of the few people to buy one of the many studies that Lady Clementina Hawarden made of her daughters day-dreaming (Fig. 38), often doubling each other as they stand together or gazing into mirrors at their reflections.[42]

Yet more startlingly, when Carroll suggests that the children can enter what he calls 'the Eerie state' and make fairyland visible, he is according them, it seems in all seriousness, an ability to travel in other dimensions, as he depicts his narrator doing, and himself has done as their interpreter and creator. Their imaginary condition as characters he has invented quivers on the border between reported fact and invented fiction: the questions the earlier Alice book had posed about fantasy are answered differently here, when Carroll implies that he himself has somehow met the children.

Transitions between worlds are performed by Carroll's story-telling without comment, and their abruptness adds powerfully to the sense of doubling: Sylvie turns into Lady Muriel from one sentence to another, just as if a wand had been waved over her. But it is with the notion of continuous time that Carroll plays the most extraordinary tricks: the story starts not merely *in medias res*, but in mid-sentence, with a long dash and a lower case letter:

—and then all the people cheered again, and one man, who was more excited than the rest, flung his hat high into the air, and shouted . . .

We, the readers, are tossed into the spate as it rushes by; the flow then twists and turns and stops and starts, with scattered verses, and sermons, and disquisitions on causes and concerns to Carroll, many of them of acute topical interest now, such as foxhunting, vegetarianism, and competition in schools. He introduces toys and games, sometimes of his own devising, including the magic

Fig. 38 All dream states, from reverie to nightmare, fascinated Lewis Carroll and his contemporaries; Clementina Hawarden, whose work he knew, posed her daughters in fancy dress mysteriously daydreaming (untitled photograph, *c.*1863–4).

reversing watch that can turn back time, and make history repeat itself, twice or more, each time differently. Magical devices which give power to characters inside the story reflect the power of narrators over the stories they are telling: writing also makes it possible to go over the same ground again, and change what happens; a writer can handle time in contradiction of physics, or describe events in dreams as if they were real. At another point in the story, a lovable inventor-type shows the children another 'impossible' object: a container with no outside or inside but only one surface: he calls it Fortunatus' Purse, and it is the three-dimensional equivalent of the better-known spatial riddle, the Möbius strip, a flat, two-dimensional band with two sides but only one surface.[43]

The *Alice* books include Carroll's exploration of dreaming, of course, as well as his structural liking for doubles projected into wonderlands from this world. But in the *Sylvie and Bruno* books, the doubling includes the events themselves, not only the characters to whom they are happening. When Carroll sets out his theory of dream projection and trance voyaging, he puts it in terms he had picked up through his membership of the Society for Psychical Research, which was founded in 1882 in Cambridge by the Cambridge moral philosopher Henry Sidgwick and his younger friend and former student, the classicist and poet Frederic Myers. Through this interest, Lewis Carroll's work reconnects us to the influence of encounters with other cultures through imperial possessions. For in their journal, the indefatigable investigators of paranormal phenomena reported copiously on alleged sightings, altered states, mediumistic happenings, and spirit photography; Sidgwick's scepticism grew more vigorous over the years, but Myers went on hoping for proof. They were both saturated in ancient Greek and Hellenistic magic as well as the beliefs of cultures explored in the wake of military conquest and colonial settlement by ethnographical researchers. The belief in spirit doubles was crucial to this new view of personality, and found expression in a language that adapted traditional spectrality to new ends: there are hundreds, perhaps thousands of books published in the nineteenth century, and of course subsequently, which argue passionately for a different concept of person, very far distant from the Judaeo-Christian integer.[44]

QUESTIONS FAR AND WIDE

F. W. H. Myers, coiner of the word 'telepathy' in 1882, exercised a considerable, but rather disregarded influence on Freud. He was the co-author of a mammoth work, *Phantasms of the Living*, which collected by post through the use of a questionnaire thousands of supernatural experiences, of examples of visits and apparitions of the dead, of premonition and other telepathic phenomena. *Phantasms* appeared in 1886, and was followed, after his death in 1901, by another huge, historical study, *Survival of Human Personality after Bodily Death* (1915).[45] There, Myers built on his eclectic reading in North American beliefs, Hinduism, and animism, as well as his own formation in Classics to put forward a secular, psychological theory, of 'the subliminal self'; this self enjoys continuity in dispersal over time and place and unconsciously carries memories which preserve its integrity over eternity; these can be awakened or recalled through mediums and other supernatural means. 'Myers's subliminal self . . .' writes Rhodri Hayward, 'operated as a kind of filter for the sacred, combining the extracarnate communication with the fragmentary memories and desires of the individual's own past. . . . The sacred was relocated within the field of memory.'[46]

Myers defined the visible self of the séance, as caught in psychic photographs, as, first, 'projections of the double'—namely the spirit of a person—and, second, 'precipitations of the *akâs*'—*akâs* being a Hindu term borrowed by the Theosophists and designating the invisible energy that flows through and unites creation.[47]

Lewis Carroll's serious proposals about fairyland, his apparent unperturbed acceptance of spirit doubles wandering about at will while the entranced body remains behind, were inspired by such ideas, and were not such a startling notion at the turn of the nineteenth century. For in the same years that Carroll was writing the *Sylvie and Bruno* books, and Myers and his colleagues in the SPR were compiling their studies of out-of-body experiences and ghostly apparitions, James Frazer was also conducting an investigation, also by post and questionnaire—worldwide. (The Victorian postal system is another of the industrial engines driving the culture.)

James Frazer, future author of *The Golden Bough*, his vast *Study in Magic and Religion* from classical antiquity to the present day, was also a fellow of Trinity, and another of the Scotsmen much concerned with magic whom we are encountering.[48] His mother's family, the Bogles, were sugar planters in the West Indies, and the adventures and travels of other relatives in India and Tibet remained alive in the Frazers' sense of their own history.[49] From 1887 onwards, James Frazer sent his *Questions* throughout the world as he saw it, and this world coincided, pretty much, with the British empire: to missionaries, colonial administrators, teachers, explorers, botanists, all of whom he convoked, notoriously never moving from his own fireside, to inquire from their native informants about the 'Manners, Customs, Religion, Superstitions, etc. of Uncivilized or Semi-Civilized Peoples'.[50] Like the ethnographers whom he had studied and copied exhaustively into his scrapbooks (including Ramón Pané via Richard Eden's translation of Peter Martyr, again), Frazer was excited by others' ideas about spirits, about ways of summoning them or controlling them, about migrating into the body of animals, and other adventures of wandering souls. His wide reading notes, forming a world tour of exotic places past and present ('The Indians of Nicaragua believe that sorcerers can transform themselves into lizards, dogs, tigers, or any other sort of animal'; 'In a dream the soul leaves the body in the form of a bird. It is dangerous to waken a sleeper . . .') gave him the background from which to draw up his list of questions.[51] He had some direct informants: Mary Kingsley, who had explored the West Coast of Africa, 'talked of spirits' with him.[52] One of her fellow travellers in the area related that 'The indwelling spirit of a man . . . may depart from him, especially in sleep, and its adventures during its absence are the things dreamed . . . the man suffers no inconvenience; it [the spirit] goes out, when he is asleep, without his knowledge; and if it should leave him while he is awake, he is only made aware of its departure by a sneeze or a yawn . . . When, however, the soul, the vehicle of individual personal existence, leaves the body, that body falls into a condition of suspended animation; it is cold, pulseless, and apparently lifeless. Sometimes, though rarely, the soul returns after such an absence, and then the man has been in a swoon or trance . . .'[53]

The intense Victorian curiosity about such psychological hypotheses, expressed in a different genre by Lewis Carroll in Oxford, inspired Frazer to publish his questionnaire in 1907. By this date, Frazer had been coaxed into showing some concern for material, economic, and political conditions. But, in keeping with the positivist neo-paganism of his contemporaries, his main interest remained with magic and demons and altered states of mind. The questions he put, for example, assume that this international survey will discover variations on metamorphosis; they are framed within an episteme that takes soul migration and spirit possession for granted, that presumes the power of objects to trap doubles, the existence of evil shadow selves and doppelgängers. For example, he asked his informants to inquire:

Does [the soul] resemble a shadow, a reflection, a breath, or what?

and

Is the soul supposed to depart from the body at death, in disease, dreams, trance, etc.?

and

Can a man's soul be extracted or stolen from his body?

and, above all,

Can a man lose [his soul] by accident? . . . Do human souls transmigrate into animals, plants etc.?[54]

This was the context—in part—in which Robert Louis Stevenson wrote his two brilliant novellas, 'The Strange Case of Dr Jekyll and Mr Hyde', in 1885, and the lesser known, but no less remarkable, 'The Beach of Falesá', in 1892.[55] Both tales grow out of the Scottish Gothic, but the later story of colonial hypocrisy and magic, set in the South Seas, reflects the anthropological interests that shaped the metamorphoses of the supernatural at the turn of the nineteenth century.[56] Another brilliant and widely travelled storyteller, Rudyard Kipling, displays possibly even more clearly this characteristic late Victorian literary cluster of concerns: empire and fairies, ghosts and modernity. Kipling's beautifully turned, poignant ghost story, 'Wireless', conveys the eerie state of another world in the metaphors of the new, disembodied means of doubling presence.

In these key works, the lurid and spooky contents of *Blackwood's Magazine* of an earlier period, embodying gruesome northern Gothic, are twined into a living oral practice of ethnographical listening, tale-spinning, and new radio broadcasting. (In 'The Beach at Falesá', the plot partly turns on tricks of sound that one of the characters uses to stage a terror scenario of revenants.) R. L. Stevenson himself, who suffered from ill-health all his life, had been terrified by his implacable nurse Alison Cunningham, to whom he dedicated the mild collection of charming poems, *A Child's Garden of Verses.* She frightened him with 'bloods', as penny dreadfuls called tales of horror; Stevenson himself declared he loved what he called 'a good crawler'. He wrote up several of her tales, including the hair-raising ghost story, 'Thrawn Janet'. Sir Walter Scott, who took Scottish yarning to even greater and more exciting amplitude with his page-turning spin on historical Gothic, was also a great aficionado of the eldritch, fey, and uncanny.

These enterprises in information-gathering and storytelling are combined in the work of another Scotsman, Andrew Lang, and his huge undertaking, the library of *Fairy Books—Blue, Green, Red, Pink,* etc.—in which he collected fairy tales from all over the world. Lang put a team of women to work under the direction of his wife, Leonora Alleyne, to revise and reshape an eclectic canon for the Victorian and Edwardian nursery, ranging from French wonder tales to the Arabian Nights. The results, published from 1889 till his death in 1912, constitute one of the richest and most influential repositories of stories made in English (Angela Carter there encountered fairy tales for the first time, for instance).[57]

The enthralled northern realm of shadows and apparitions, in which James Hogg's characters wandered and became lost, as we saw, joins the brighter terrain which produced Andrew Lang's *Fairy Books* in one of the most curious and interesting pieces of fairy lore, the Revd Kirk's book *The Secret Common-Wealth of Elves, Fauns, & Fairies,* a rare and remarkable document about fairyland which provides the crucial missing ancestor for the eighteenth century uncanny and new, contemporary models of personhood. Kirk probably wrote it in 1689 and published it two years later, but the work remained largely unknown until Sir Walter Scott took an interest, soon: this was again picked up by Andrew Lang in his introduction to the book in 1893, right in the middle of the most productive period for supernatural tales of fetches, ghosts, and doubles.[58]

The Revd Robert Kirk had been stolen by the fairies, the story went, when he was walking near a fairy hill one evening in his nightshirt; he collapsed, and was soon buried, in Aberfoyle churchyard. But after this death, he reappeared, to one of his relations, and told him that he was no ghost, but still alive, and a prisoner in fairyland. He gave him an urgent message, that when his posthumous child was being christened, he would appear again, and that one of his relatives present, Graham of Buchray, should throw a knife at the phantom over his head. By this method, the spell would be broken, and Kirk set free.

But when Kirk did indeed appear, as promised, his kinsman was so astounded, that he missed his moment and the vision vanished.

The Revd Robert was never seen again. His coffin was believed to be filled with stones, Walter Scott reported, and Andrew Lang repeated, and Robert Kirk was said to be a captive of the fairies still, a Tam O'Shanter who did not get away, a night walker who had no Fair Janet to hold him till dawn.

In his edition of Kirk's wonderful, eccentric book, Lang comments on 'the worldwide diffusion' of such beliefs and offers some comparative thoughts, drawing on his own anthropological reading: 'We may regard him . . . as an early student in folk-lore and in psychical research—topics which run into each other . . .', he writes.[59] Later, he cites H. J. Bell's 1889 work on *obeah* magic in Haiti, and adopts Myers's phrase 'the subliminal self': 'Whatever hallucination, or illusion, or imposture, or the 'subliminal self' can do today, has always been done among peoples in every degree of civilization . . .'[60] (This use of the transitive verb 'can do' interestingly supports the entranced and delusory states he is describing.) He goes on, 'Thence Mr Kirk glides into that singular theory of savage metaphysics which somewhat resembles the Platonic doctrine of Ideas. All things in Red Indian belief have somewhere their ideal counterpart or "Father" . . . Now the second-sighted behold the "Double-man," " Doppelgänger", "Astral Body," "Wraith," or what you will, or a living person, and that is merely his counterpart in the abstruse world.'[61] He cites the 17,000 reports of incidents gathered by the Society for Psychical Research, and offers some vivid alternative local expressions for doubles: *co-walkers* or 'joint-eaters' or *reflex-men.*

The term reflex-man contains hints of duplication by reflection, or by casting a shadow or an image, as in a 'reflex camera', or catoptrical gadget such as Kircher explored.

Media of reproduction have proliferated since Daguerre invented his way of capturing images, and since Lewis Carroll used photography figuratively and literally to tell his stories, and with their burgeoning the forms of the double in current culture have also flourished. In the autumn of 2001, the very week I was giving my lecture on 'Doubling', genetic engineers claimed to have cloned a human embryo for the first time so that they can 'harvest stem cells' and grow material to help certain degenerative diseases. In order to understand the excitement, compounded of fear, marvelling, and horror that this new possibility stirs, the history of doubles provides a context, for cloning in its popular cultural manifestations continually ponders possible states of personal identity: the copy—the you who is not you but is yet another you—challenges the premiss of individual integrity; it also performs, it seems, a daemonic act of metamorphosis from inanimate to animate that in mythology often discloses divine operation.[62] But this is not the place to debate the issue of medical cloning, except to put the argument that the stories of the past offer divining instruments for present grounds of anxiety and terror.

I tried to show in my second chapter, 'Hatching', that the cycle of insect gestation helped naturalize metamorphosis as a principle of unity in discontinuity, of identity in difference over time; here I want to suggest that changes in the means of representation have also contributed to spreading, through literature as well as within the media themselves, a plural idea of consciousness that installs the double or doubles in the ordinary way of things. Metamorphic storytelling, with its fantastic and prodigious suspension of apparent and apprehensible realities, once described a vision of natural mutation and change. The uncanny literature of spirit thefts and doublings grasped and contended with psychological, inner demons; the entertainment of horror on the one hand and of fairyland on the other domesticated the ghostly. Now it seems to me metamorphosis embodies the shifting character of knowledge, of theories of self, and models of consciousness that postulate the brain as an endlessly generative producer of images and of thoughts, selected from and connected through fantasy, observation, and memory.[63] But the objects of these faculties, in the epistemological confusion of new communications, are not always easy to distinguish. As Dubravka Ugrešić writes in her novel *The Museum* of *Unconditional Surrender*, the narrator ponders how '"dreamed reality" began to unravel before our eyes'. She goes on to ask, 'Did my acquaintance dream the horrors of war, which then actually happened or had the horrors of war already occurred some time in the future, and she just dreamed them?'[64]

Contemporary writers are increasingly plotting their fictions against the normative models of the unified self, as we shall see in my brief, concluding thoughts.

Epilogue

In the tremendous vision of transmigration which closes Plato's *Republic*, the dead are able to choose their fate in their future lives: Socrates describes how a warrior called Er was taken for dead and entered the other world, but, on his funeral pyre, came back to life and then was able to describe how he saw, in the afterlife, in 'a certain demonic place', the souls of Homeric heroes taking on their next existence—in the form of a new daemon. The dead were told, 'A demon will not select you, but you will choose a demon. Let him, who gets the first lot make the first choice of a life to which he will be bound by necessity.'[1] As Er watches the redistribution of lives after death, Orpheus chooses a swan, Ajax singles out a lion, and Agamemnon an eagle. This next incarnation responds to their past character, often in ironical ways, as contrary and yet as revelatory as a shadow double. Atalanta, the swift runner, chooses to become a male athlete, for example; Epeius, who made the Trojan horse, opts to become a female artisan, while Thersites the buffoon becomes an ape. Exhausted Odysseus rejects his former brilliant life of exploits and wanderings: he wants to be a private man who minds nothing but his own business and 'with effort it [his soul] found one lying somewhere, neglected by the others. . . .' Thankfully, Odysseus picks this ordinary life out of the pile.[2]

The core of this strange and ghostly myth offers the promise of another chance at happiness; the souls of the dead are immortal and return in a change of outward shape and terrestrial identity, over which, in this story, they exercise some kind of power (after the lots have been cast for precedence); as in Ovid's later poem, their deathless souls may be housed in animals, live on, transmogrified, in 'all kinds of mixtures'.[3] The oblique, almost witty matches between the past and the future imply personal responsibility for the fate ahead. Though Er does not expand on the appropriateness of the metempsychosis, the souls' earlier conduct impinges on the range of desirable, potential selves.

Plato closes with Socrates' enigmatic words, that this myth, which 'was saved and not lost . . . could save us, if we were persuaded by it'. At least one contemporary writer of myths, Philip Pullman, has responded directly to this promise. In *His Dark Materials*, his trilogy of novels, he has vividly reimagined the Platonic daemons. Like the *Alice* books, this teeming and ambitious metaphysical fiction was written and published for children, but has sprung clear of the confines of the genre after remarkable word-of-mouth success with readers of all ages.[4] Pullman continues to develop the relation between metamorphosis as truth-telling about people, through an extraordinary dramatic device, a personal daemon accompanying every character, a kind of external soul.

The first volume, *Northern Lights*, opens with the sentence: 'Lyra and her daemon moved through the darkening Hall . . .' Her daemon is called 'Pantalaimon', and they are figured as two persons in one, forming a single entity that has a dual aspect. In this opening scene, Pantalaimon 'was currently in the form of a moth, a dark brown one so as not to show up in the darkness of the Hall'. Daemons here belong to the opposite gender of their owner— a Jungian idea of anima or animus—and it is absolutely taboo to touch someone else's daemon, though your own may curl up in your lap, live on your shoulder, and express your innermost thoughts, ones that lie concealed from your own consciousness. These daemons possess the power of protean metamorphosis during the years of childhood, but once adulthood is reached the daemon acquires fixed form; and daemons reveal personality—they are appropriately metamorphic, like Lycaon turning into a werewolf, or Arachne the weaver into a spider, as in Ovid.

'"Why do daemons have to settle?"' asks Lyra. '"I want Pantalaimon to be able to change for ever. So does he."' But she is warned, '"And when your daemon settles, you'll know what kind of a person you are."'[5] This potentiality provides the plot line: for the wicked Mrs Coulter wants to extract and use for her own purposes the polymorphous energies of child daemons.[6] Her plan involves splitting the daemons from their owners, and there is a powerful scene when Lyra attempts to rescue her friend, a boy who has been captured and operated upon in this fashion, but too late and he has—the well-known consequences of splitting—been evacuated of selfhood and become a zombie. In the last volume, Lyra goes down into the underworld, in the steps of Odysseus and Dante and Orpheus, to find him, not to bring him back—because Pullman faces hard realities—but because she feels implicated in his fate, and she wants to make amends by taking her farewell properly.

It is significant that *His Dark Materials* recasts the individual in this doubled, daemonic form, for it also mounts a decisive attack, in the unmanacled spirit of William Blake, on the bigotry and corruption of institutionalized Christianity—especially the Catholic Church. Pullman's materialism is nevertheless saturated in metaphysical poetry, spliced with wide knowledge of the latest theories in new physics and utopian biology. In short his trilogy reveals clearly how literary adventures with metamorphosis have now fashioned a new, compelling way of presenting the self, as constantly shadowed by another, an unconscious incarnate, in animal shape. But although the sequence *His Dark Materials* contains, in keeping with its title, much that is perplexing and distressing and demanding, the trilogy generally converts the negative uncanny of doppelgängers, and the stain on pagan metamorphosis, into a paeon to the pure virtuality of transformation as energy itself.

Interest in different ideas of persons as no longer unified, but split, doubled, or even multiple—haunted by an evil genius, or illuminated by a familiar daemon—have combined with new instruments of perception and knowledge, to reconfigure character and story in contemporary fiction. Philip Pullman has brilliantly invented another world—or rather several other worlds—but he is not the only children's writer who is generating new metamorphoses for our time; and although children's writers are uncommonly prodigal in their gifts at the moment[7] (J. K. Rowling, with the *Harry Potter* series, is not innovatory, but rather belated) many of the most successful fiction writers for adults also operate in this metamorphic and supernatural territory: Salman Rushdie, Margaret Atwood, Toni Morrison. A secular agnostic like Rushdie constantly flourishes fantastic prodigies—meteorological (the earthquake in *The Ground Beneath Her Feet*), and psychological (numerous portents, twins, devils, dolls, puppets, many shamanic flights), as does Toni Morrison, through the poltergeist in *Beloved* (1997) for example, and the returning dead in *Paradise* (1998); Margaret Atwood explicitly evokes a revenant, who works through spirit possession as the avenging motive force in *Alias Grace*, her fictional treatment of the first murder committed by a woman in Canada. In all three cases, the writers are paying homage to the muted voices of past histories, and invoking a nearly obliterated legacy of belief. But they are also engaged, as are the illusionists of the era of phantasmagoria, with making the impossible happen through acts of mimetic language and projection. As Rushdie comments, through his hero the singer Ormus Cama: 'Everything must be made real, step by step . . . This is a mirage, a ghost world, which becomes real only beneath our magic touch, our loving footfall, our kiss. We have to imagine it into being, from the ground up.'[8]

This has become the vision of the novelist's art: it is the world that is the *fata morgana*, the spectral vision which cannot come into being, except through imagination's acts. In Rushdie's next novel *Fury* (2001), the protagonist has actually become a doll-maker. This theme has a long tradition. The difference now is that the Christian supernatural, with its terror of pagan concepts of metamorphosis, no longer obtains in quite the same way as it did for the readers of James Hogg, for example, or indeed, for Hogg himself. For it must be admitted that the two approaches to the mythic in twentieth-century fiction—political acts of recovered memory, and divine literary omnipotence—do not address the ontological issue, raised by the use of the uncanny now. There's an element of parody, literary jokes and echoes, and, of course, play. But I would suggest that the template lies, again, in models of consciousness, and is nourished by the growing fallout from such concepts as the sub-liminal self, with its connections to spirit voyaging, to revenants, and teleporting souls, to animism and metempsychosis, to a vision of personal survival through dispersed memory, in life and in death, rather than to Freud's unconscious, and its hopes for poten-tial individual integration. In a rather flip way, Toni Morrison catches this thought when she writes, 'God is not a mystery. We are.'

The French writer Marie Darieussecq first produced a Swiftian fable of moral and political degradation in her book *Truismes*, trans-lated into English as *Pig Tales*, about a woman who (jubilantly) turns into a sow. Then, in *La Naissance des phantômes* (*My Phantom Husband*), she moved as it were naturally from this Circean scenario of bestial transmogrification to the language of quantum physics, to create a gripping story of a man who vanishes into thin air (into a black hole) when he goes out to buy some bread for breakfast one morning.[9] Darieussecq's career embraces both poles, the interest in self-disclosure and self-fashioning through animal transform-ation at one end, and, at the other, the impact of impalpable and inscrutable forces on the stability of individuals.

Technologies have historically interacted with magic in the processes of transformation, and some varieties of external shape-shifting have now travelled beyond the scope of spectral media into ever-expanding zones of medical and cosmetic possibility. But with this instrumental realization of physical metamorphosis comes a deeper dread of obliteration and evacuation, of shattered and dis-persed selves. Kafka created his memorably denatured hero at the beginning of the last century; at the beginning of this one, the shape-shifting self is most at risk of vanishing, into virtual worlds, as in Darieussecq's and Ugrešić's novels. The beauty and the energy of metamorphosis, celebrated in Ovid's Pythagorean theory of eternal rebirth, and then, later in Renaissance paganism, as Leonardo revels in in his images of Leda's hatchlings, will never become time regained, not at least for us. The desire to exploit the possibilities of self-transformation may burn bright in the cosmetic and surgical industries, but stories disclose a growing unease with the menace of different selves taking over the real self, beyond bidding or control.

Tales of metamorphoses express the conflicts and uncertainties, and in doing so, they embody the transformational power of story-telling itself, revealing stories as activators of change. They can help us respond to the fundamental question, Why tell stories? The great granary—to borrow Keats's phrase—of Hellenic and Roman narratives has fed us for millennia: there is indeed a fresh surge of hunger for revisionings, attested by many con-temporary writers' inventions and versions—they are continuing Shakespeare's way of plundering and mining and recasting. I am thinking of Christopher Logue's *War Music*, of Seamus Heaney's *The Cure at Troy*, a play which translates Sophocles in order to throw into sharp relief affinities with the Troubles in Northern Ireland; of Ted Hughes and the phenomenal best-selling *Tales from Ovid*, which brought *Metamorphoses* to a huge new readership and Ovid himself fresh fame. The popular success of Ted Hughes's book came about, partly, because his method enhances the cinematic immediacy of Ovid's storytelling, in a language of material presence that partakes of hard-boiled genre writing as well as epic grandeur. For all Hughes's commitment to the eternal horizon of mythic meanings, and his endeavour, alongside his close friend Seamus Heaney, to propel poetic language beyond the earthly into time zones of eternity, his diction and his narrative style belong to today's world.

A single episode from Ovid's poem, the cruel and magnificent scene when Minerva and Arachne contend at their weaving, has spiralled out in long shining threads into the work of writers such as A. S. Byatt, who has claimed Arachne as the pre-eminent figure of women's work.[10] The American poet, Gjertrud Schnackenberg, meditates elegiacally on the story of Oedipus, in *The Throne of Labdacus*, in which she enters the mind of the oracular god Apollo.[11] The Canadian poet and classicist Anne Carson continues her engagement with myth, in her recent verse novel, *Autobiography of Red*, about a gay love affair between Heracles and the ancient (and Dantesque) monster Geryon, who, in her imagining, is an adolescent boy with hidden, red, bat's wings. In these reworkings of ancient material, the physical conditions of ordinary existence simply do not obtain: characters are free to fly, to shape shift, to see far into the beyond, and these breaches in the order of reality enhance the psychological intensity of the depiction of human states of being, they press into new forms ways of telling the self—recasting literature's familiar materials, anguish, passion, lust, pity. This list of writers could be added to, of course; it is the lineage within which I would like to place myself, as someone who writes fiction and thinks about the life of stories.

We continue to demand that stories be *told over and over*, we want them to metamorphose themselves from the recipes of the manuals into drama and poems, into novels and texts, we want them not only for themselves, but for how they seed storytellers' imaginations, how they make other stories, how they change in different poets' or novelists' or playwrights' hands into works—into opera, and indeed operas, into *poesis*. As Jonathan Bate has wonderfully perceived, in his fine book *Shakespeare and Ovid*, Shakespeare's Sonnets revisit the Ovidian shape-shifting universe and re-enact its transformations within the text of the Sonnets and their language. Stories are truly still *made*, made over, made again, shape-shifted. Elias Canetti sharply remarked, about a book he did not like, 'It hasn't any transformations in it.'[12]

One of the things that we want from stories, it seems, is orientation, with regard to the powers that we imagine govern our destinies, call them gods or fate or providence or chaos or relativity. The marvellous geography I travelled in order to write this book took me through variable terrain, where anxiety and pleasure, perplexity and discovery took different shapes, like beckoning figures in a dream. It would be stupid to suggest stories invariably enlighten; but stories do offer a way of imagining alternatives, mapping possibilities, exciting hope, warding off danger by forestalling it, casting spells of order on the unknown ahead. Rape in a story, as told in Arachne's web, tells us rape happens, but also can perform an apotropaic act by speaking of it, by conjuring it in fantasy. These overlapping qualities and effects contribute to the pleasure, the sheer enjoyment that so much of the literature of fantastic metamorphoses can give.

At times during this book, I have felt rather like the Old Man of the Sea in Ovid, as he tries to grasp the ever-changing body of Thetis, the sea nymph; and she twists from him, now in the shape of a bird, a tree, even a spotted pard. Stories of metamorphosis, in poetry, art, and fictions, born at moments of historical and cultural metamorphosis, leaped and shifted with their own vitality and fantasy, but I tried to hold on long enough to communicate to you some of their pleasure and power, the ways they convey ideas about ourselves and enact processes that move and structure imagination.

Notes

Introduction

1 Ovid, *Metamorphoses*, trans. Frank Justus Miller, rev. G. P. Goold (Cambridge: Loeb Edition, 1916, 1977, hereafter abbreviated as *Met*/Loeb); trans. Rolfe Humphries, *Ovid's Metamorphoses* (Bloomington, 1983) (abbr. *Met*/RH); trans. Ted Hughes, *Tales from Ovid* (London, 1997). *Met*/RH, p. 3; my understanding of Ovid has been greatly helped by Jonathan Bate's fine study, *Shakespeare and Ovid* (Oxford, 1993); the collection of essays, *Shakespeare's Ovid: The Metamorphoses in the Plays and Poems*, ed. A. B. Taylor (Cambridge, 2000); Sarah Annes Brown, *The Metamorphosis of Ovid: From Chaucer to Ted Hughes* (London, 1999); Raphael Lyne, *Ovid's Changing Worlds: English Metamorphoses 1567–1632* (Oxford, 2001).

2 Book XV, lines 165–8; *Met*/RH, p. 370.

3 Impossible to be inclusive, but among my most well-thumbed resources: Jean-Pierre Vernant, *Myth and Society in Ancient Greece*, [1974] trans. Janet Lloyd (London, 1980); id., *Entre Mythe et politique* (Paris, 1996); P. M. C. Forbes-Irving, *Metamorphosis in Greek Myths* (Oxford, 1990); *The Metamorphoses of Antoninus Liberalis*, ed. and trans. Francis Celoria (London, 1992); Richard Buxton, *Imaginary Greece: The Contexts of Mythology* (Cambridge, 1994); Margaret Anne Doody, *The True Story of the Novel* (London, 1997).

4 Book XV, lines 158–9; *Met*/RH, p. 370.

5 To take only recent examples, James Lasdun and Michael Hofmann's *After Ovid* (London, 1994), which inspired Ted Hughes to continue his 'translation', published as *Tales from Ovid*. See my conclusion for more examples.

6 Book XV, lines 456–8; *Met*/RH, p. 379.

7 *Metamorphoses*, Book VI, line 369. See Paul Muldoon's version, 'The Lycians', in *After Ovid*, ed. Lasdun and Hofmann, pp. 151–3; this is the story with which I begin my novel, *The Leto Bundle* (London,

2001), though in my story, Leto turns into an ordinary woman, in flight from crisis to crisis, until she appears in the here and now, a refugee with her bundle of babies and few scraps of possessions.

8 Ted Hughes, Introduction, *Tales from Ovid*, pp. ix–x; see also Marina Warner, 'Hoopoe', in Nick Gammage (ed.), *The Epic Poise: A Tribute to Ted Hughes* (London, 1999).

9 *Metamorphoses*, Book XI, lines 221–42; *Met*/Loeb, ii. 137; *Met*/RH does not catch the wordplay on writing itself; cf. Mestra, or Hympermestra, the daughter of Erysichthon, who also possesses the gift of protean disguise (Book VIII).

10 Richard Buxton, in a talk I heard at Oxford, to be published in *Greek Metamorphoses: Myth, Religion and Belief*, spoke very interestingly about the ambiguity of metamorphosis, in Greek literature and in art.

11 Charles Taylor, *Sources of the Self: The Making of Modern Identity* (Cambridge, 1989); Ian Hacking, *Rewriting the Soul: Multiple Personality and the Sciences of Memory* (Princeton, 1995).

12 Peter Hulme, *Colonial Encounters: Europe and the Native Caribbean 1492–1797* [1986] (London, 1992), 93. Hulme is drawing on James Smith, *Shakespearian and Other Essays* (Cambridge, 1974), 159–261, and Charles Frey, 'The Tempest and the New World', *Shakespeare Quarterly*, 30 (1979), 33.

13 Peter Lamborn Wilson, *Pirate Utopias: Moorish Corsairs and European Renegadoes* (New York, 1995) 177.

14 For example, Stephen Greenblatt, 'cracking apart of contextual understanding in an elusive and ambiguous experience of wonder', quoted Lyne, *Ovid's Changing Worlds*, 255–6.

15 Paul Gilroy, *The Black Atlantic: Modernity and Double Consciousness* (London, 1993).

16 William Pietz, 'The Problem of the Fetish, I', *Res*, 9 (Spring 1985), 5–17, 5; id., 'The Problem of the Fetish, II', *Res*, 13 (Spring 1987), 23–45, 24.

17 Ashis Nandy, *The Intimate Enemy: Loss and Recovery of Self under Colonialism* (Delhi, [1983], 1992), 2.

18 See for example, Peter Hulme and William H. Sherman (eds.), '*The Tempest' and its Travels* (London, 2000), esp. Part III, 'Transatlantic Routes', pp. 171–263, for recent, helpful approaches to, and bibliography of, the literary history.

19 Toni Morrison, *Playing in the Dark: Whiteness and the Literary Imagination* (Cambridge, 1992).

20 *The Greek Alexander Romance*, trans. Richard Stoneman (London, 1991); see also Peter Dronke, 'Introduzione', *Alessandro nel Medioevo Occidentale*, ed. Mariantonia Liborio, Piero Boitani, et al. (Verona, 1997), pp. xv–lxxv; Paul Muldoon, *To Ireland, I* (Oxford, 2000), 136.

21 Roger Caillois, *La Pieuvre: essai sur l'imaginaire* (Paris, 1973), 230.

22 Debbie Lee, 'Certain Monsters of Africa: Poetic Voodoo in Keats' "Lamia"', *Times Literary Supplement*, 27 Oct. 1995; see also Debbie Lee, 'Poetic Voodoo: Keats in the Possession of African Magic', in Robert Ryan and Ronald A. Sharp (eds.), *The Persistence of Poetry: Bicentennial Essays on John Keats* (Amherst, 1998), 132–52.

23 *Le Cabinet des fées*, ed. Charles Joseph Mayer, 41 vols. (Paris, 1785–9). See Marina Warner, *From the Beast to the Blonde: On Fairytales and their Tellers* (London, 1994) for a fuller discussion of this tradition.

24 Jan Potocki, *The Manuscript Found in Saragossa* [?1797–1815], trans. Ian Maclean (London, 1995).

Chapter 1 *Mutating*

1 Ramón Pané, 'Scrittura di Fra Roman delle Antichità degl'Indiani . . .', in *Le historie della vita e dei fatti di Cristoforo Colombo per D. Fernando Colombo suo figlio*, ed. Rinaldo Caddeo (Milan, 1930), 2 vols, ii. 34–54; Fray Ramón Pané, *An Account of the Antiquities of the Indians*, ed. José Juan Arrom, trans. Susan C. Griswold (Durham, 1999). Neil L. Whitehead has written critically of this last edition and translation, questioning Arrom's conflation of various sources (for example Peter Martyr) and the concept of a discrete Taino culture, in 'Fray Ramón Pané's *An Account of the Antiquities of the Indians*', 1999, unpublished, kindly lent by Peter Hulme.

2 See Tzvetan Todorov, *La Conquête de l'Amérique: la question de l'autre* (Paris, 1982); Kirkpatrick Sale, *The Conquest of Paradise: Christopher Columbus and the Columbian Legacy* (New York, 1991), 215.

3 The anthropologist José R. Oliver, in a remarkable, structuralist analysis of Taino myths, has persuasively linked the journey of

Guahayona to the relative values of precious metals in Taino culture, and, above all, to the ranking of the alloy *guanín* over gold in their system and thence to the ceremonial ornaments of the Jamaican *caciques*, or chiefs. See José R. Oliver, 'Gold Symbolism among Caribbean Chiefdoms: Of Feathers, *Çibas*, and *Guanín* Power among Taíno Elites', in Colin McEwan (ed.), *PreColumbian Gold: Technology, Style and Iconography* (London, 2000), 196–219.

4   Pané's name is given in the Italian form Fra Roman Pané in the first extant published version; thereafter he appears as Pan or even Ponç. See German Arciniegas, 'Our First Anthropologist', in *Americas* (Washington), 23/11 and 12 (1951), 2–10.

5   Las Casas, quoted by Arrom, *Account*, 56.

6   See *Americas Lost 1492–1713: The First Encounter*, ed. Daniel Levine (Glasgow, 1992), esp. *The First Encounter with the Americas*, 28–53. Peter Hulme, in his book (forthcoming) explores the surviving descendants, all over the Caribbean, of Taino and Carib. He writes (private communication; 26 August 2001) 'The whole question of indigenous survival . . . isn't really grammatical but semantic— what do terms like survival and vanishing mean any longer? There are Garifuna communities all over the Americas, amounting to tens of thousands of people, and all descending in some fashion from Caribs; and there are lots of Taíno-identifying people.'

7   'Io mi son faticato per intendere che cosa credono e se san dove vadano dopo morti . . .' *Le historie*, i. 33.

8   Pané, *Account*, ed. Arrom, p. 41.

9   By Alfonso Ulloa.

10 See Arrom's edn. of Pané, *Account*, for a bibliography of the tangled history of publication, pp. 68–70.

11 Peter Martyr de Angleria, *De Orbe Novo* (*Of the New World . . .*) (1504); trans. Richard Eden (and Richard Willes), in *The History of Travayle in the West and East Indies . . .* (London, 1577); Arrom, edn. of *Account*, 46–53, calls him Pietro Martire d'Anghiera, and reprints part of his letter to cardinal Ludovico of Aragon, in which he abridged Pané's report, which became the ninth chapter of the first *Decade, History of Travayle*, 47–54. See also Olmedilla de Pereiras, Maria de Las Nieves, *Pedro Martir de Angleria y la Mentalidad Exoticisca* (Madrid, 1974), 53 ff., 221.

12 Peter [the] Martyr (1205–52) belonged to the missionary order the Dominicans; he was born into a Cathar family but became a zealot in his pursuit of heresy—the Inquisition, in which he took an active part in Lombardy, was founded by the Dominicans. His moral and religious activities won him many enemies, and he was murdered: he is traditionally depicted with an axe through his skull, as in the Prado altarpiece, and, canonized the year after his death, is revered as the Dominicans' first martyr. In many ways, he makes a highly appropriate forerunner for his namesake Peter Martyr de Angleria.

13 Sale, *Conquest of Paradise*, 222.

14 Shakespeare in *The Tempest* uses both first names of this chronicler for characters.

15 See Arrom, edn. of *Account*, 54–67.

16 Bartholomé de Las Casas, *Apologética Historia de Las Indias* (Madrid, 1909), ch. 19, pp. 321–2, trans. Helena Ivins; see Arrom, edn. of *Account*, 54–67.

17 Arrom, edn. of *Account*, 66.

18 For example, Prospero's phrases about his spirit spectacles echo a passage in Richard Eden's translation of the Spanish account of the customs of the islanders of Hispaniola: the king's followers kill themselves at its death, he reports, in order to accompany him in the afterlife. 'All that refuse so to doe, when after they dye by theyr naturall death or otherwyse, theyr soules to dye with theyr bodyes, *and to bee dissolved into ayre, and become nothyng,* as doe the soules of Hogges, Byrdes, Fyshes, or other brute beastes: and that only the other may enjoy the priviledge of immortalitie for ever, to serve the kyng in heaven.' Later, Eden passes on from describing the idols worshipped by the Indians, to the phenomenon of hurricanes, and the local devils' special role in raising these terrible tempests. Eden, *Mistory of Travayle*, 194^v–195.

19 Joseph Leo Koerner, 'Hieronymus Bosch's World Picture', in Caroline A. Jones and Peter Galison (eds.), *Picturing Science, Producing Art* (New York, 1998), 297–323; see also id., 'Bosch's Contingency', in *Kontingenz*, ed. Gerhart v. Graevenitz et al., *Poetik und Hermeneutik*, XVII (Munich, 1998), 245–84; Paul Vandenbroeck writes that the painting should be called 'The Grail or The False Paradise', see Paul Vandenbroeck, 'Hieronymus Bosch: The Wisdom of the Riddle', in

Jos Koldeweij, Paul Vandenbroeck, Bernard Vermet et al., *Hieronymus Bosch: The Complete Paintings and Drawings* (Amsterdam, 2001) (Catalogue of exhibition at the Boysmans-van-Beunigen Museum, Rotterdam), 100 ff.; the dating has been complicated by dendrological analyses carried out on six planks in the panels on which it is painted, which give a date for the wood of 1460/66, earlier than expected. However while this of course gives a *terminus ante quem*, other considerations point to a later execution of the painting. See Bernard Vermet, 'Hieronymus Bosch: Painter, Workshop or Style?', ibid., pp. 84–98, where Vermet reviews the evidence, and concludes that 'it remains difficult to accept that the Garden of Earthly Delights could be an early work', ibid. 98.

20 *Inferno* XXV, in *The Divine Comedy of Dante Alighieri*, ed. John D. Sinclair (London, 1958), lines 143–4.

21 Ibid., line 77.

22 Ibid., lines 68–9.

23 Ibid., lines 97–102. My translation. John Sinclair gives: 'Let Ovid be silent about Cadmus and Arethusa; for if in his lines he turns him into a serpent and her into a fountain, I do not grudge it to him, for two natures face to face he never transmuted that both kinds were ready to exchange their substance.'

24 See Kenneth Gross, 'Infernal Metamorphoses: An Interpretation of Dante's "Counterpass"', in *Modern Language Notes* 100/1 (1985), 42–69; Caroline Walker Bynum, *Metamorphosis and Identity* (New York, 2001), 182–5.

25 Stuart Clark has most compellingly reviewed this argument in his book, *Thinking with Demons: The Idea of Witchcraft in Early Modern Europe* (Oxford, 1997), see esp. pp. 31–93.

26 Bynum, *Metamorphosis and Identity*, 185.

27 See Hein. Th. Schulze-Altcappenberg, *Sandro Botticelli: The Drawings for Dante's Divine Comedy* (Royal Academy, London, 2000).

28 The dating of the drawings to *The Divine Comedy* is confused, but the favoured time scheme, proposed by Schulze-Altcappenberg in the catalogue to *Botticelli: The Drawings*, suggests a long process of creation, from a start in 1480 to the artist's death in 1510, with the major work done around 1494–5, that is several years after the great *poesie*

painted for the same patron, Lorenzo di Pierfrancesco de' Medici, a younger cousin and rival of Lorenzo the Magnificent.

29 See for example the stupefying *Ovide moralisé: poème du commencement du quatorzième siècle*, ed. C. De Boer (Amsterdam, 1915).

30 IC.41148; also another copy, not coloured, published by Antoine Verard in Paris, 1507.

31 E. De Jongh, 'A Heathen Poet Christianized and Moralized', in *Questions of Meaning, Theme and Motif in Dutch Seventeenth-Century Painting*, trans. and ed. Michael Hoyle (Leiden, 1995), 232.

32 The London Library has this edition: Ovid, *Metamorphosis Englished, Mythologiz'd and represented in figures* (London, 1640). See also Ovid, *Metamorphoses*, commentary by Raphael Regius (Lyon, 1510), 2 vols. (BL 654.c.17).

33 *Purgatorio*, XII, lines 43–5.

34 '. . . tous avaricieux, baillifs, prevosts, usuriers, robeurs et tous marchands dedans a temp lesquelz tous sont prejudiciables au pauvre peuple.' *La Bible des poètes* (Paris, 1493), fo. clxvii.

35 '. . . lequel oyseau de sa propre nature a le bec dur et longue langue Tellement quil la boute entre fourmiz et quant il les sent dessus il les engloutit en retirant icelle . . . Disons donc que cette Circe plaine de venin signifie le dyable ou le pechie de luxure.' *La Bible des poètes*, fo. xiv.

36 Francesco Bardi (pseud. Giovanni Palazzi), *Metamorfosi di P. Ovidio N . . . Brevemente spiegate* (Venice, 1676), 35.

37 'Laquelle chose et opinion ia soit ce quell soit erronee et non creable touteffois si fut celle opinion merveillable estre di ete de ung payen Car desia il sentoit lame estre immortelle comme elle est mais non pas muable en la maniere quil oppinoit. Ses dis sont fort especiaux et plains de grant mistere pour quoy ie ny entens riens moraliser fors seulement que par les exemples y mises il appert clerement que toutes choses en cestuy monde sont et gisent dessoubs vanite et quil ny a riens de estable.' *La Bible des poètes*, fo. clxxix verso.

38 Dirk Bax, *Hieronymus Bosch: His Picture Writing Deciphered* [1949] (Rotterdam, 1979); Wilhelm Fraenger, *Le Royaume millénaire de Jerome Bosch*, trans. Roger Lewinter (Paris, 1966); Laurinda Dixon, *Alchemical Imagery in Bosch's Garden of Delights* (Ann Arbor, 1981).

See Paul Vandenbroeck's helpful survey article on Bosch in *The Macmillan Dictionary of Art*, iv. 445–55; Koldeweij et al., *Bosch*. Cf. Michel de Certeau, *The Mystic Fable*, vol. i: *The Sixteenth and Seventeenth Centuries*, trans. Michael B. Smith (Chicago, 1995), 49–72, 51: 'The painting organizes, aesthetically a loss of meaning'; 'The Garden cannot be reduced to univocity. It . . . offers a multiplicity of possible itineraries, the traces of which, as in a labyrinth, would constitute so many stories, until one comes to a dead end that marks a forbidden meaning. But there is something more here. The painting seems both to *provoke and frustrate* each one of these interpretative pathways. It not only establishes itself within a *difference* in relation to all meaning; it produces its difference in *making us believe that it contains hidden meaning.*' Ibid. 50.

39 See Nicola Bown, *Fairies in Nineteenth-Century Art and Literature* (Cambridge, 2001), 118–19, 155 ff. for insights into the miniaturization in the Victorian fairy paintings of Anster FitzGerald and Richard Dadd, who were influenced by Bosch.

40 De Certeau, *Mystic Fable*, 50.

41 Katrina Porteous, 'Charlie Douglas', a poem in Scots, includes the phrase 'berried hens' for female lobsters carrying eggs. Quoted in Andrew Motion (ed.), *Here to Eternity: An Anthology of Poetry* (London, 2001), 147–9, at 148.

42 Koerner, 'Hieronymus Bosch's World Picture', 297–323; see also id., 'Bosch's Contingency', 245–84.

43 See *Botticelli: The Drawings*, 326–34.

44 See also the devils at the Gates of Dis, *Inferno*, VIII and IX, pp. 54–9, and *Inferno*, XVI, pp. 78–9.

45 A reduced copy of the painting, made in the 1550s, now in the Wellcome Institute, London, interestingly renders the nudes more sensually, with stronger, Italianate, moulding and highlighting of the flesh.

46 '. . . full scale alchemical conjunction, and the ensuing multiplication of the prima materia. Allegorically this stage of the operation was known as "child's play", when the elements joyfully coupled in imitation of the first parents . . . Bosch's scene shows the process of transmutation as first a "mixture of various things" which gradually "change and go out from one nature and take on

another nature . . ." ' Laurinda Dixon, quoting from Abu'L-Qasim Muhammad's twelfth-century treatise, *The Book of Knowledge*, in *Alchemical Imagery*, 25.

47 Ernst Gombrich, 'The Earliest Description of the Triptych', and ' "As it was in the Days of Noe" ' in *The Heritage of Apelles: Studies in the Art of the Renaissance* (London, 1976), 79–90; see also Vandenbroeck, 'Riddle', in Koldeweij et al., *Bosch*, pp. 107–8; Certeau, *Mystic Fable*, 68–9.

48 Peter Dronke, 'Earthly Paradises', in *Imagination in the Late Pagan and Early Christian World*, ch. 4 (Florence, 2003), kindly lent by the author.

49 Hesiod, *Works and Days*, lines 105–7 in *Hesiod and Theognis*, trans. Dorothea Wender (Harmondsworth, 1982), 62.

50 Ovid, *Metamorphoses*, Book XV, lines 96–103, *Met/RH*, 368.

51 Ovid, *Metamorphoses*, Book XV, lines 158–9; *Met/RH*, p. 370.

52 Lyne, *Ovid's Changing Worlds*, 202–3.

53 Ovid, *Metamorphoses*, Book I, lines 89–115, trans. Hughes, pp. 9–10; emphases added.

54 Cf.: 'that golden worlde wherein men lived simplye and innocently without enforcement of lawes, without bookes, without quarrelling, iudges, and libelles, content only to satisfie nature' in Eden, *History of Travayle*, 15.

55 Michel de Certeau confidently identifies the thistle-like blossom on the left, the one dusting the surface of the transparent globe in which the pair of lovers are sitting, as the flower of the pineapple. The pineapple was a native plant of the Americas, and so, if this were the case, this would constitute a deliberate reference within the painting to that particular Other World. Certeau, *Mystic Fable*, 61.

56 Arrom, edn. of *Account*, 52.

57 Las Casas, *Historia apologética*, 64.

58 Andrew Marvell, 'Bermudas'.

59 Eden, *History of Travayle*, 24, see Robert Ralston Cawley, 'Shakspere's Use of the Voyagers in *The Tempest*', *PMLA* 41 (1926), 688–726, 704.

60 Richard Eden, *History of Travayle*, p. 194.

61 Pané, *Historie*, ii. 37; my translation. Arrom translates 'natura' as sex, meaning the genitals. I think that the repetition might imply an early distinction between sex and gender, with *natura* as sex in a wider sense than the different organs. The ungrammatical shift from

singular to plural is characteristic of the sloppiness, either of Pané or the translator Alfonso Ulloa.

62 Ibid. 37–8 (my translation).

63 Quoted Lyne, *Ovid's Changing Worlds*, 231.

64 Sandys, *Metamorphosis Englished*, folio edn. (London, 1640), 266. (There is an earlier, quarto vol., 1626, in the Wellcome too, but without commentary.)

65 Lyne, *Ovid's Changing Worlds*, 249 ff., 254–5.

66 Pané, *Historie*, 40.

67 Ibid. 40–1.

68 Arrom, edn. of *Account*, 18.

69 *The Garden of Earthly Delights* might have been commissioned by Count Hendrick III of Nassau, whose wife was Spanish: Mencia de Mendoza, Marquesa de Cenete, assembled a collection of Bosch paintings in his lifetime. See Vandenbroeck, 'Riddle', in Koldeweij, et al., *Bosch*, 110, also id. in *Macmillan Dictionary* article, Vol. IV, pp. 446, 452. Cardinal Ludovico of Aragon might provide another link between Spain and the Netherlands; it is his secretary, Antonio de Beatis, who provides the earliest description of the painting. See *The Travel Diary of Antonio de Beatis 1517–1518*, trans J. R. Hale and J. M. A. Lindon, ed. J. R. Hale (London, 1979), 94; André Chastel, *Louis d'Aragon: Un Voyageur princier de la Renaissance* (Paris, 1986), 55–6.

70 Sigüenza does not discuss Pané, though he does mention the later evangelizing visit of Hieronymites to Hispaniola in 1519. *Historia del Orden de San Geronimo*, vol. iii (Madrid, 1605), Book I, ch. 25, p. 125.

71 The *madroño* (arbutus, strawberry tree) coincidentally features on the coat of arms of the city of Madrid, along with a bear; the story goes that the bear used the prickly fruit to relieve itchy eyes (!). I am very grateful to Eric Southworth, of St Peter's College, Oxford, for bringing this association to my attention. This symbolism dates from medieval times, and Pliny, whom Las Casas, for one, often quotes, explicitly tries to clear up muddles in this respect. He suggests the arbutus' affinities with paradise, for the tree bears flowers and fruits at the same time: 'The flesh of the ground strawberry (*terrestribus fragis*) is different from that of the strawberry-tree which is related to it, the strawberry being the only fruit that grows at the same time on a bush and on the ground. . . . the fruit takes a

year to mature, and the following crop flowers side by side with the earlier crop when it is ripening . . . The Greeks describe it by the two names . . . which shows there are two varieties . . . with ourselves it has another name, the arbutus.' The arbutus fruit is edible, but tasteless. However, the entire class of berries, including blackberries, is singled out by Pliny for its fleshiness: 'Reliqua carnosi sunt generis . . .' (The remaining fruits belong to the fleshly class . . .'); this was almost certainly not intended figuratively, but could have been read so. Pliny the Elder, *Historia Naturalis*, Book XV, ch. 28, ed. H. Rackham (Loeb edition), iv. 356–7.

72 Koerner, 'Bosch's World Picture', 300.

73 Sandys, *Metamorphosis Englished*, 521, quoting the Spanish chronicler José de Acosta, translated by Edward Grimston (1604) quoted Lyne, *Ovid's Changing Worlds*, 248.

74 Bernard Picart, *The Ceremonies and Religious Customs of the World*, abridged by Robert Huish (London, 1828), 787.

75 The Dragon Palm (*Dracaena draco*) is so called because when cut, it drips blood; dried as powders, the blood has restorative powers, especially on men's potency. Does its presence in Eden point to the sinful pursuit of pleasure? Bosch probably drew on *The Nuremberg Chronicle*, itself dependent on Charles de L'Ecluse's botanical work, *Rarorum . . . per Hispanias* (Antwerp, 1576), according to Laurinda Dixon, *Alchemical Imagery*, 19.

76 Hesiod, *Works and Days*, lines 105–26 in *Hesiod and Theognis*, ed. Wender, p. 62.

77 Bosch's triptychs characteristically feature a visionary in the central panel, whose experiences are represented by the painter— St Anthony, for example. James Walmsley, of All Souls College, Oxford, proposed, after hearing my lecture in October 2001, that the signifying figure in the corner, pointing at the woman half buried in the ground, is indicating that the scene is anchored in her consciousness, that she, the 'Eve' or 'Pandora' figure, is imagining it or being assailed by its temptations. In this case, the pleasures represented in the *Garden* would communicate her erroneous idea that such pursuits could be without sin. The garden would then become a false dream, not a lost paradise. This interpretation would line up with sixteenth-century fears of the devil's ability

to pervert understanding, to conjure illusion; the Indians' ideas would then fall to his sphere of influence. The whole teeming scene would become a phantasmagoria. The virtue of this line of argument lies in its relationship to Bosch's interest in demonology and witchcraft.

78 Some 15th- and 16th-century millenarianists held that the reign of lust would return again, at the end of the world: some commentators claim that 'Bosch supported this view "historically".' Vandenbroeck, *Dictionary* article, iv, p. 449.

79 Jonathan Bate, *The Song of the Earth* (Oxford, 2000), 25–6; quoted Laurence Coupe, 'Bate & Leavis: An Ecocritical connection?', *Green Letters*, 2 (Autumn 2000), 14–15.

80 Ibid.

Chapter 2 *Hatching*

1 Pliny, *Natural History*, ed. W. S. Jones (Cambridge, Mass., 1963), Book XXVIII, ch. 5, p. 282, echoed by Reginald Scot, *The Discoverie of Witchcraft* (1584), see Iona Opie and Moira Tatem (eds.), *A Dictionary of Superstitions* (Oxford, 1989), 135–6.

2 See Marina Warner, *No Go the Bogeyman: Scaring, Lulling and Making Mock* (London, 1998), 44–5, 182–3, Pls. 9–10.

3 In the National Gallery of Prague, an unusual painting of Saint Christopher, from the circle of the Master of Frankfurt, shows a sable-skinned homunculus hatching upside down from an eggshell at the giant's feet, possibly an allusion to the giant saint's life as a savage heathen before his conversion. A drawing in the Louvre, Paris, attributed to a follower of Van Eyck, resembles this painting, and so postulates an older model. See *Chefs-d'œuvres de Prague 1450–1750: Trois siècles de peinture flamande et hollandaise* (Bruges, 1974), 24–5; an enigmatic *Allegory* by Giovanni Bellini, in the Accademia, Venice, possibly symbolizes envy, and shows a serpentine figure writhing upside down as he emerges out of a conch shell.

4 'He [Homer] does not trace Diomedes' return right back to the death of Meleager, or the Trojan War to the twin eggs of Leda. All the time he is hurrying on to the crisis, and he plunges his hearer

into the middle of the story . . .' Horace, *Ars Poetica (On the Art of Poetry)*, 148 ff., in *Classical Literary Criticism*, trans. T. S. Dorsch (London, 1965), 84.

5 Pliny, *Natural History*, Book X, para. 145, pp. 77–8 'Umbilicus ovis a cacumine inest, ceu gutta eminens in putamine.' (Du côté de la pointe de l'œuf renferme le germe, espèce de goutte qui surnage à l'intérieur de la coquille.' For French edition, see n. 26 below.)

6 Moscus, *Turba Philosophorum* (12th century). As the model for obtaining the longed-for philosopher's stone, alchemists preferred to invoke the egg and its development rather than the gestatory cycle of human reproduction: 'the interior fire of matter, excited by the outer fire, just as the interior fire of the egg, excited by the heat of the hen, becomes reanimated little by little and gives life to the matter of which it is the soul, from which the philosophical child is born . . .' Antoine-Joseph Pernety, *Dictionnaire mytho-hermétique* [1787] (Paris, 1972), 258.

7 Pernety, *Dictionnaire*, 258.

8 *L'Alchimie et son livre muet [Mutus Liber]* [La Rochelle, 1677], ed. Eugène Canseliet (Paris, 1967), Figs. 8, 19, 11, 13; pp. 99–111.

9 Sir Hans Sloane, *A Voyage to the Islands* (London, 1707–25), vol. i, 1, pp. 54–6, vol. i, 2, Plate 21.

10 Sloane, ibid., i, 1, pp. 54–6; i, 2, Plate 21.

11 In 1786, an advertisement for the the museum of Sir Ashton Lever announced that it contained 'a Specimen of The ELASTIC or FLEXIBLE STONE. From the Brazils'. In J. H. C. King, 'New Evidence for the Contents of the Leverian Museum', *Journal of the History of Collections*, 8/2 (1996), 167–86, 172. Of course these collectors might be describing coral, and mistaken not in its organic origins, but in its stony character.

12 Lucius Apuleius, *The Golden Ass*, trans. Robert Graves [1950] (Harmondsworth, 1988); id., *The Golden Ass*, trans. R. G. Walsh (Oxford, 1994); see also Margaret Anne Doody, *The True Story of the Novel*, 113–24.

13 Franz Kafka, *The Metamorphosis* [1915], trans. Stanley Corngold (New York, 1972); Vladimir Nabokov, *Nabokov's Butterflies*, ed. Brian Boyd and Robert Michael Pyle (Boston, 2000); 'Christmas', trans. Dimitri Nabokov, in *Collected Stories* (London, 1997), 131–6.

14 See Londa Schiebinger, *Nature's Body: Gender in the Making of Modern Science* (Boston, 1993), 203–5; Natalie Zemon Davis, 'Maria Merian', in *Women on the Margins: Three Seventeenth Century Lives* (Boston, 1995), 140–202, and useful bibliographical notes.

15 Maria Merian, *Dissertatio de Generatione et Metamorphosibus Insectorum Surinamensium* (Paris, 1726), note to Plate XV (my trans.).

16 Aristotle, *De Animalium Generatione*, 735^{a}18–23.

17 On the history of silkworms, see the beautiful last chapter of W. G. Sebald, *The Rings of Saturn*, trans. Michael Hulse (London, 1998).

18 See Marina Warner, *The Leto Bundle* (2001) for speculation that a medieval merchant may have had the idea before.

19 Londa Schiebinger, *The Mind Has No Sex* (Cambridge, Mass., 1989), 69–78.

20 The word metamorphosis is also used in the title of her first books in Dutch, and by Jan Goedaert (1660–9), the entomologist.

21 John Ray, *Methodus Insectorum* (1705) and *Historia Insectorum* (1713).

22 There were thirty volumes in all; see Bernadette Bucher, *Icon and Conquest: A Structural Analysis of the Illustrations to De Bry's Great Voyages*, trans. Basia Miller Gulati (Chicago, 1981).

23 Davis, 'Maria Merian', 152.

24 Vladimir Nabokov, *Speak Memory* [1951], in *Nabokov's Butterflies*, ed. Boyd and Pyle, pp. 83–4.

25 Aristotle, *De Animalium Generatione*, 733^{b}12 f.; see Anton Bitel, 'Quis ille Asinus aureus? The Metamorphoses of Apuleius' Title, and its Entomological Subtext', *Ancient Narrative*, vol. O (*sic*) (2000), preliminary version, for entomological refs.

26 Pliny, *Histoire naturelle*, trans E. de Saint Denis (Paris, 1961), Book X, ch. 68, pp. 93–4; cf. Aristotle, *De Animalium Generatione*, 539^a.

27 John White, the English artist who accompanied Walter Raleigh to Virginia in 1585, made a lovely watercolour study of a swallowtail butterfly, but all on its own. See Paul Hulton, *America 1585: The Complete Drawings of John White* (London, 1984), Plate 58, p. 183.

28 e.g. Jan Swammerdam, *The Book of Nature*, trans. Thomas Floyd (London, 1758).

29 A hundred years earlier, George Hoefnagel, and his son Joris Hoefnagel, had conjured the vanity of life through mementoes of mortality such as a dead chick in its shell, butterflies, and moths,

and attached pious mottoes such as: 'Let us not too curiously examine divine works with human reason, but having been led along let us admire their artificer.' Joris Hoefnagel, *Archetypa Studiaque Patris Georgii Hoefnageli, Jacopus F . . . ab ipso Sculpta* (Frankfurt, 1592); see Thomas Da Costa Kaufmann, *The Mastery of Nature* (Princeton, 1993), 187.

30 This was Constantijn Huygens (1596–1687), civil servant and early supporter of Rembrandt; see Rudolf Dekker, *Childhood, Memory and Autobiography in Holland: From the Golden Age to Romanticism* (London, 2000), 23–30.

31 Apuleius, *The Golden Ass*, trans. Graves, pp. 42–3.

32 See Marzio Dall'Acqua, Gianni Guadalupi, Franco Maria Ricci, *Fontanellato* (Milan, 1994) for beautiful photographs of the paintings, and some wild theories as to its meaning. The case for its relation to *The Golden Ass* will be made fully when I have researched the interesting circle of writers and poets around the Sanvitale family in Fontanellato in my forthcoming study of magic.

33 *The Golden Ass*, 234.

34 Ibid. 241.

35 See Bitel, 'Quis ille Asinus aureus?'.

36 I used the separate edition: Apuleius, *Cupid & Psyche*, ed. E. J. Kenney (Cambridge, 1990). I have written elsewhere about this tale, so my account here is very compressed. See Marina Warner, *From the Beast to the Blonde*, 143–5, 223–4, 273–8, *et passim*.

37 e.g. Martianus Capella, *De Nuptiis Philogiae et Mercurii*; see D. C. Allen, *Image and Meaning: Metaphoric Tradition in Renaissance Poetry* (Baltimore, 1960), 28 ff.; see also Harold Bloom, 'Muiopotmos, or The Fate of the Butterflie', in *Shelley's Mythmaking* (New Haven, 1959).

38 Aristotle, *Historia Animalium*, 551^a14.

39 See Ulisse Aldovrandi, *De Animalibus Insectis* (Bologna, 1602), 255; *Nabokov's Butterflies*, 472.

40 Plato, *Phaedrus*, 249A.

41 In the Pergamon Museum, East Berlin, 1684. Malcolm Davies and J. Kathirithamby, *Greek Insects* (London, 1986), 106–7.

42 Thorvaldsen Museum (1929), no. 504 from A. B. Cook, *Zeus: A Study in Ancient Religion*, 3 vols. (Cambridge, 1914–40), 2 (1), p. 645, Fig. 563.

43 Anthony Preus, 'Science and Philosophy in Aristotle's "Generation of Animals"', *Journal of the History of Biology*, 3/1 (Spring 1979), 23–6.

44 Davies and Kathirithamby, *Greek Insects*, 106–7 for further references.

45 See one of Maria Merian's mentors: Jan Goedaert, *Metamorphosis Naturalis* (1660–9) iii, Plate C. It is interesting, in this respect, that 'larva', meaning in Latin a fright, a spectre, a hobgoblin, or mask, was attached by Linnaeus to the grub stage, thus extending the mask metaphor: *OED* cites John Ray (1692), again, for the first use in English.

46 Francesco Colonna, *Hypnerotomachia Poliphili: The Strife of Love in a Dream* [Venice, 1499], trans. Joscelyn Godwin (London, 1999); see also Peter Dronke, Introduction to facsimile of Francesco Colonna, *Hypnerotomachia Poliphili* (Zaragoza, 1981) (*Colección Mnemosine* 1), 7–75, repr. in id., *Sources of Inspiration: Studies in Literary Transformations, 400–1500* (Rome, 1997) (*Storia e letteratura; Studi e Testi* 196), 161–240. In 'Leda and the Swan: The Unbearable Matter of Bliss', in *Poetry and Philosophy in the Middle Ages: A Festschrift for Peter Dronke*, ed. John Marenbon (Leiden, 2000), I published some earlier thoughts on this theme.

47 Colonna, *Hypnerotomachia Poliphili*, trans. Godwin, pp. 182–3.

48 Aldus was liberally supported by Greek fugitives from the Fall of Constantinople in 1454, and his finest vernacular production reflects the hellenism of Byzantine humanist scholarship. I am grateful to Enrico Palandri for this observation—indicating another example of enriching points of convergence.

49 Colonna, *Hypnerotomachia Poliphili*, trans. Godwin, p. 164.

50 Ibid. 'Uni gratum mare alterum gratum mari': I wonder if it is possible that the engraver omitted letters, and that the message should read 'Uni gratum *a*mare alterum gratum *a*mari'? This does not entirely fit the destinies of Helen and Clytemnestra, but could possibly refer to the selfless refusal of Pollux to enjoy immortality if Castor was denied it. The flame rising from the egg would not then point forward to burning Troy, but rather evoke the pointed flames of a torch of victory, or a heart on fire.

51 Ibid. 166; Leda is identified as 'Theseus' daughter', which is perhaps a misprint of the typesetter, or simply a mistake on the part of the

author, for *Thestios'* daughter. See Apollodorus, *The Library of Greek Mythology*, trans. Robin Hard (Oxford, 1997), 120–1.

52 Ovid, *Metamorphoses*, Book VI, line 109.

53 Colonna, *Hypnerotomachia Poliphili*, trans. Godwin, p. 184.

54 Edgar Wind, *Pagan Mysteries in the Renaissance* [1958] (Harmondsworth, 1967), 168.

55 Leda's myth in the ancient sources only appears in fragments, or brief notes by the mythographers. The Vatican Mythographer asserts that Leda laid one egg, from which Castor, Pollux, and Helen were born. Other writers pair the twins by sex, the two girls in one egg, the two boys in another. Several vase paintings show Leda discovering the egg, sometimes with Tyndareus observing from the sidelines, looking sceptical and raising his arms in exclamation. See Lilly Kahil, Noelle Icard-Gianolio, 'Leda' in *Lexicon Iconographicum Mythologiae Classicae* (abbreviation *LIMC*) (Zurich, 1992), vi, 1, 231–46, ii, Plates 1–133.

56 In the version given by Apollodorus in *The Library*, Leda herself is a substitute, and becomes the twins' mother after the goddess Nemesis, pursued and raped by Zeus, changes into a goose to fly from him, but Zeus, taking on the shape of a swan, flies after her and pins her down. Nemesis then drops the egg in the lap of Leda, who sleeps with her husband Tyndareus that same night; she then bears one pair of human children to him, and raises the other divine progeny of Zeus as her own. This twist provides an explanation for the human mortality of two of the siblings (Castor and Clytemnestra) and the immortality of Helen and Pollux.

57 Euripides, *Helen*, in *The Bacchae and Other Plays*, trans. Philip Vellacott [1954] (Harmondsworth, 1972), 135–6.

58 Hyginus can't decide which of the four children are Tyndareus': he makes him Helen's father as well at one point. Hyginus, *Poetica Astronomica*, ed. and trans. Mary Grant (Lawrence, 1960), 73–6, 193–4.

59 Homer, *Odyssey*, trans. E. V. Rieu [1946] (Harmondsworth, 1982), Book XI, lines 177–8.

60 Cf. Marina Warner, *The Leto Bundle*.

61 Maurice Merleau-Ponty, *Le Visible et l'invisible*, ed. Claude Lefort [1964] (Paris, 1979), 189–204, 302–15.

62 Oliver Taplin, *Comic Angels and Other Approaches to Greek Drama through Vase-Painting* (Oxford, 1994), 82–3; reproduced, Plate 19.20; see also Richard Buxton, *Imaginary Greece: The Context of Mythology* (Cambridge, 1994), 35.

63 Formerly attributed to the 'Master J B with the Bird' but now to Giovanni Battista Palumba, fl. 1500–20.

64 Edmund Spenser also describes the loves of Jupiter as depicted on a tapestry, including Leda:

> Then was he [Jove] turned into a snowy Swan,
> To win faire Leda to his lovely trade:
> O wondrous skill! and sweet wit of the man,
> That her in daffadillies sleeping made
> From scorching heat her daintie limbes to shade;
> Whiles the proud Bird, ruffing his fethers wyde
> And brushing his faire brest, did her invade . . .
> *The Faerie Queene*, Book III, Canto XI, lines 28–46.

65 Hesiod, *Theogony*, ed. M. L. West (Oxford, 1966), lines 572 ff., p. 133, 326.

66 See J. Wilde, 'Notes on the Genesis of Michelangelo's *Leda*', in *Fritz Saxl: Memorial Essays*, ed. D. J. Gordon (London, 1957), 270–80; Michael Hirst, *Michelangelo and his Drawings* (New Haven, 1988), 73–4.

67 P. Bober and R. Rubinstein, *Renaissance Artists and Antique Sculpture: A Handbook of Sources* (London, 1986), 52–3, Plates 3–4.

68 The episode lent itself to bawdy, too. The 'Mallard Song', first written down after 1650, is sung at All Souls College, Oxford, twice a year by the Fellows; it offers an alternative identity for the god's disguise:

> The Poets fain'd Jove turn'd a Swan,
> But lett them prove it if they can.
> To mak't appeare it's not attall hard:
> Hee was a swapping, swapping mallard . . .
> Hee was swapping all from bill to eye,
> Hee was swapping all from wing to Thigh;
> His swapping tool of Generation
> oute swapped all ye wingged Nation.

Martin West writes, 'this "indecent verse" was tacitly removed in the 1821 edition of *The Oxford Sausage . . .*'; he helpfully glosses the rare word 'swapping' as having 'acquired the colloquial sense of "whopping great" from 1589 to the nineteenth century'. Martin West, *The All Souls Mallard: Song, Procession, and Legend* (Oxford, 2000), 3–6.

69 It was in Lorenzo's cabinet in Florence after 1471, and then went to Pope Clement VII and thence to the Farnese. Bober and Rubinstein, *Renaissance Artists*, 52–3, Plates 5b–c.

70 Bernard Berenson, *The Drawings of the Florentine Painters*, 3 vols. (Chicago [1938], 1970), 180.

71 Martin Kemp, *Leonardo da Vinci: The Marvellous Works of Nature and Man* (London, 1981), 277.

72 The smiling, inclined Venus, from Correggio's *School of Love*, in the National Gallery, London, recalls the pose of Leonardo's Leda.

73 Kemp, *Leonardo*, 275–7. Leonardo was fascinated, the compositions reveal, with doubling as a form of generation, with likeness and reflection as reproductive, facsimile forces. The twinning of the babies in his Leda images recurs in his cartoon of the Virgin and Saint Anne and the doubling of John the Baptist and Jesus as a child. (In the British Museum.) Walter Pater was not being only fanciful when he alluded to both Leda and Saint Anne in his famous purple passage on the Mona Lisa: 'and as Leda, [she] was the mother of Helen of Troy, and as Saint Anne, the mother of Mary . . .'. Walter Pater, 'Leonardo da Vinci' [1869], in *The Renaissance: Studies in Art and Poetry* (London, 1873).

74 Conrad Lycosthenes, *Liber Prodigiorum* (Basle, 1557), 12–13.

75 Aristotle, *De Animalium Generatione*, $735^a18–23$.

76 Michelangelo's *quadrone da sala* was taken to France, to be offered for purchase to François I by one of the artist's *garzoni*, Antonio Mini. There it somehow got lost. The Leonardo seems to have been also taken to France by the artist in 1516, where it too disappeared at some point after 1625, when Cassiano del Pozzo mentions seeing it. Correggio's *Leda and the Swan* painting suffered many misadventures too: commissioned by Federico Gonzaga in Mantua, it then passed into the collection of Philip II of Spain. In 1603 Rudolph II of Prague acquired it; subsequently, as part of the booty carried off by

the Swedes in 1648, it finally passed into the hands of the Orléans family in Paris. Louis, son of Philippe, Duc d'Orléans, Regent of France during Louis XV's minority (1715–23), was so enraged by the image that he attacked the painting. It is thought that François Boucher may have also had a hand in the restoration too (now in Berlin), but art historians are agreed that a copy in the Prado, made by Eugenio Cajes before the mutilation, gives a much more convincing account of Correggio's original than the restoration. See Alberto Bevilacqua and A. C. Quintavalle, *L'Opera completa di Correggio* (Milan, 1970), 109–10; David Ekserdjian, *Correggio* (London, 1997), 288–91.

77 Colonna, *Hypnerotomachia Poliphili*, trans. Godwin, p. 184.

78 See for example a relief of *Leda and the Swan* from the fifth century, now in the Coptic Museum in Cairo, showing a very large, dynamic bird preceding the figure of Eros, in a *mise-en-scène* that foreshadows the role of both the Holy Ghost and the Angel Gabriel in the Annunciation; Lilly Kahil and Pascale Linant de Bellefonds, *Commentary*, *LIMC* vi, 1, 246.

79 See, for example, *The Coronation of the Virgin* by the Rubielos Master, Cleveland Museum of Art.

80 Yeats was working for Francis Dutton. R. F. Foster, author of *W. B. Yeats: The Apprentice Mage* (Oxford, 1996) and the forthcoming second volume, recalled this most interesting connection in a personal communication, for which I am most grateful.

81 Foster, ibid. i. 556.

82 *The Collected Poems of W. B. Yeats* (London, 1950), 241.

83 Ibid. 281–2; see Edward Larissy, *W. B. Yeats* (Plymouth, 1998), 51; also Elizabeth Butler Cullingford, *Gender and History in Yeats' Love Poetry* (Cambridge, 1993), 140–64 for a highly perceptive historical essay on the political, religious, and social context in which Yeats wrote these aggressive lyrics.

84 Cullingford, 'Swans on the Cesspool: Leda and Rape', in *Gender and History*, 140–64.

85 Ibid. 164.

86 *The Magic Toyshop* was powerfully adapted for the stage by Bryony Lavery, in a touring production by Shared Experience, directed by Rebecca Gatward and very effectively designed by Liz Cooke; I saw it at the Oxford Playhouse in October 2001. The predatory, savage

swan with his bobbing, prehensile neck and broad, strong wings, harked back to the tradition in Italian prints; onstage the costume was cleverly calibrated to begin preposterously and only then, in 'that white rush' become deeply alarming.

87 The subsequent vicissitudes of sexual liberation have however profoundly altered this chemistry, again, and twenty years later, the critic Maud Ellmann, in a complex probing of Yeats's rape scenarios, criticizes the poet's procedures though she arrives at a Carteresque conclusion (she does not mention *The Magic Toyshop*): 'Because the sexes flicker, tremble, deliquesce, it takes a sacred crime, a counter-natural event, to institute them . . .'. Maud Ellmann, 'Daughters of the Swan', *m/f: a feminist journal* (1986), 49–62, 60.

88 Kafka, *Metamorphosis*, in *The Complete Short Stories*, ed. Nahum N. Glatzer (London, 1999), 89.

89 Hermann Pongs, quoted Stanley Corngold (ed.), *The Metamorphosis by Franz Kafka* (New York, 1981), 98.

90 Nabokov, *Lectures on Masterpieces of Modern Fiction* (Ithaca, NY, 1951) in *Nabokov's Butterflies*, 473–5.

91 *Nabokov's Butterflies*, 449.

92 Nabokov, *The Annotated Lolita*, ed. Alfred Appel, Jr. (New York, 1991) 9.

93 Ibid. pp. 332–3.

94 Dr John Ray (1627–1705), *Methodus Insectorum* (1705) and *Historia Insectorum* (1713) 'based on the concept of metamorphosis', according to Appel, *The Annotated Lolita*, 326 and esp. 338–9.

95 Cornell Lectures, 1951, in *Nabokov's Butterflies*, 472–3.

96 Nabokov, 'Christmas', trans. Dimitri Nabokov, in *Collected Stories*, 131–6. I am most grateful to Michael Wood for pointing me to this wonderful story.

Chapter 3 *Splitting*

1 Robert Southey, *History of Brazil*, 3 vols. (London, 1810, 1817, 1819), vol. iii, ch. 31, pp. 25–6.

2 Ibid. 28.

3 Southey calls Da Rocha Pitta 'a meagre and inaccurate work' while discussing his sources. Ibid., Preface, no pp.

4   See, for example, Tim Fulford, *Landscape, Liberty and Authority: Poetry, Criticism and Politics from Thomson to Wordsworth* (Cambridge, 1996) and Nicholas Roe, *John Keats and the Culture of Dissent* (Oxford, 1996).

5   Quoted in Nigel J. T. Thomas, 'Zombie Killer'—website: www.calstatela.edu/faculty/nthomas/zombi-k.htm

6   Simon Blackburn, *Think: A Compelling Introduction to Philosophy* (Oxford, 1999), 52–4.

7   See Kenneth Gross, *The Dream of the Moving Statue* (Ithaca, 1992), 200–4 on Wittgenstein's question, 'Could one imagine a stone's having consciousness?'

8   Dante, *Inferno*, ed. Sinclair, Canto XXXIII, lines 109–50.

9   See Beongcheon Yu, *An Ape of Gods: The Art and Thought of Lafcadio Hearn* (Detroit, 1964).

10 See R. F. Foster, Foreword, in Paul Murray, *A Fantastic Journey: The Life and Literature of Lafcadio Hearn* (Folkestone, 1993), pp. vi–ix.

11 For example, *Creole Sketches* (Boston, 1924), written in New Orleans 1878–81.

12 Lafcadio Hearn, *Gombo Zhèbes: Little Dictionary of Creole Proverbs Selected from Six Creole Dialects* (New York, 1885).

13 Lafcadio Hearn, *Trois fois bel conte . . .* trans. Serge Denis (into modern French), *avec le texte original en Créole Antillais* [Paris, 1932] (Vaduz, 1978). *Two Years in the French West Indies* [1890] (Oxford, 2001).

14 See Hearn, 'A Midsummer Trip to the West Indies', repr. from *Harper's Monthly*, 1887–8 (Trinidad, 1891); also Elizabeth Stevenson, *Lafcadio Hearn* (New York, 1961), 160–1.

15 Hearn, *Midsummer Trip*, no pp.

16 Raphaël Confiant, Foreword, Hearn, *Two Years*, pp. x–xi.

17 'L'impossible est beaucoup plus étroitement apparenté à la realité que la plus grande partie de ce que nous dénommons le vrai et l'ordinaire. L'impossible n'est peut-être pas la vérité toute nue, mais je crois que c'est souvent la vérité masquée et voilée, sans doute, mais éternelle. Celui qui prétend ne pas croire aux fantômes ment dans son propre coeur.' From 'L'Eternelle hantise', quoted by Serge Denis, Introduction, *Trois fois bel conte*, 29–30.

18 Hearn, *Two Years*, 291; cf. Aimé Césaire, in 1942: 'Everything is zombi. Be watchful, suspicious of everything. Their charming or reassuring forms? A snare! A trap! Beware the over-friendly and

over-seductive woman: zombi, zombi, I tell you! . . . You are afraid. You are suspicious. Of what? Of everything. Of evil affirming itself, like the evil that disguises itself. Beware of being; but at the same time beware of appearance . . .' Aimé Césaire and René Menil, 'An Introduction to Martiniquan Folklore', in *Refusal of the Shadow: Surrealism and the Caribbean*, trans. Michael Richardson, ed. Michael Richardson and Krzysztof Fijalkowski (London, 1996), 101–4.

19 Hearn, *Trois fois bel conte*, 76.

20 'Le Rocher, c'etait la table où le Diable les enduisait de graisse et de serpent, d'huile des trépassés, de phosphore, et des mille ingrédients qui, la nuit, donnent à Zombi sa clarté.' Ibid. 98.

21 'C'est maintenant la tendre feuille du bananier . . .' Ibid. 102.

22 'Le Diable la dévora comme une chevrette.' Ibid. 102.

23 Hurston also published another study in folk tales and religion, *Mules & Men* (1935); the stories she collected for this book, phonetically set down with vivid directness, were only rediscovered in 2001, and published as *Every Tongue Got to Confess: Negro Folktales from the Gulf States*, with a Foreword by John Edgar Wideman, ed. and introd. Carla Kaplan (New York, 2002). See also Robert Hemenway, *Zora Neale Hurston: A Literary Biography*, with a Foreword by Alice Walker [1977] (London, 1986).

24 Zora Neale Hurston, *Tell My Horse: Voodoo and Life in Haiti and Jamaica* [1938] (New York: Harper & Row, 1990), 179.

25 Ibid. 183.

26 Ibid. 43–4.

27 I am indebted to Darryl Pinckney, who in his response to the photograph, helped me see the difficulties it presents.

28 *Obeah Simplified, The True Wanga! What It Really Is, and How It Is Done! By* Prof. Dr Myal Djumboh Cassecanarie (Port of Spain, *c*.1895). In spite of its uncertain status, between burlesque, satire, and document (the author's name means Broken Pot in creole), this short book includes much that seems well informed and many anecdotes about spells and cures, dated from 1849 onwards.

29 Andrew Lang, introd. to Robert Kirk, *The Secret Commonwealth* (London, 1893), p. xxv.

30 There are numerous other early spellings. *OED* cites James Grainger's poem 'Sugar Cane' (1764), for example; and John Gabriel

Stedman (1796). See n. 35 below. Edward Long uses *obeah* in his *History of Jamaica* (1774). In 1889, H. J. Bell published a study of voodoo in Haiti, called *Obeah*, which Jean Rhys might also have read. The British Library copy has been mislaid, so I have not been able to read this work.

31 See Carlo Ginzburg, 'On the European (Re)discovery of Shamans', *Elementa*, 1 (1993), 23–9.

32 Bernard Picart, *The Ceremonies and Religious Customs of the World* (London, 1733–9), 4 vols.; another edition, in nine vols., appeared in Amsterdam, 1733–6; an abridged version, in a single volume, by Robert Huish, was published as *The Religious Ceremonies and Customs of Every Nation of the World* (London, 1828).

33 I first saw one on exhibition in the British Museum; see J. H. C. King, *Human Image* (London, 2000), 20–1.

34 Richard Eden with Richard Willes, *The History of Travayle in the West and East Indies . . . a Translation of De Orbe Novo by P. M. Anglerius . . .* (London, 1577), 193ᵛ–194.

35 John Gabriel Stedman, *Narrative of a Five Years Expedition against the Revolted Negroes of Surinam, from the Year 1772 to 1777*, 2 vols. (London, 1796), i. 263.

36 Eden and Willes, *History* (after *De Orbe Novo*), Decade II, Book VI, ch. 2, 162; Olmedilla de Pereiras, Maria de Las Nieves, *Pedro Martir de Angleria y la Mentalidad Exotisca* (Madrid, 1974).

37 In the endmatter of Picart's tomes, the author included an open letter addressed to Pierre-Daniel Huet, Bishop of Avranches, one of the most brilliant and independent-minded men of the early eighteenth century, 'Concerning the Metempsychosis'. In this, the Jesuit correspondent was evidently struck by the strong affinity of 'savage metaphysics' with Pythagorean and Platonic theories: the 'Footsteps of the Doctrine . . .' he writes, 'may very visibly be traced among the Americans'. He does however conclude that they 'bear no finall Resemblance'. Picart, *Ceremonies*, iv. 159–87.

38 Jean Baptiste Du Tertre, *Histoire générale des Antilles habités par les Français*, 4 vols. (Paris, 1667–71), ii. 372.

39 Picart, *Ceremonies*, iii. 141.

40 Du Tertre, *Histoire*, ii. 370.

41 Sven Loren, *Origins of the Tainan Culture, West Indies* (Goteborg, 1935), 126–7.

42 Père [Jean-Baptiste] Labat, *Nouveau Voyage aus (sic) Isles de l'Amérique*, 2 vols. (The Hague, 1724). The first edition was published in Paris, 1722, in 6 vols.; another, in 12 vols. was published in Paris in 1742.

43 See *Memoirs of Père Labat 1693–1705*, trans. and abridged by John Eaden (London, 1931), introd. Philip Gosse.

44 'These pirates had pillaged the ships of the Great Mogul laden with women, merchandise and enormous treasure from Mexico, and they had loaded their great ship with an incredible quantity of the richest Indian silks and muslins. . . . The pirates had circulated through the Islands a great quantity of precious stones and gold coins of Asia . . .

   'I used all the money I had, and 200 écus more that I borrowed, to buy as much of these materials as I could . . .' *Memoirs of Père Labat*, 202–3. Philip Gosse in his introduction, identifies the ship: 'There is no doubt whatever that the plunder was actually the one taken by the famous pirate Captain Kidd from the ship the Quedagh Merchant, and left by him at St Thomas on his way to New York to face the accusations of piracy which awaited him and which led eventually to his trial and execution' (p. xiv). The legend of this booty in turn excited the ready imagination of Edgar Allen Poe: the immense treasure hoard that features so malignantly in 'The Gold-Bug', his classic brew of dark enchantments, code-breaking hokum, and bizarre entomological mutations, written in the 1840s, was buried, the narrator tells us, by the fugitive Captain Kidd. *The Complete Tales and Poems of Edgar Allen Poe* (London, 1982), 42–70, esp. 62–3.

45 Labat, *Nouveau Voyage*, ii. 163–7 (my translation); Hearn, *Two Years*, 131 gives a slightly shorter, different version.

46 Hearn, *Two Years*, 131.

47 Including reports of 'Milk-white Indians' with diamond-shaped eyes: 'Their eyelids bend and open in an oblong Figure, pointing downward at the corners, and forming an Arch or Figure of a Crescent with the points downwards . . . we us'd to call them Moon-ey'd. For they see not very well in the sun . . . when Moonshiny nights come, they are all life and Activity . . . skipping about like Wild Bucks.' Lacento [their chief] told Wafer, 'Twas through the force of the Mother's imagination looking at the Moon at the time of conception . . .' Lionel Wafer, *A New Voyage and Description of the Isthmus of America* (London, 1699), 137–8.

48 See Patrick O'Brian, *Joseph Banks: A Life* (Chicago, 1987), 179–86, 190–1 for a highly entertaining account of Omai's visit to England; Sir Joshua Reynolds's portrait of Omai (1776), from Castle Howard, was sold at auction for a record price in November 2001; see *Important British and Irish Pictures*, 29 November 2001 (Sotheby's, London, 2001), reproduced on cover, and pp. 36–45. Incidentally, many of the books I read, in the British Library, while doing the research for this book, once belonged to Sir Joseph Banks, one of the founders of the Library, and bear his lovely signature on the flyleaf.

49 See Richard D. Altick, *The Shows of London* (Cambridge, 1978), 120–7 on De Loutherbourg's innovatory entertainments.

50 See Ruddiger Joppien, 'Philippe Jacques de Loutherbourg's Pantomime, "Omai, or, A Trip round the World" and the Artists of Captain Cook's Voyages', in *British Museum Yearbook*, 3 (1979), 81–118; Iain McCalman, 'Spectacles of Knowledge: OMAI as Ethnographic Travelogue', in *Cook & Omai: The Cult of the South Seas* Exhibition catalogue (Canberra, 2001), 8–15; Christa Knellwolf, 'Comedy in the OMAI Pantomime', ibid. 16–21. I am very grateful to Jenny Newell of the British Museum for these references.

51 John O'Keeffe, *A Short Account of the New Pantomime called Omai, or a Trip around the World . . . with the Recitatives, Airs, Duetts, Trios and Chorusses* [sic] . . . (London, 1785).

52 O'Brian, *Joseph Banks*, 95–7 does not endorse this exactly, but see Colin Roderick, 'Joseph Banks, Queen Oberea and the Satirists', in Walter Veit (ed.), *Captain James Cook: Image and Impact* (Melbourne, 1972), 67–89. I am indebted to Debbie Lee for pointing me to this gossip.

53 See William Huse, 'A Noble Savage on the Stage', *Modern Philology*, 33 (1935–6), 303–16; McCalman, 'Spectacles of Knowledge', 10–13; see also J. C. H. King, *Artificial Curiosities from the Northwest Coast of America: Native American Artefacts in the British Museum collected on the Third Voyage of Capt. James Cook and Acquired through Sir Joseph Banks* (London, 1981), 37; Adrienne L. Kaeppler, *Artificial Curiosities* (Honolulu, 1978) catalogues the exhibition of Captain Cook's collection of 'native manufactures collected on the three Pacific voyages'.

54 *The Daily Universal Register*, soon to become *The Times*, quoted Altick, *Shows*, 120.

55 O'Keeffe, *Omai*.

56 Antoine Galland, *Les mille et une nuits: contes arabes* (Paris, 1702); 'The Story of "Ala Al-Din and the Magic Lamp"', in *The Arabian Nights*, trans. Husain Haddawy (London, 1995), ii. 81–163, 90–1.

57 Robert Irwin, 'There's the rub . . . and there too', *Times Literary Supplement*, 24 December 1993, pp. 14–15; id., *The Arabian Nights: A Companion* (London, 1994), 17–18; for his admirable survey of the complicated history of the *Nights*' transmission, see 'A Book without Authors', ibid. 42–62.

58 Sir Richard Burton, 'Alaeddin; or, The Wonderful Lamp', in *The Book of the Thousand Nights and a Night* (London, 1893), x. 137; Burton reads the Master in the egg as a Lady. He adds a note that he knows someone who links this wizard's mother to 'our "rook" meaning beak or parson'.: Husain Haddawy: 'bird of prodigious size which inhabits the peak of Mount Caucasus in Arabian myth.'

59 George Sloan, *Aladdin: A Fairy Opera in Three Acts* (London, 1826), 65, emphasis added.

60 Richard Burton, whose translation indulges in enough orchidaceous archaizing to make Swinburne austere, renders it, 'Now this Darwaysh (for dervish) was a Moorman from inner Marocco and he was a magician who could upheap by his magic hill upon hill . . .' From *The Arabian Nights*, vol. iii, *Supplemental Nights to the Book of the Thousand and a Night*, trans. Richard F. Burton (Kamashastra Society edition, London, 1894), x. 34–5.

61 'The Story of "Ala Al-Din and the Magic Lamp"', 81–163, 90–1.

62 Henry Weber, 'Aladdin, or The Wonderful Lamp', in *Tales of the East Comprising the most Popular Romances of Oriental Origin . . .* , 3 vols. (Edinburgh, 1812), 340–81, 345.

63 John O'Keeffe, *Aladdin Songs: The Recitatives, Airs, Choruses in Aladin* [sic]; *or, The Wonderful Lamp. A Pantomime Entertainment. Performed at the Theatre Royal, Covent Garden. The music composed by Mr Shields* (London, 1788).

64 Edward Long is the first user of the word 'myal', counter-magic to *obeah*, in his *History of Jamaica* (1774), according to the *OED*. This

concept has been revisioned and reclaimed in Erna Brodber's highly original, compressed lyrical novel *Myal* (London, 1988).

65 Such as *Obi, or Three-Finger'd Jack* (1800), which draws directly on the account the doctor Benjamin Moseley gave of local *obeah* medicine, starred the black actor Ira Aldridge, and was performed 'with Songs and Choruses' at the Theatre Royal, Hay Market around 1800: Other titles in this odd, mixed genre branch of entertainment include *Pizarro* (1814), *The Black Princess* (1814—featuring the heroine Jettiana and the Usurper O'erwhelmo), *The Slave* (1816), *Paul and Virginia* (1818), *Inkle and Yarico* (1819); Debbie Lee, 'Grave Dirt, Dried Toads, and the Blood of a Black Cat: How Aldridge Worked His Charms', forthcoming in *Romantic Praxis*, kindly lent by the author.

66 I am very grateful to Julie Anne Lambert of the John Johnson Collection at the Bodleian Library Oxford, for help with the collection of playbills.

67 Henry R. Bishop, *Songs, Recollections, Duels, Choruses, in the Fairy Opera of Aladdin,* Theatre Royal Drury Lane, 29 April 1826, p. 18.

68 See Alan Richardson, 'Romantic Voodoo: Obeah and British Culture, 1797–1807', in Margarite Fernandez Olmos and Lizabeth Paravisini-Gebert (eds.), *Sacred Possessions: Vodou, Santería, Obeah, and the Caribbean* (New Brunswick, 2000), 171–94.

69 Geoffrey Thorn, *Aladdin, or The Saucy Young Scamp who Collared the Lamp* (London, 1889–90).

70 Southey, *History of Brazil,* iii, ch. 31, p. 24.

71 In this respect, the critic Alan Richardson has offered a most interesting reading of a ballad included in Wordsworth and Coleridge's volume of 1797, but placing it against the background of imperial terror, of Caribbean slavery's disruptions to both person and polity. 'Goody Blake, and Harry Gill', which significantly is subtitled 'A True Story', tells a cautionary tale how one bitter winter, young Harry Gill lies in wait for an old vagrant woman, who is stealing firewood from his hedge, and beats her; she prays 'O may he never more be warm!' Her words come true: 'He went complaining all the morrow | That he was cold and very chill . . .' 'A-bed or up, by night or day; | His teeth they chatter, chatter still . . .' The figure of the hexed landowner here conveys, Richardson argues, the terror of black rebellion, and the imagined

revenge the oppressed may take by means of witchcraft. Like homegrown witches, those who have been treated as if they have no souls—this was one of the arguments for slavery, after all—are not always weak: they have residual power to do harm, to curse, to suck out another's being, and make their targets in their own likeness. Samuel Taylor Coleridge and William Wordsworth, *Lyrical Ballads*, ed. R. L. Brett and A. R. Jones (London, 1968), 54–8; Richardson, 'Romantic Voodoo: Obeah and British Culture, 1797–1807'.

72 'The Three Graves', in Samuel Taylor Coleridge, *Poems*, ed. J. B. Beer [1963] (London, 1970).

73 Barron Field, *Memoirs of Wordsworth*, ed. Geoffrey Little (Sydney, 1975), 100–1, quoted in John Spencer Hill, 'Coleridge, Wordsworth and the Supernatural', in id., *A Coleridge Companion* (London, 1983), 126; emphasis added.

74 'The Three Graves', lines 532–7, in Coleridge, *Poems*, 144–58.

75 Ibid. 144.

76 Bryan Edwards, *The History, Civil and Commercial, of the British Colonies in the West Indies etc.* (London, 1793–4); id., *An Historical Survey of the French Colony of the Island of San Domingo* (London, 1798) was written during the turbulence. Edwards belongs to the pro-slavery lobby. Samuel Hearne, in *A Journey from Prince of Wales's Fort in Hudson's Bay, to the Northern Ocean* (London, 1795) describes metamorphoses in dream experiences, as well as certain healing ceremonies performed by 'conjurers', pp. 189, 194; he shows a mixture of admiration and scoffing: 'the confidence which they had in the supernatural power of the conjurors, which induced them to believe, that talking lightly or disrespectfully of any thing they seemed to approve, would materially affect their health and happiness in this world . . .' (p. 344). Hearne was helped by a ghostwriter, who may have been William Wales. Wales had travelled with Captain Cook, no less, as the astronomer on board, and then, in his capacity as a school-master, taught Coleridge mathematics at Christ's Hospital—and what else besides, one might wonder? See Tim Fulford, 'Slaves, Shamans and Superstition: The Ancient Mariner Goes Native', forthcoming in Lucy Newlyn (ed.), *A Companion to Coleridge* (Cambridge, 2002), 45–58.

77 Interestingly, the poet expands an optical metaphor to situate the mystery in perception: in what sounds very like an actual moment in one of the poets' walks, the three victims observe closely the phenomenon of prismatic refraction, naturally occurring:

> The sun peeps through the close thick leaves,
>   See, dearest Ellen! See!
> 'Tis in the leaves, a little sun,
>   No bigger than your ee;
>
> A tiny sun, and it has got
>   A perfect glory too;
> Ten thousand threads and hairs of light,
> Make up a glory, gay and bright,
>   Round that small orb, so blue.'
>
> And then they argue of those rays,
>   What colour they might be;
> Says this, 'they're mostly green'; says that,
>   'They're amber-like to me.' (lines 505–17)

The attempt to settle the question of what they each see, even at close quarters, in this spirit of scientific empiricism, fails: when the mind is twisting and turning, all becomes metamorphic.

78 Coleridge, *Poems*, 195–210, lines 265–9.

79 See *A Choice of Coleridge's Verse*, ed. and introd. Ted Hughes (London, 1996), 67–74.

80 Coleridge, *Poems*, 'Christabel', lines 457–8.

81 Ibid., lines 619–20. For another dramatic case of spellbound personality in the context of imperial encounters, see Debbie Lee's eloquent and incisive article, 'Poetic Voodoo in Lamia: Keats in the Possession of African Magic', in *The Persistence of Poetry: Bicentennial Essays on Keats*, ed. Robert Ryan and Ronald Sharp (Amherst, 1998), 132–52.

82 Jean Rhys, *Smile Please* (London, 1979), 30.

83 Hearn, *Two Years*, 118. Labat died of snakebite, according to another story, of a *fer de lance*, allegedly imported by plantation owners to police runaways; another version says that, as he embarked to leave the island, he cursed it for its ingratitude. Ibid. 119. (In fact he died in his bed in Paris in 1738, 33 years after he left Martinique.)

84 Hearn, *Two Years*, 140.

85 Carole Angier, *Jean Rhys* (London, 1992), 371–2; Lucretia Stewart, 'Pearls of the Antilles', *Times Literary Supplement*, 27 July 2001.

86 *Wide Sargasso Sea* (London, 1966), 42.

87 Ibid. 38.

88 Ibid. 88–9. There is no record of such a book that I can trace.

89 Raphaël Confiant, Foreword, to Hearn, *Two Years*, p. x.

90 Angela Carter left a synopsis for *Adela: A Romance*, describing the young girl's many adventures as she searches for her identity: her mother, in France, becomes a heroine of the Commune, Adela turns on Mr Rochester for not telling her he is her father, and is eventually reconciled with Jane Eyre. As Angela Carter writes, the planned fiction 'plays some tricks with history; *Jane Eyre* is set in the 1820s, after all. But, then, it *is* a novel . . . ' My thanks to Susannah Clapp for letting me see this outline.

Chapter 4 *Doubling*

1 Heinrich Heine, 'Still ist die Nacht' (*Die Heimkehr*, no. 20) in *The Fischer-Dieskau Book of Lieder*, ed. and trans. George Bird and Richard Stokes (London, 1976), from the programme of Alfred Brendel: Seventieth Birthday Series, Royal Festival Hall, London, 3 June 2001, where I heard it sung by Matthias Goerne, with Brendel at the piano. The version I played in the lecture at Oxford is sung by Anthony Rolfe Johnson.

2 Rainer Maria Rilke, 'Primal Sound' [1919], in *Rodin and Other Prose Pieces*, trans. G. Craig Houston (London, 1986), 127–32, 128; see also Steven Connor, *Dumbstruck: A Cultural History of Ventriloquism* (Oxford, 2000), *passim*.

3 See Karl Miller's ground-breaking *Doubles: Studies in Literary History* (Oxford, 1985); also Wendy Doniger's two effervescent studies of many doublings and redoublings in *Splitting the Difference: Gender and Myth in Ancient Greece and India* (Chicago, 1999), and *The Bedtrick: Tales of Sex & Masquerade* (Chicago, 2000).

4 The plot goes like this: the King reveals to his wicked prime minister that a wizard has given him the magic power to migrate into a

corpse—animal or human—and reanimate it and then go about in that shape at his pleasure; this absolute disguise allows him to penetrate the secrets of his subjects in order to rule justly. The prime minister of course begs to be let in on the secret formula, and, even though his evil intent is obvious to all, the King unwisely demonstrates the spell on a hunt, and glides into the body of a stag he has killed, leaving behind his own body for dead; the vizier pounces in his turn and steals the prone body of the King; he then orders the death of the stag and when one of the bystanders, a feeble old man, refuses, kills him in anger. The King's spirit is able to escape from the dying stag in the nick of time and squats instead in the body of the Feeble Old Man. Now occupying the King's body, the vizier wreaks his evil will, though the virtuous queen, on whom he has obvious designs, recoils from the unrecognizable behaviour and changed character of the King's double. Eventually, the tangle gets untangled, with some uncompromisingly cynical aspersions on ambition, deceit, and abuse of power. Carlo Gozzi (1720–1806), *Il re cervo* (1762); see also *Le memorie inutili* (*Useless Memoirs of Carlo Gozzi*), trans. John Addington Symonds, ed. Philip Horne (London, 1962). I saw a not entirely successful production, by the American Repertory Theatre, with designs by Julie Taymor, as part of the Bite Festival, 2001, at the Barbican, London.

5 Emily Dickinson, *The Complete Poems*, ed. Thomas H. Johnson [1970] (London, 1986), no. 670, p. 333.

6 Advertisement for Visa credit cards, *New Yorker*, 4 June 2001.

7 Mark Dorrian, 'On the Monstrous and the Grotesque', *Word & Image*, 16/3 (2000), 310–17, 310.

8 Eden, *History of Travayle*, 195.

9 Michael Taussig comments, 'Note the *replicas*. Note the magical, the soulful power that derives from replication. For this is where we must begin; with the magical power of replication, the image affecting what it is an image of, wherein the representation shares in or takes power from the represented—testimony to the power of the mimetic faculty through whose awakening we might not so much understand that shadow of science known as magic . . . but see anew the spell of the natural where the reproduction of life merges

with the recapture of the soul.' Michael Taussig, *Mimesis and Alterity* (New York, 1993), 2.

10 Stuart Clark, *Thinking with Demons: The Idea of Witchcraft in Early Modern Europe* (Oxford, 1999), 80 ff.

11 Gabrielle Suzanne de Villeneuve, *La Belle et la bête*, trans. Carolyn Kunin (Pasadena, *c*.1999), unpublished, kindly lent by the translator, pp. 6, 26.

12 Ovid, *Metamorphoses*, VI, 104; Met/RH, 132.

13 Iain Wright, 'All done with mirrors: politics, magic and theatrical illusion in *Macbeth*', paper given at Shakespeare symposium, Humanities Research Centre, Australian National University, Canberra, June 1998, forthcoming in study of *Macbeth*, 2002.

14 Cf. Steven Connor, 'Fascination, skin and screen', *Critical Quarterly*, 40/1 (1998), 9–24.

15 See Joel Snyder, 'Picturing Vision', *Critical Quarterly*, 6 (1980), 499–526; see more on this in Marina Warner, Introduction, *The Inner Eye: Art beyond the Visible*. Catalogue of exhibition, Manchester, Brighton, Swansea, Dulwich Picture Gallery (London, 1996–7); id., 'The Structure of the Imagination' in Wendy Pullan and Harshad Bhadeshia (eds.), *Structure: In Science and Art* (Cambridge, 2000), pp. 163–91; id., 'Spirit Visions 1: Figuring the Invisible', in *Tanner Year Book* 22 (1999–2000) (Utah, 2001), 67–100.

16 See the splendidly comprehensive and stimulating study *Devices of Wonder: From the World in a Box to Images on a Screen*, by Barbara Maria Stafford and Frances Terpak (Los Angeles: Getty Research Institute catalogue, 2001).

17 Cesare Carena, *Tractatus de Officio Sanctissimae Inquisitionis* (Cremona, 1641), 217–18, quoted in Maurice Slawinski, 'Marino, le streghe, il cardinale', *Italian Studies*, 54 (1999).

18 Richard Holmes, *Coleridge: Early Visions* (London, 1989), 229–31.

19 From Coleridge, *Poems*, ed. Beer, pp. 311–12; emphasis added.

20 Coleridge, *Verse*, ed. Hughes, p. 6.

21 James Hogg, *The Private Memoirs and Confessions of a Justified Sinner*, ed. John Carey (Oxford, 1999), 182; a new edition, by Peter Garside (Edinburgh, 2001) was not yet available to me, but see Karl Miller's review, 'The Demons of Division', *TLS* 10 Aug. 2001, 3–4.

22 Hogg, *Private Memoirs*, 56. In an article 'Nature's Magic Lantern', Hogg reviews his own experience of meteorological illusions, and he discussed them with Sir David Brewster, the physicist, inventor of the kaleidoscope and, even more significantly, of the theory that led to stereoscopic photography. However Hogg disclaims Brewster's explanation: 'Sir D. Brewster, who, of all men I ever met with, is the fondest of investigating everything relating to natural phenomena: [he] pretended to account for it by some law of dioptrical refraction, which I did not understand.' James Hogg, 'Nature's Magic Lantern', *Chamber's Edinburgh Journal*, 28 Sept. 1833, 273–4. Karl Miller most kindly sent me the text from *The Worlds of the Ettrick Shepherd: Tales and Sketches*, ed. Thomas Thomson (Edinburgh, 1873), 459.

23 Hogg, *Private Memoirs*, 39–40.

24 Ibid. 41–2. In the second half of the novel, where Robert gives a first person account of his misdeeds, he also describes the violent encounter in the clouds: he goes there, at the urging of his evil genius, to kill his brother. He too there suffers visions: a woman in white appears to him out of the mist, and upbraids him for his evil intentions, but Robert's 'prince' and 'counsellor' rematerializes on the instant, and in archaic, lofty tones orders his minion not to be so faint-hearted, but to throw his wretch of a brother from the pinnacle into 'the foldings of the cloud'. Robert goes, but at the crucial moment, fails to push George over the edge; we have his word for it that his soul rebelled.

25 Thomas De Quincey, 'Suspiria de Profundis', in *Confessions of an Opium-Eater and Other Writings*, ed. Grevel Lindop (Oxford, 1996), 156.

26 Ibid. 156–7.

27 Carlo Ginzburg, 'On the European (Re) discovery of Shamans', *Elementa*, 1 (1993), 23–9.

28 De Quincey, 'Suspiria de Profundis', 87.

29 See Brian Coe and Mark Haworth-Booth, *A Guide to Early Photographic Processes* (London, 1983), Plates 1–3. I am most grateful to Mark Haworth-Booth for his help showing me the collection in the Victoria and Albert Museum, London, and discussing their characteristics with me.

30 R. L. Stevenson, *The Strange Case of Dr Jekyll and Mr Hyde*, ed. Jenni Calder (London, 1979) 37–8.

31 Ibid. 40.

32 Ibid. 56.

33 Ibid. 81.

34 Lewis Carroll, *Sylvie and Bruno* [1889], ed. Martin Gardner (London, 1988); with *Sylvie and Bruno Concluded* [1893], in *The Complete Sylvie and Bruno*, ed. Thomas Christensen (San Francisco, n.d.), 389.

35 Carroll was a member of the Society for Psychical Research; he also once sought out a man who had painted a ghost who had appeared to him: 'a pretty she-ghost, in fact, who had been quite willing to pose for her portrait'; in *Phantasmagoria and Other Poems*, edited with *Lettres à ses Amies-Enfants*, by Jean-Jacques Mayoux, trans. Henri Parisot (Paris, 1977; originally published London, 1869), 58.

36 Lewis Carroll, *Through the Looking Glass and What Alice Found There*, ed. Hugh Haughton (London, 1998), 241.

37 Roger Taylor, ' "Some Other Occupation": Lewis Carroll and Photography', in Lewis Carroll, catalogue, British Council Touring Exhibition, London, 1998.

38 James Atherton, *The Books at the Wake* (London, 1989), 124–36, esp. 128.

39 Carroll, *Sylvie and Bruno*, 192–5, 212–13.

40 Helmut Gernsheim, *Lewis Carroll Photographer* [1949] (London, 1969), Plate 23.

41 See Morton N. Cohen, *Lewis Carroll: A Biography* (London, 1995), 146, 152, 163.

42 See Virginia Rodier, *Clementina Lady Hawarden* (New York, 1999), *passim*, and Marina Warner, 'The Shadow of Young Girls in Flower', Introduction, ibid.

43 Carroll, *Sylvie and Bruno Concluded*, ch. 7, pp. 233–4.

44 See Pamela Thurschwell, *Literature, Technology and Magical Thinking, 1880–1920* (Cambridge, 2001).

45 F. W. H. Myers, with Frank Podmore and Edmund Gurney, *Phantasms of the Living* (London, 1886), 2 vols.; F. W. H. Myers, *Human Personality and its Survival of Bodily Death*, 2 vols. (London, 1903); John Beer, 'Myers's Secret Message', in *Providence and Love* (Oxford, 1998), 116–88.

46 Rhodri Hayward, 'Popular Mysticism and the Origins of the New Psychology 1880–1910' (Lancaster Ph.D. thesis, 1995), 157, 186.

47 F. W. H. Myers, 'Note', First Report of the Committee of the Society for Psychical Research (SPR) . . . [on] Marvellous Phenomena . . . ', *c.*1884–5, Myers archive, Harry Price Library, Senate House, University of London.

48 See Robert Fraser, Introduction to J. G. Frazer, *The Golden Bough: A Study in Magic and Religion*, ed. Robert Fraser (Oxford, 1994), p. xiii for Frazer's relationship with Andrew Lang.

49 Ibid., p. xi; see also John B. Vickery, *The Literary Impact of The Golden Bough* (Princeton, 1973), and David Richards, *Masks of Difference: Cultural Representations in Literature, Anthropology and Art* (Cambridge, 1994), ch. 5, 'Do they Eat their Enemies or their Friends? Cambridge and Buganda 1887–1932', pp. 145–88; id., 'Making Pre-History: Mycenae, Pausanias, Frazer', in Maureen Bell, Shirley Chew, et al. (eds.) *Re-Constructing the Book: Literary Texts in Transmission* (Aldershot, 2001), 112–23.

50 Richards, *Masks*, 150–3. The original 187 questions expanded to 213 in 1889, and then, for publication in 1907, to 507.

51 J. G. Frazer, *The Native Races of America: A Copious Collection of Passages for the Study of Social Anthropology from the Ms. Notebooks*, ed. Robert Angus Downie (London, 1939), 206, 288.

52 Ibid. 347–8. Mary Kingsley was the influential author of *Travels in West Africa* (London, 1897) and *West African Studies* (London, 1900) and *The Story of West Africa* (London, 1899), in the *Story of the Empire* series—'No English Schoolroom should be without them' (*The Times*); she gave a collection of her findings to the British Museum.

53 Frazer, *Native Races*, 409–10, quoting A. B. Ellis, *The Ewe-Speaking Peoples of the Slave Coast of West Africa* (London, 1890).

54 J. G. Frazer, *Questions on the Customs, Beliefs, and Language of Savages* (Cambridge, 1907), 38–42.

55 Stevenson, 'Dr Jekyll and Mr Hyde', ed. Jenni Calder (London, 1979).

56 For a discussion of 'The Beach of Falesá', see Marina Warner, 'Siren/Hyphen; or, "The Maid Beguiled"', *New Left Review*, 223 (May/June 1997), 101–13, repr. in *Caribbean Portraits: Essays on Gender Ideologies and Identities*, ed. Christine Barrow (Kingston, 1998); coinci-

dentally, 'The Beach of Falesá' was first published under the title 'Uma', which picks up an echo from Lafcadio Hearn's successful novel of 1890, *Youma*; then collected, three years later, in *Island Nights' Entertainments*, a different nod, this time to the storytelling tradition of *The Arabian Nights*. See Calder, Intro., 25.

57 Personal communication: we were talking about Lang, because the *Fairy Books* were my childhood reading, too, as for so many others. The prolific Lang also edited, in 1890, the Elizabeth translation by Robert Dallyngton of Francesco Colonna's *The Strife of Love in a Dream.*

58 The legend about Kirk being taken by the fairies was first written down by Patrick Graham in 1812; Walter Scott, in his *Letters on Demonology and Witchcraft* (London, 1830) repeated it.

59 Robert Kirk, *The Secret Commonwealth*, with Comment by Andrew Lang (London, 1893), p. xv.

60 Ibid.

61 Ibid., p. xxv.

62 Kenneth Gross, himself a twin, is writing about twinship for a forthcoming book, in which he explores the ordinariness of being one. And a clone is only a twin, after all. See Kenneth Gross, 'Ordinary Twinship', forthcoming, *Raritan*, 22/3, Winter 2003.

63 See Gerald M. Edelmann, 'Building a Picture of the Brain', *Daedalus* (Spring, 1998), 37–69; I discuss this more fully in 'Le Mythe et la féerie: reécriture et recupération', *Actes du colloque Où en est-on avec la théorie littéraire?* (Paris VII, 1999), ed. Julia Kristeva et Evelyne Grossman, *Textuel*, 37 (April, 2000), 85–97.

64 Dubravka Ugrešić, *The Museum of Unconditional Surrender*, trans. Celia Hawkesworth (London, 1999), 202–3.

Epilogue

1 Plato, *The Republic*, 617E, ed. and trans Allan Bloom [1968] (New York, 1991), 300.

2 Ibid., 620A–D, pp. 302–3.

3 Ibid., 620D, p. 303.

4 Philip Pullman, *His Dark Materials*, vol. i: *Northern Lights* (London, 1995); vol. ii: *The Subtle Knife* (London, 1997); vol. iii: *The Amber Spy-Glass* (London, 2000). Pullman has since been awarded the Whitbread Prize, the first children's book to win overall.

5 *Northern Lights*, 167.

6 Ibid. 143.

7 For example, Joan Aiken, Michael Morpurgo, Alan Garner, Melvyn Burgess, David Almond.

8 Salman Rushdie, *The Ground Beneath Her Feet* (London, 1999), 268.

9 Marie Darieussecq, *Pig Tales*, trans. Linda Coverdale (London, 1996); id., *My Phantom Husband*, trans. Helen Stevenson (London, 1999).

10 For example, the short story 'Arachne', in *Ovid Metramorphosed*, ed. Philip Terry (London, 2000), 131–57.

11 Gjertrud Schnackenberg, *The Throne of Labdacus* (Newcastle, 2001).

12 My source is Mary Douglas, in conversation over lunch she kindly gave me, 12 February 2001.

Picture Sources

Frontispiece, I, II, III, 12, 13 Bridgeman Art Library

IV, 1, 2, 4, 30, 31 By permission of the British Library (IC 411198; IC 41148; IC 41148; 1001.c.12; 878.L2; 567.h.16)

V © National Gallery, London

VI, 27 The Wellcome Library, London

VII, 14, 15, 16, 17, 18 All Rights Reserved © Prado Museum, Madrid

3, 5, 22, 24, 37 Private Collection

6 By permission of the castle of Fontanellato (Parma), Italy

7, 19 Photographs courtesy of Magdalen College, Oxford

8 AKG London

9 Bibliothèque Nationale de France, Paris

10, 11 Kupferstichkabinett, Berlin

20 Thorvaldsens Museum, Dept. of Greek and Roman Antiquities, Copenhagen (Inv. No. I. 1510)

21 Photograph: Warburg Institute, London

23 Soprintendenza Archelogico della Basilicata, Potenza

25, 29 © The British Museum

26 Devonshire Collection, Chatsworth. Reproduced by permission of the Duke of Devonshire and the Chatsworth Settlement Trustees

28 From Zora Neale Hurston, *Tell my Horse*, 1990 Harper & Row, © 1938 by Zora Neale Hurston. Renewed 1966 by Joel Hurston

32 Bodleian Library, University of Oxford (Opie C 389)

33, 34 The London Library

35, 36 Courtesy of the Bill Douglas Centre for the History of Cinema and Popular Culture

38 V & A Picture Library

Index

Note: page references in *italics* indicate illustrations